Staking Her Claim

Staking Her Claim

. . . .

Women Homesteading the West

. . . .

Marcia Meredith Hensley

HIGH PLAINS PRESS

COVER PHOTOGRAPH (also on page 232): used by permission of the Colorado
   Historic Society and colorized by Marty Petersen Artwork and Design.
TITLE PAGE PHOTOGRAPH: two unidentified young women, courtesy of the
   Wyoming State Archives, Department of State Parks and Cultural Resources.
PAGE 16 PHOTO: Rock River, Wyoming, train station on the Union Pacific
   Railroad, from the Stimson Collection at the Wyoming State Archives.
PAGE 44 PHOTO: A page of Cecelia Weiss's *Sunset* magazine article, June 1916.
PAGE 282 PHOTO: Esther Dollard's homestead patent courtesy of Jean
   Skaife-Brock.

Library of Congress Cataloging-in-Publication Data

Hensley, Marcia Meredith
   Staking her claim : women homesteading the West / Marcia Meredith Hensley.
      p. cm.
   Includes bibliographical references.
   ISBN-13: 978-0-931271-89-2 (cloth : alk. paper)
   ISBN-13: 978-0-931271-90-8 (trade paper : alk. paper)
   1. Women pioneers--West (U.S.)--Biography. 2. Single women--West (U.S.)--
Biography. 3. Women--West (U.S.)--Social life and customs--20th century. 4.
Frontier and pioneer life--West (U.S.) 5. West (U.S.)--Social life and customs--
20th century. 6. West (U.S.)--History--1890-1945. I. Title.
   F595.H45 2007
   978'.030922--dc22
   [B]

2007035752

HIGH PLAINS PRESS
403 CASSA ROAD
GLENDO, WYOMING 82213

CATALOG AVAILABLE
www.highplainspress.com

. . . .

To my mother, Frances Griffin Meredith, who nurtured my love of books and understood when I needed to move west.

To my daughters, Robyn and Wendy, who caught the pioneering spirit and are now conquering their own frontiers.

To my husband, Mike, who shares and enhances the journey.

. . . .

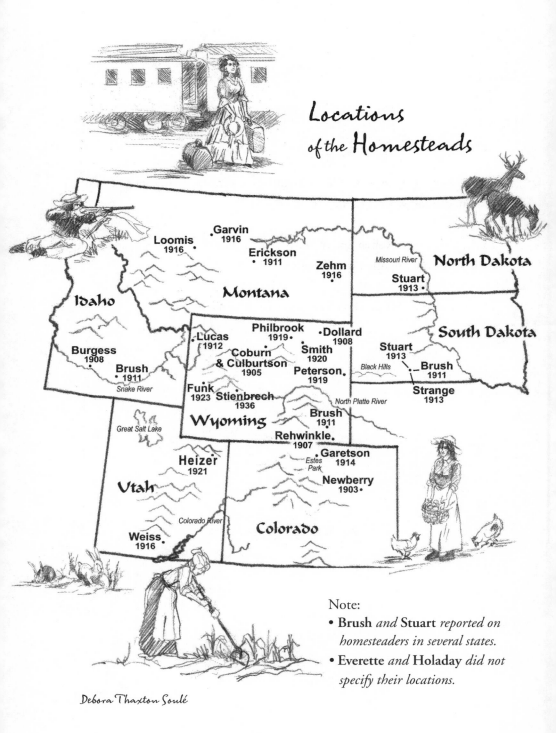

Locations *of the* Homesteads

Idaho

Montana

- Loomis
  1916
- Garvin
  1916
- Erickson
  1911
- Zehm
  1916

Missouri River

North Dakota

- Stuart
  1913

South Dakota

- Burgess
  1908
- Brush
  1911

Snake River

- Lucas
  1912
- Philbrook
  1919
- Dollard
  1908
- Coburn
  & Culburtson
  1905
- Smith
  1920
- Peterson
  1919
- Stuart
  1913
- Brush
  1911

Black Hills

- Funk
  1923
- Stienbrech
  1936
- Strange
  1913

Wyoming

North Platte River

- Brush
  1911
- Rehwinkle
  1907

- Heizer
  1921

- Garetson
  1914
- Newberry
  1903

Estes Park

Utah

Great Salt Lake

- Weiss
  1916

Colorado River

Colorado

Note:

- **Brush** *and* **Stuart** *reported on homesteaders in several states.*
- **Everette** *and* **Holaday** *did not specify their locations.*

Debora Thaxton Soulé

Contents

· ·

Acknowledgments

· ·

My interest in single women homesteaders has evolved over many years, and numerous people have helped along the way. My first debt is to those historians whose assertions about reluctant pioneer women caused me to question and prompted me to look for evidence to the contrary. I was encouraged to discover evidence of women eager to come west in Susanne George Bloomfield's book about Elinore Pruitt Stewart, *The Adventures of the Woman Homesteader*, and Dee Garceau-Hagen's book *The Important Things of Life: Women and Work in Sweetwater County*. Reading about North Dakota single women homesteaders in Elaine Lindgren's *Land in Her Own Name* stimulated my interest in their counterparts in the Rocky Mountain region. My colleagues in the Western American Literature Association provided a receptive audience for numerous papers I presented about single women homesteaders at the organization's conferences.

All the following provided much appreciated research assistance: the Wyoming State Archives; University of Wyoming Library and American Heritage Center; the Washakie Museum in Worland, Wyoming; the Homesteaders Museum in Torrington, Wyoming; the Homesteader Museum of Powell, Wyoming; Colorado Historical Society; Denver Public Library; Estes Park Historical Museum; University of Montana at Missoula; Idaho State Historical Society; Boise State University Library Special Collections; and Iowa State University Library Special Collections. At Western Wyoming Community College's Hay Library, interlibrary loan librarians Fern Stringham and Sharon Dolan were especially helpful.

Other organizations contributed to the book's creation. While on the Wyoming Council for the Humanities Speakers Bureau in 2001–2003, I discovered people were not only interested in single women homesteaders, but also that they had information to share. Receiving the Wyoming Arts Council's Neltje Blanchan Memorial Writing Award gave me confidence not only that I could write a book, but also that people might actually want to read it. I also appreciate the encouragement of fellow writers in the Eden Valley History Project, Barbara Smith's creative writing class at Western Wyoming Community College, and Wyoming Writers, Inc.

To the families of single women homesteaders who shared information with me and allowed me to include their stories and photographs, I am deeply grateful. Thank you Wynona Breen, Jean Skaife Brock, Patience H. Hillius, Liz Howell, Faith Mullen, Fern K. Nelson, Molly Rozum, Robert Blake Smith, Lynn Thorpe, and Marjorie Vandervelde. I am also grateful to publishers who granted permission to reprint single women homesteaders' stories in my book: Jack Zumwinkle of the *Allenspark Wind*, the Sublette County Artists' Guild, and the Prairie County Historical Society.

I've been fortunate to have the encouragement of accomplished writers and editors along the way. At Linda Hasselstrom's Windbreak House Retreat, I began thinking of myself as a writer. Betsy Marston of *High Country News* bolstered my confidence and honed my editing skills. Because Nancy Curtis, High Plains Press publisher, listened to and found merit in my early notions of the book, I persevered. I thank her for her patience in waiting for the book to progress and especially for publishing it. My good friend since college and fellow English teacher, Barbara Clarke, who has her own editing business, Windswept Works in Tulsa, Oklahoma, played an invaluable role in artfully pruning an early version of the book. Judy Plazyk, editor for High Plains Press, deserves much credit for reshaping the book into its final form. I am grateful that these talented people shared their expertise as well as their enthusiasm for the subject.

I also thank friends and family who contributed to the book in various ways. Tammie McCallister typed documents to free my time for writing. Artist Deborah Soule created the map of women homesteaders' locations. Conversations with friends and colleagues with kindred interests, Susan Bates, Barbara Bogart, Chris Kennedy, Karen Love, and Kayne Pyatt, were catalysts during the writing process. My daughters, Robyn Meredith and Wendy Berry, were cheerleaders for the project. Wendy was always a good listener and sounding board, and Robyn shared her journalist's skills in both writing and revising. Most of all I thank my husband, Mike. Without his understanding, patience, and encouragement this book would not have come to be.

All these people have helped shape the book. I deeply appreciate their contributions and hope the book lives up to their expectations.

Introduction: The Legacy of Single Women Homesteaders

. . . .

The legacy of single women homesteaders is a rich, if well hidden, vein of stories about their lives, stories that must be mined like precious nuggets from the larger vein of the American West's history and literature. In the early 1900s, accounts of girl homesteaders did find their way into magazines and newspapers. That these accounts were overlooked as the West's past was excavated and omitted when major western histories were written is likely attributable to three main factors. The first reason might be the relatively small percentage of single women homesteaders—about 12 percent of all homesteaders. Because these few stepped outside the boundaries of conventional behavior for women, their stories may have been discounted. Secondly, perhaps their experiences were thought to be identical to those of homesteading men and their families; thus their uniqueness was underestimated. Finally, an unconscious cultural bias may have existed that assumed women's roles in settling the West were insignificant except as helpmates to men. It is likely that all of these factors contributed in some degree to muting the stories of single women homesteaders.

Although magazines such as *Sunset, Overland Monthly, Atlantic Monthly, The Independent,* and *Collier's* gave single women homesteaders their day of fame by publishing their accounts, more often the homesteaders' stories are self-published, recorded in oral histories, or found in family lore or community records. Their surviving letters and diaries were saved primarily as personal memorabilia within families. The few published stories went largely unnoticed for several generations. Thus many women have grown up unaware that single women homesteaders existed.

Without adventuresome role models like women homesteaders, women may have sublimated their longing for adventure by identifying with the masculine heroes in literature and popular culture. No doubt many girls growing up during the mid-twentieth century were riveted to Saturday afternoon matinees at the local movie theater, imagining themselves riding into the landscape of adventure like Roy Rogers, Gene Autry, or the other heroes of B westerns. These same women may have identified with Huck Finn who "lit out for the territory ahead of the rest" rather than with the unpleasant female civilizers in Twain's novel. Yet, they were taught that nice girls did not light out for the territory on their own; they stayed home, got married, had children, and put down roots. The women's movement in the 1970s began to liberate women from that stereotype, empowering more of them to become journey-takers, motivating a reexamination of history to unearth stories of women's lives overlooked before, and freeing contemporary women to write their own journey stories.[1]

From the time they staked their claims, single women homesteaders quietly played a part in these social and literary changes. They were models of independence in their time. The popular magazines of the early twentieth century that touted their accomplishments suggested that any woman could do the same. Even if a woman didn't choose to homestead, reading the stories of women who did might have planted a seed that grew into other forms of independence. Single women homesteaders demonstrated a take-charge-of-your-own-life attitude and proved that a woman could be a successful entrepreneur in the enterprise of homesteading. They were both examples of the changing roles of women in the early twentieth century and agents of that change. As role models for their friends, their sisters, and eventually their daughters, they continued the work initiated by suffragettes in eroding restrictive codes of behavior and increasing women's options.

In *Westering Women and the Frontier Experience 1800–1915*, Sandra Myres asserts that the values of modern western women differ from women in other parts of the country, revealing "their frontier heritage in their personal values and attitudes" (1982, 270). She cites as evidence a 1943 survey that compared western women with northern and southern women. The survey found the following:

> [Western women] were far better educated, held a wider variety of jobs, and were more likely to continue working [after marriage], were less prone to adhere to traditional religious and denominational beliefs, were more excited and more optimistic about their lives, were more open to change, and were more likely to approve equal standards for men and women (270).

Myers concludes that "the westering experience continued to influence Western women's values and attitudes long after the passing of the frontier" (270).

The westering experiences of single women homesteaders shaped their life choices, paving the way for equality in their marriages and in their work roles. A woman who owned her own property had clout in the community, and she was more likely to be considered an equal partner in a family ranch if her name was on the homestead patent granting ownership. Being a landowner might even have given her an advantage in finding a marriage partner, if she wanted one. Or if she didn't marry, she knew she could take care of herself. If she married, her daughters probably saw a different family dynamic than she had seen in her own parents. Mother likely had a say in what happened on her land, and she worked as hard on it as Father, even doing such formerly masculine work as horseback riding, operating farm equipment, and branding cattle.

This anthology of their stories illustrates that single women homesteaders contradict what historian Elaine Lindgren calls the "marriage, madness, marginality" stereotype (1996, 210). Lindgren explains that according to this outdated view, "women are portrayed as depending on marriage for fulfillment, unable to cope with severe adversity, and as marginal or secondary contributors to the important business of society" (210). Recent scholarship is breaking down that stereotype and broadening our understanding of the variety of women's experiences in the West, showing that many women who confronted the frontier shared what Gretel Ehrlich describes as the ability to see the emptiness of the West not as a void but as a "geography of possibility" (1985, 9).

The reader is not likely to have previously encountered the twenty-four single women homesteaders' stories this book includes. While Elinore Pruitt Stewart's widely read stories do not appear here, my reading of her *Letters of a Woman Homesteader* (1914) and *Letters on an Elk Hunt* (1915) kindled my interest in single women homesteaders and motivated my search for more of their narratives. I found the stories of these women in musty periodicals and oral history files in library stacks, in local histories of small communities, and in long out-of-print books. Providing access to their stories is the primary goal of this anthology, and in chapters three through six, they speak for themselves. In all cases, the texts appear exactly as they did originally, with all idiosyncrasies of spelling and usage preserved.

In addition to creating an awareness of single women homesteaders and their stories, this book provides a frame of reference for these women, with the hope that others will continue to explore their accomplishments. Chapter one offers historical and literary context to explain the significance of writing by and about single women homesteaders and how one may read the writing of these women as literature as well as historical documents. Chapter two provides statistics on the backgrounds, experiences, and success rates of single women homesteaders.

The time parameters of this study grew naturally out of the stories themselves. Transportation improvements, increasing acceptance of women's independence, and generous revisions in the homestead laws coincided at the beginning of the twentieth century, providing an impetus for single women to homestead. Their first-hand accounts began to appear in publications in the early 1900s. Their memoirs were published as late as the 1960s.

The stories also determined the geographical parameters of the book. By the 1900s lands opening for homesteading were often those previously passed over in less promising agricultural areas in Colorado, Wyoming, Montana, Idaho, Utah, North Dakota, and South Dakota. As a result, many single women homesteaded in those regions. Thus, stories from these areas best represent the experiences of single women homesteading at the beginning of the twentieth century, although some single women also homesteaded at the same time in the other western states.

The book includes only the nonfiction writing of women homesteaders to limit the book's length and because fewer examples of fiction and poetry exist from which to draw a representative sample. Nonfiction writing by and about single women homesteaders exists in several genres: magazine articles, personal correspondence, memoirs, and historical accounts. The book devotes a chapter to each of these genres.

"Heroines of the Popular Press," chapter three, includes the stories of adventure and success homesteading women wrote in popular magazines of the day. At the same time, newspapers and popular magazines dispatched reporters to the mountains and plains to describe for their readers the unusual phenomena of single women homesteaders. Written during the time women were actually homesteading or shortly after they had "proved up," these accounts are consistently optimistic, focusing on useful information about homesteading and giving glowing reports of its rewards.

Chapter four, "Please Answer Soon: Letters of Single Women Homesteaders," documents yet another type of literary legacy: the letters women wrote home to family and friends telling about daily life on their claims. More than any other genre in which they wrote, their letters allow today's readers to get to know them in a personal way. One can sense their growing independence and confidence as they discarded Victorian expectations and took on whatever kinds of work needed to be done to support their claims.

"Looking Back: Single Women Homesteaders' Memoirs," chapter five, presents accounts of their homesteading lives in retrospect as these women created a record for posterity. In their memoirs, women often glossed over the unpleasant aspects of the experience, focusing on the culturally approved message that homesteading was a vehicle for personal achievement and happiness.

"Rediscovered: Single Women Homesteaders in Historical Records," chapter six, includes the stories of single women homesteaders rediscovered by relatives examining their family histories, communities collecting stories of their past, oral historians documenting individual's stories, and by researchers probing historical records.

My research failed to uncover any diaries of single women homesteaders. This may be because a woman who homesteaded alone had limited time to write and used what time she had to correspond with family and friends rather than keep a diary. If she did have a diary, its personal nature might have prompted her to destroy it eventually. For the same reason, a family member who inherited a diary might be reluctant to share it.

As a whole, this collection of writing creates a vivid montage of single women homesteaders' experiences, documents their place in western history, and brings to life their spirited journeys of self-determination. As a quilt made of varied shapes, colors, and patterns becomes a beautifully coherent whole, the unique stories of each single woman homesteader becomes an archetypal story about women achieving independence and individuality.

No doubt more narratives by and about single women homesteaders remain to be found, but, until then, the articles, memoirs, letters, oral histories, and remembrances in this collection serve as a representative sample of the whole remarkable community of women who homesteaded alone.

1. Single Women Homesteaders: Their Place in History & Literature

. . . .

◊ Their Place in History

The stories of single women homesteaders in the American West have been overlooked in both American history and American letters. In fact, women's stories in general were overlooked in western studies that took place before the 1970s. Sandra Myres points out that the early twentieth century historian Frederick Jackson Turner, who emphasized the importance of the frontier in shaping American character, wrote as if those frontiers were "devoid of women," and "succeeding generations of historians" greatly influenced by him "continued to interpret the westering movement in masculine terms" (1982, 8). The stories of explorers, mountain men, miners, and cowboys dominate our national fascination with the West. Their adventures, struggles, and conflicts with the native inhabitants provide fodder for countless western fantasies in print and film from *Leatherstocking* and *The Great Train Robbery* to *All the Pretty Horses* and *Dances with Wolves*. Though not totally invisible, women are certainly portrayed as minor players in most western dramas.

Until recently, even those western historians who made attempts to discuss women often made assumptions based on limited research. For example, a section in Walter Prescott Webb's 1931 book, *The Great Plains*, has this heading: "What has been the Spiritual Effect of the American Adventure in the Great Plains on Women?" (505–506). Webb first characterizes this spiritual effect on men who went west, concluding that they found "zest in life, adventure in the air and freedom from restraint," and they were insensitive to the hardships and lack of refinement. In contrast, Webb cites Beret Hansa, the down-trodden homesteader's wife in Ole Rolvaag's fictional *Giants in the Earth* as evidence that women who went west were "crushed to the soul" by the vast, treeless landscape. Webb's concluding words in this section of his book ask, "Who can tell us how the Great Plains affected women, and why?" (1931, 506). Any woman reading that question could see how obvious the answer is. Ask the women. But at the time Webb was writing, diaries and journals of ordinary women were not yet being consulted. Ironically, in 1931, when Webb's book was first published, historians could have found the answer to that question by asking homesteading women who were still alive rather than relying on conjecture.

The result of these attitudes was to silence or at least mute the stories of single women homesteaders. In her analysis of the "silencing" of Helga Estby's historically significant but virtually ignored transcontinental walk in 1896, Linda Lawrence Hunt explains that a story may be overlooked through a combination of sanctions. For example, if a woman's story is perceived as "breaking the code" of standard behavior, it may be discounted or ignored (2003, 245). Even at the turn of the twentieth century when women's roles were less confined than in the Victorian era, homesteading was seen primarily as the work of men and families, not of single women; thus, women homesteader stories could be viewed as breaking the code, as aberrations from the norm and thus not worthy of serious consideration.

According to Hunt, "underestimating the worth" is another sanction that may have led to the muting of single women's stories (2003, 246). Because women's experiences received less attention than men's in historical studies until the 1970s, the worth of single women homesteaders' experiences was underestimated. The devaluing may have arisen from the women homesteaders' families themselves, influenced by societal norms to see the story of the woman's experience as something a little too strange and thus ignoring or minimizing it in the family's history.[1]

One of the first to note the dearth of women in western historical studies, Wyoming historian T.A. Larson set out to survey the extent to which women were included in western history textbooks in use in the early 1970s. He found that one book had devoted only two sentences to the role of women in the West, while another text had more generously allotted a half page to the subject, including seven words about woman suffrage in Wyoming. Larson concludes that "standard textbooks used in college and university courses in Western History come close to ignoring women entirely. Were women really that insignificant in the West?" (1974, 4). The publication of Larson's essay "Women's Role in the American West" marked a new direction. The essay quotes from women writing about their western experience and looks at demographics as well as the kinds of work women actually did in the West. Larson notes the fallacy of expecting to

Many homesteaders lived in dugouts or sod cabins such as this one. (*Colorado Historical Society*)

correct the historical imbalance by simply inserting into history books the names of a handful of great women. While a woman such as Sacajawea certainly deserves her honored place in history, Larson argues that the contributions of ordinary western women should be taken into account.

The Stereotype. In view of increasing attention to women's issues in the 1970s, it is surprising to find a woman historian asserting in 1976 that "[t]here are few, if any, women who could imitate Huck Finn and 'light out for the territory'; few literary or real life models for women to begin a solitary odyssey of searching and exploring" (Sochen 1976, 38). Sochen theorizes that accepting her role as a self-sacrificing, compromising helpmate, the pioneer wife put her own qualms and fears aside and went west with her husband. This image of the reluctant pioneer woman became the stereotype perpetuated in art and literature.

But the accounts of single women homesteaders in this book show that some women did indeed "light out for the territory." Unmarried women who went west because they wanted to and who were not burdened with providing care for a husband and children differ from the image of the reluctant pioneer wife. As single women making their own decisions, going west became a chosen adventure rather than an imposition of someone else's will. Compare with the stereotype this account of women going west from Elaine Lindgren's book *Land in Her Own Name*:

> Mary, Helen, Christine and I packed our suitcases. I took my mandolin, Christine took hers and her rifle. The boys paid us our share of the farm and away we went by train to St. Paul. On August 20, 1905 we were on our way to Minot. . . . The trains were packed. Everyone was very friendly and we met people from all over, all talking of the adventure of going to a new country opening up for settling (1996, 11).

The reluctance that some historians attribute to women going west does not appear in the account of Alice Day Pratt, who homesteaded in eastern Oregon in 1910. In her account, she recalls how she felt the day she boarded the train to go west. She felt no regret at leaving behind "extremes of gayety and misery . . . competition . . . life at high pressure" but rather anticipation that before her lay "calm . . . freedom . . . limitless spaces . . . hope and opportunity" (1993, 3).

Or consider the story of Florence Blake Smith, a twenty-one-year-old bookkeeper for the Federal Reserve in Chicago. When she heard about Wyoming homesteading opportunities from a young man in Chicago who had tried it, she said, "I was immediately taken with the idea. Since I was free, white, female and just twenty-one, I decided right there that I could do it if he could. I was so thrilled, so eager" (1962, 1).

The Cultural Setting. Dee Garceau observes that in the nationwide debate "about woman's place . . . the American West was like a laboratory of change, where migration, relocation, and new settlement underscored the processes of reconstructing a new social identity" (1997, 2). By the 1880s some states and territories had already granted women the right to vote and hold office. According to Katherine Harris's study of Colorado homestead families from 1873 to 1920, "woman suffrage may have had a subtle effect," which led to the "muting of gender-role distinctions" (1993, 169). There was nothing subtle about woman suffrage in Wyoming, which had given women the right to vote and hold office when it was made a territory in 1869. Wyoming was a model proving to the rest of the nation that woman suffrage could succeed (Sprague 1972).

The activism of suffragettes created a more egalitarian atmosphere in which woman had a wider range of life choices. While their urban sisters were bobbing their hair and wearing short skirts to celebrate their new freedom, single women homesteaders broke away from confining roles in a different way. By the time the Nineteenth Amendment was ratified in 1920, many single women homesteaders had already filed on claims successfully and become western landowners. They were part of a new generation of women, independent from male authority and self-supporting, women who exercised control over their personal, social, and economic lives.

Women and Landownership. Landownership in the American West had always embodied mythic qualities of renewal, offering a chance to redefine one's identity and one's place in society. This reinvention of self must have resonated strongly for women during the early twentieth century as limiting attitudes about women's sphere eroded. As early as 1840, many states had passed the Married Women's Property Act, making it legal for one segment of the female population to own and manage property. Another liberating moment occurred when the Homestead Act was ratified in 1862, opening the door for both men and single women to become landowners. According to the act, any "head of household" could "prove up" on 160 acres of land by paying a modest filing fee and improving the land while residing on it for seven months out of each of five years. Requirements for improving the land varied depending on the time and place one homesteaded but generally required the building of a structure and making the land productive in some way.

Between 1862 and 1890 two million people had taken advantage of the Act, and by the middle of the twentieth century, "285 million acres of the public domain had been transferred from the government to private hands through the Homestead Act" (Hine 1984, 177). Although some historians have suggested the Homestead Act was little better than a scam luring unsuspecting settlers to poor, arid land that destined many to failure, others have called it one of the great democratic measures in history. Certainly, the fact that it did not discriminate on the basis of gender was significant. For a woman homesteader, however, there was a caveat. A single woman could file on land because she was considered a "head of

This reconstruction of a boxcar-style claim shack at the Homestead Museum in Torrington, Wyoming, is typical of claim shacks built in eastern Wyoming. (*Mike Hensley*)

household," but if she married between the time of filing and proving up, she would no longer be the head of household; thus ownership of her property reverted to her husband.

Studies of actual practice show that interpretation and enforcement of this provision varied and some exceptions were made. For example, the claim of Mrs. Della Myers Landers in Idaho's Payette National Forest was questioned, but Forest Supervisor E. Grandjean noted, "In view of the fact that the entrywoman is practically separated from her husband, and must support her children and make this her permanent home, raising vegetables to support herself and her children, and must derive an income by leasing part of the land for pasture use, I would recommend that no protest be made in this case" (Reddy 1993, 7). Differing legal decisions and legislation between 1875 and 1914 generally recognized the rights of women who married after filing but before proving up.

When the Revised Homestead Act of 1909 increased the amount of land one could homestead to 320 acres and the Revised Homestead Act of 1912 decreased the residency requirement from five to three years while still permitting an absence of five months each year, the prospect of homesteading for a single woman became more attractive. She could own more land with a smaller investment of her time. Most stories of women who homesteaded alone take place after 1909, suggesting that these two revisions encouraged single women to homestead.

Transportation Improvements. Transportation advances at the beginning of the twentieth century increased the feasibility of homesteading for single women. By 1869 the transcontinental railroad spanned the country, opening western lands earlier accessible only by horseback, wagons, or stage coaches. After that, many railroads expanded into more remote lands of the West and became active promoters of homesteading. For example, an undated brochure promoting railroad travel, titled "Wonderful Opportunities for Homesteader or Investor,"[2] not only paints a rosy picture for western land investment but also seems aimed at a female audience, as this poem in the brochure illustrates:

Mary Had a Little Farm
Mary had a little farm,—as level as the floor;
She placed on it a fancy price, and struggled to get more.
She kept the land until one day the country settled up,
And where the wilderness had been there grew a bumper crop.
Then Mary rented out her land (she would not sell you know)
And waited patiently for the prices still to grow.
They grew as population came, and Mary raised the rent;
With common food and raiment now she could not be content.
She built her up a mansion fine, had bric-a-brac galore—and every time
The prices rose, she raised the rent some more.
"What makes the land keep Mary so?" the starving people cry.
"Why Mary keeps the land you know." The wealthy would reply.
And so each one of you might be "Wealthy, refined and wise."
If you bought some land and held it for the rise.

Heading west on a passenger train with a trunk load of possessions in the freight car was something a single woman could do more easily than venturing west in a covered wagon. One enterprising young woman even

Union Pacific Railroad distributed brochures such as this one to encourage homesteading in the West. (*Colorado Historical Society*)

shipped her claim shack, a nine by twelve foot portable garage purchased in Chicago, after the salesman assured her that a woman could easily assemble it by herself (Smith 1962). Traveling by train, an aspiring homesteader could arrive at her destination in days rather than months. The dangers and hardships she faced, if any, would not be a result of the trip. In fact the trips Lindgren chronicles in her book about single women homesteaders in North Dakota were enjoyable social events (1996). Once she arrived at the railhead nearest her destination, a single woman homesteader usually faced another day or two in a wagon or stage to get to a small community near her homestead site. For example, after Elinore Pruitt Stewart's train trip from Denver to Green River, Wyoming, she and her young daughter, Jerrine, faced another day's drive by wagon to Burnt Fork, Wyoming, a journey made more interesting by the flirting of the wagon driver (1914).

Another transportation innovation of the early twentieth century, the Model-T Ford, sometimes made traveling to remote homesteads easier. Common practice when homesteaders arrived at the town closest to their claims was for a land locator to take them into the outlying area where he helped them find their designated property. By 1908, land locators often transported clients in Model-T Fords. Florence Blake Smith tells how her land locator confidently started out in his Model-T with three young women to find their claims. After the party was a considerable distance from town, the car became hopelessly stuck in the mud. The chagrined locator left the three women alone all day while he walked back for help. The women were eventually rescued and taken back to spend the night at a nearby ranch. Not surprisingly, they began their search for their claims the next day on horseback (Smith 1962).

Country Life and Back-to-the-Land Movements. Single women homesteaders were doubtless influenced in their decisions to move west by a growing national infatuation with country life. In the first decade of the twentieth century, country life became a popular theme in the magazines of the time, causing widespread "dreaming of, talking of, planning for, and oftentimes actually undertaking a move from the city to the farm" (Layton 1988, 18). This back-to-the-land movement had its origins in the Commission on Country Life, established by Theodore Roosevelt as a result of a concern about the exodus of population from farms to cities. The Commission's goal was to study the problems of the

Reconstruction of a homesteader claim shack interior at the Homestead Museum in Torrington, Wyoming. (*Mike Hensley*)

country's farms and to improve them. Its report coincided with the passage of the Enlarged Homestead Act of 1909, which doubled the amount of land one could acquire.

Stanford Layton's study of homesteading history quotes G. Walter Fiske's 1912 textbook *The Challenge of the Country: A Study of Country Life Opportunity*: "the city sapped the strength and virtue of those who ventured within it, giving nothing in return" (Layton 1988, 15). Fiske and numerous magazine and newspaper writers of the time promoted country life as a boon to both physical and psychological well-being. Fiske argues, "For centuries country people had made their way without cities. They could do so again. The cities, on the other hand, could not survive a month without sustenance from the country" (Layton 1980, 15). Evidence that single women were encouraged to participate in this movement appears in a 1913 article in *The Independent* magazine lauding the new "lady honyokers"—

its term for homesteading single women. The article's author, Mabel Lewis Stuart, concludes as follows:

> Instances might be multiplied of the ennobling work of our young women in the new West, and of their fine courage and determination. Surely they are to be congratulated upon the opportunity thus wisely seized upon— to become stable factors in the economic life of the nation—and upon their adaptability, energy and perseverance in triumphing over the trying conditions of pioneer life (1913, 137).

Second Generation Pioneer Women. Another reason homesteading by single women increased by the time of the Enlarged Homestead Acts of 1909 and 1912 is that by then the daughters of families who homesteaded in the late 1800s were coming of age. These young women had acquired skills needed to homestead while growing up on their parents' homesteads farther east and were no strangers to the hard work they were undertaking. A study of women homesteaders in Utah found that single women who filed were generally first and second generation descendents of Utah pioneers whose mothers "had been directly involved in the settlement of Utah's frontier lands and in many cases provided a role model that did not focus entirely on domestic duties" (Warnick 1985, 73–74). Single daughters of homesteaders and ranchers also became homesteaders to enlarge the family property. Marie Jordan Bell is a good example. She took out a homestead "up in the meadow near a tiny stream" near the family ranch. Her father fixed up a "little old house" for her and she lived there for the three years it took to prove up on her claim. Her father then leased the land from her, paying her every year, but eventually she sold it to him for a thousand dollars. Marie, married by then, used the money to fix up her new home (Jordan 1992, 26). Thus Marie helped increase the size of the family ranch and profited herself.

Of course, not all single women homesteaders grew up on farms or ranches; many were from cities or small towns and had no previous homesteading experience. These women found encouragement in the popular magazines of the day. Between 1913 and 1928 magazines such as *Sunset*, *Overland Monthly*, and *Atlantic Monthly* published how-to articles and testimonials of success by established single women homesteaders. The articles give specific advice about how to find land and file on it, what to bring along, and the cost of homesteading. Most of all, these articles enthusiastically endorse homesteading for single women. Dee Garceau points out that these "literary homesteaders presented their experience as a vehicle for developing emotional self-reliance, economic autonomy, and political clout" (1997, 123).

◊ Their Place in Literature

Single women homesteaders' stories are literary documents as well as historical records. The women wrote nonfiction narratives, but their real-life experiences often read like fiction. Thus it is useful to consider them from literary perspectives such as point of view, setting, style, character, plot, and theme as well as the interplay of mythic and realistic elements.

Point of View.

Women homesteader stories generally use the first person point of view because the woman describes her own experiences. The point of view may change subtly depending on whether the woman is writing at the time of homesteading or writing her memoir many years later. In stories written and published at the time they homesteaded, women write personal testimonials, providing details about how they actually accomplish homesteading. They confess some of their worries and brag a little about their accomplishments.

In letters, their first person point of view provides a more intimate and revealing picture of the writer, although the letters too include practical details of everyday life. In memoirs, the first person point of view often becomes reflective and philosophical. This book also includes third person accounts written about single women homesteaders for newspapers and magazines of the time.

Setting: Mountain and Plains Landscapes.

This book includes accounts by women from the Rocky Mountain states—Wyoming, Montana, Colorado, Idaho, and Utah—as well as the plains of North and South Dakota. Although the presence of mountain terrain and vistas influenced their perceptions of the land, most homesteaders found themselves in the valleys, basins, and plains at the foot of the mountains. Homesteaders of the early twentieth century ventured into arid, previously unproductive areas that the government had opened up to encourage the development of productive farm lands. Thus, they wrote more of sagebrush than of pine trees in their accounts, described vast expanses rather than sheltered mountain valleys, spoke more of irrigation, springs, and creeks than of rivers.

After arriving in Wyoming and discovering that the region has "just three seasons—winter and July and August"—Elinore Pruitt Stewart gave up her romantic notion of living "on the peaks among the whispering pines" and homesteaded in the valley below. On a trip to the county seat in Green River, she wrote to her friend Mrs. Coney that "for the whole sixty miles there was but one house, and going in that direction there is not a tree to be seen, nothing but sage, sand, and sheep" (1914, 6). A description of a sunset she witnessed later on that trip reveals her discovery of the beauty of such lonely places:

> It seemed as if we were driving through a golden haze. The violet shadows were creeping up between the hills, while away back of us the snow-capped peaks were catching the sun's last rays. On every side of us stretched the poor, hopeless desert, the sage, grim and determined to live in spite of starvation, the great, bare, desolate buttes (10).

Any twenty-first century reader who has driven the Interstate 80 corridor can relate to Stewart's description of Wyoming's landscape with its miles and miles of "bare, desolate buttes" and "grim and determined" sagebrush (1914, 10). In the narratives of single women homesteaders, as in all western literature, landscape has overriding importance. It is the stage on which women homesteaders play out their dramatic adventures. The land and its attendant climate can even be seen as characters in that drama, sometimes the woman's adversary, sometimes her friend, but certainly her ever-present companion.

Characters. Although the woman homesteader is the protagonist, other characters inhabit her accounts. Perhaps it is the sister or friend who has accompanied the woman on her adventure. Perhaps it is the mother at home to whom she writes her letters, or the man she has hired to help her do the hard physical labor on her claim. The extent to which the woman allows other characters to people the story of her homesteading suggests the importance of the person to her and to the success of the project. Although we seldom become as intimately acquainted with those characters as we do with the protagonist, these characters provide conflict and color in the stories just as they did in real life.

Plot. The plots in their stories grow naturally out of a retelling of the events in single women homesteaders' lives. As in fiction, their accounts have beginnings that set the scene and establish the conflicts, middles in which complications arise and conflicts escalate, and endings when the resolution, proving up her claim, results in personal empowerment. Occasionally, a writer begins with proving up and writes the rest of the story by using a flashback technique explaining how she did it, but for the most part the homesteading stories have linear plots. Although plots are not discernible in individual letters, patterns of action do emerge when one considers a woman's correspondence from beginning to end.

One of the most recognizable plots in American literature—the initiation story—dominates the narratives of single women homesteaders. In initiation stories the protagonist undergoes a trial or testing and emerges from it a better, wiser person. In these stories, a solitary woman ventures into unknown territory, tests herself against daunting conditions, and not only prevails but also wins the prizes of personal and economic independence. Every article, letter, and memoir written by a single woman homesteader reads like a testimonial to the benefits of homesteading for single women and exudes a sense of pride in accomplishment such as in the following glowing assessment by Metta Loomis:

> As for myself, I know of no other way by which, in five year's time, I could have acquired such riotous health, secured much valuable property, experienced so much joy in living, and infused so much of hope and buoyancy into life, and no other way to provide such cheering prospects for my old age (1916, 64).

Their initiations made women homesteaders realize and cherish their independence. Their testimonials weigh the tangible rewards of property ownership, financial security, and improved health equally with the intangible rewards of independence, freedom, patriotism, status, and a sense of hope for the future. Joy in living seems to have been as valuable a payoff as was the deed showing that they had proved up on their claims.

Style. Whether they were writing letters to an audience of family and friends or writing for publication to wider audiences, single women homesteaders crafted their stories carefully to create their own distinctive voices. Numerous stylistic variations occur to surprise and delight the reader as in Katherine Garetson's descriptions of autumn at her mountain homestead when "leaves lie pale and motionless on dark pools under skies of deep blue" and the "crispness and brilliancy of atmosphere dance me through November until I am bound by the snows of December" (1989, 66).

Although sections of single women homesteaders' stories may have the factual, practical style of an instruction manual, the writers also employ literary devices to enhance the readability of their accounts, including personification, allusion, figurative language, and sentence variety to paint vivid pictures of their surroundings, their experiences, and their emotions.

Theme. Several themes emerge in the body of literature written by single women homesteaders. The desire for freedom, independence, and escape from the pressures of their former lives as well as the hope of economic gain and security are some of the reasons single women homesteaded, and these themes surface in every account. The importance of cooperation also emerges as an underlying theme in virtually every story by or about a women homesteader. Examining these themes sheds light on a question readers of their narratives inevitably ponder: why did single women homestead?

Freedom, Escape, Independence. Women homesteaders' stories reveal that the open, unsettled land of the West had the same magnetic appeal to single women homesteaders as it had to the masculine explorers and pioneers who ventured west before them: it offered freedom, escape from repressive circumstances, and independence. In her article in *Sunset* magazine, "The Lure of the West for Women," May Holaday observes that for her the chief appeal of the West was its independent spirit:

> In fact I began to feel it in the air while crossing the Rockies and straight away my former ideas of the importance of class distinction and the observance of social conventions seemed to fall from me like a heavy cloak, which had long been a burden—and I was free (1917, 61).

In their search for freedom, escape, and independence, single woman homesteaders naturally began with a journey, thus their stories become part of a tradition of journey literature in which a protagonist embarks on a quest for self-fulfillment and home-founding. America's history and literature are replete with such journey stories. Think of Daniel Boone, Huck Finn, or the Joad family in *The Grapes of Wrath*, who assume heroic qualities through their journeys west (Stout 1983). While women homesteaders were unlikely to have been following this tradition purposefully, they were likely to have seen their journeys in a positive light because those themes are so pervasive in American culture.

Economic Security. Single women homesteaders realized that the independence they desired required them to earn their own way and to provide their own financial security. Like many others, these women were likely influenced by the enormously popular nineteenth century stories of Horatio Alger in which economic gain is the reward for hard work. As women in the early part of the twentieth century gained confidence in their ability and right to be independent, they must have believed that the Horatio Alger success story need not be limited to men. Single women homesteaders' stories show that they were entrepreneurs willing to take a risk that led to improvement of their financial standing, although their goals were economic security rather than great wealth. This concern with economic matters is evident in the fact that their writings often contain careful accounting of the costs involved and the profits earned. Even women with good teaching jobs such as Metta Loomis and Alice Newberry had no retirement pensions. They saw their homesteads as investments that would provide for their old age if they never married. The belief that homesteading would provide financial security previously possible to women only if they made good marriages appears often in the their accounts.

Cooperation. Although the desire for independence was certainly a factor in a woman's decision to homestead, the fact of the matter is she also required assistance occasionally; therefore, the theme of cooperation makes an appearance often in these stories. Most of the women hired men to build their claim shacks, break sod for their crops, and help with the harvest. Without this cooperation, a single woman homesteader's experience, though not impossible, was much more difficult.

Another form of cooperation the stories describe is the practice of pooling their resources with other women to cope with the difficulties of homesteading. A colleague from her Iowa school joined Metta Loomis in the homesteading venture, which proved quite successful. Other women did the same. Helen Coburn and Mary Culbertson moved from Carroll, Iowa, together, filed on adjacent claims near Worland, Wyoming, and built a claim shack that straddled their property lines ("Experiences of Miss Mary Culbertson" 1936). Thus they could live in the same house while proving up. In one instance four women homesteading in Wyoming filed on four adjoining parcels of land and built adjacent one-room cabins at the corner where all four properties came together. Local cowboys who stopped by to socialize named the area Calico Hill (Bauman 1986). Women recognized the advantages of pooling their resources, having someone to share the work, and having companionship during the seven months of each year they were required to live in relative isolation on their claims. Cooperation with sisters, friends, masculine relatives, and hired help increased the odds that single women would succeed in homesteading.

Myth or Reality? Another question facing those who explore single women homesteaders' writing is to what extent did each woman write fact or create fiction? The articles, memoirs, and letters in this book are broadly defined as nonfiction writing; yet, even writers of nonfiction creatively select, omit, emphasize, or minimize to shape experience into story.

On the whole, women who wrote about their experiences homesteading alone told positive stories. Their magazine articles stress the feasibility of homesteading for women and illustrate how capable they were of assuming work roles formerly considered suitable only for men. Their optimistic stories of frontier achievement must have inspired many young women to stretch the limits of their circumstances whether or not they homesteaded. An idealized perception of the single woman homesteader emerges from these popular magazine accounts of the time and later is echoed in homesteaders' memoirs. It goes something like this: Single women homesteaders were courageous and optimistic. Although homesteading was difficult, they achieved success and had many enjoyable adventures as well. Women could do most of the work themselves, but, if necessary, they could count on help from neighbors, family, or one of the many men in the vicinity.

Common sense suggests, however, that not every single woman who took out a claim had a positive experience. Statistics compiled about single women homesteading in Wyoming show that approximately one in three women who filed on land actually proved up on their claims (Bauman 1986). Understandably, those two out of three who did not succeed were less likely to write articles or books about their experiences.

In a 1921 article about her homesteading experience in northeastern Utah, Kate Heizer includes a section titled "Not All Roses" in which she cautions that for the typical homesteader without much money "the first two or three years . . . are usually accompanied by privation and hardship." She lists such difficulties as the high cost of freighting supplies in and having your claim "contested" if you were absent for very long. Her "greatest torments were the rabbits and prairie dogs" that destroyed gardens in spite of "scarecrows, guns and poison" (1921, 37).

Looking back on her homestead experience, Dr. Bessie Rehwinkle tempers her account of the exhilarating experience of becoming a Wyoming landowner with the admission that "it is not as easy or glamorous as the storybooks about the westward trek of the covered wagon often picture it. It is a slow process and a hard day-by-day struggle, and only the strongest are able to survive" (Rehwinkel 1963, 57).

Although there is less talk of fear than one might expect in their stories, some women admitted to being fearful on their claims alone. No harm came to any of the women whose homesteading accounts I have read. Occasionally, however, their stories reveal that they were vulnerable to various dangers while living alone in isolated places. Perhaps some of the women who did not succeed, and therefore did not write about their homesteading experiences, were not so fortunate. Even though in most single women's accounts of homesteading the writers do not admit openly to having difficulties or fears, when one reads between the lines of their optimistic accounts, one can reasonably infer the reality that their homesteading experiences were not all a "bed of roses."

2. Getting Acquainted: Meet the Single Women Homesteaders

· ·

Once I was asked to do a twenty-minute reading from this manuscript. As I skimmed the pages looking for an excerpt that would capture the book's essence and the audience's attention, I found it nearly impossible to make a choice. Each woman's story was special; each story was unique. It was as if after a long silence, once I had gathered them together, they all clamored to tell the stories of their homesteading years. I could almost see them waving their hands in the air like a class of eager students and hear them shouting out "Choose me! Choose me." It made me realize how alive these women were to me. I had spent the previous four years searching for and discovering them, then getting to know them through reading and rereading their words. I had spent more time with them than with most of my friends who, when we did get together, had to endure my excited retelling of whatever women homesteader story I was currently researching.

Are the women in this anthology representative? I can't be certain. But I do know that, at least by default, they have taken on the role of spokespersons for all women who homesteaded alone because they were the ones who described their experiences.

◊ Numbers Don't Lie

People are often surprised to discover how many single women actually did homestead. The twenty-one women profiled, along with the dozen or so mentioned by journalists in this anthology, are a small but vociferous sample of single women homesteaders. According to statistics provided by the National Homestead Monument, two million people attempted to earn a patent on land through the Homestead Act. Homesteading became possible in 1862 and continued to 1976 when the Federal Land Policy and Management Act repealed it in all states except Alaska, which was allowed a ten-year extension (National Park Service 2007). There are no nationwide statistics documenting how many of the two million homesteaders were unmarried women, but my research suggests that as many as 200,000 women may have attempted to homestead, and, of those, as many as 67,500 may have successfully proved up.[1]

A 1911 *Collier's* article asserts that "men who handle the statistics of the Land Office hazard the guess" that single women homesteaders are "two thousand strong" (Brush 1911, 16). Unfortunately the article fails to say whether those numbers refer to state, regional, or national homestead records. A 1915 article in the *Denver Times* headlined "Women Are Taking Up Much Land in Colorado" reports that "almost 50 percent of the homesteads now are taken up by women" (2). Even without a nationwide compilation of statistics, data from several states where homesteading was popular in the late nineteenth and early twentieth centuries reflect reliably the percentages of women homesteaders throughout the West. Sheryll and Gene Patterson-Black researched land office records in Lamar, Colorado, and Douglas, Wyoming, for the years 1887, 1891, 1907, and 1908. They found 11.9 percent of those who filed were women and the percentage of women increased as years passed, varying from 4.8 percent in Douglas in 1891 to 18.2 percent in Lamar in 1907 (1978). In her study of single women homesteaders in six Wyoming counties between 1888 and 1943, Paula Bauman also found that nearly 12 percent of the entrants were women (1986).

Elaine Lindgren's research in nine North Dakota counties resulted in the same estimate: 12 percent of homesteaders were single women (1996, 51). When Jill Thorley Warnick surveyed Bureau of Land Management records of Land Claims in Utah, she found that 13.5 percent of Utah's land claimants were women (1985, 36). Warnick then conducted a more detailed search in tract entry books in three areas of the state in which homesteading took place. This search found similar numbers of single women homesteaders: 12.9 percent in the Cedar City area; 12.5 percent in the Logan area; 9.9 percent in the Monticello region (1985, 47–48). In a study of Washington and Logan counties of northeastern Colorado, Katherine Harris found that before 1900, single women made up 12 percent of those who homesteaded, and after 1900, the percentage rose to 18 percent (1993, 20).

◊ *Success Rates*

Readers may question how successful single women were in actually proving up on their claims. When Bauman addressed this question in her study, she found that in Wyoming 42 percent of women who filed on land successfully proved up compared with a 37 percent success rate for men who filed (1986, 48). Warnick's study of Utah women homesteaders showed remarkably similar success rates for men and women. In the three areas she studied, Warnick found success rates for women of 42.7 percent in the Cedar City area, 31.9 percent in the Logan area, and 39 percent in the Monticello area, almost identical to the success rates of male home-steaders in the same regions (1985, 56). Harris's study of northeastern Colorado homesteaders found the success rates of men and women to be "nearly identical—in the neighborhood of 50 percent" (1993, 21). In her comparison of homesteaders in North Dakota, Lindgren also found similar rates for both male and female homesteaders. In one of the two North Dakota counties she studied, 28 percent of men canceled their rights compared with 24 percent of women. In the other, 29 percent of men and 32 percent of women failed to prove up their claims (1996, 224). As Cecelia Weiss comments in a *Sunset* article, "There have been times when it has been very hard to stay, but I have never even thought of quitting, though scores of men in this vicinity have been unable to hold on" (Armstrong 1916, 25).

As much as I admire the successful single women homesteaders in this anthology, I am also aware that they are the lucky 42 percent. I am troubled by the thought of the other 58 percent, the single women who just as optimistically claimed homestead land but failed to prove up. The stories in this anthology offer few clues to why a woman would give up her claim. Was it fear? Kate Heizer spends a frightening Christmas vacation alone on her claim, wondering whether the howling wolves circling her cabin could break in. Cecelia Weiss tells of barricading her cabin door on at least one occasion, fearing human intruders. Animals from mice to porcupines terrorize Madge Funk alone in her cabin. Did loneliness and hardship defeat some women? Katherine Garetson writes of wintering in her mountain home, an isolation that caused her companion homesteader to leave after the first winter. Florence Blake Smith and many others remark on the frustrations of trying to grow crops in less-than-ideal soil and weather conditions. Then there was the problem of earning enough money to make required improvements on the land. And as Bessie Rehwinkle points out, the romance and glamour of the idea of homesteading soon gave way to the reality of a hard day-to-day struggle.[2] Although the women in this

This elegantly appointed claim shack of homesteader Mary Bonertz Dugan in Perkins County, South Dakota, shows how women homesteaders could transform crudely constructed claim shacks into inviting and efficient living spaces. (*The Virginia Dugan Rozum Family Collection*)

book don't mention it, perhaps some women were made to feel unwelcome by fellow homesteaders who might have seen an unmarried woman homesteading alone as peculiar.

Lindgren also studied the length of time women homesteaders stayed on their land. She found that "60 percent stayed little longer than the time required to meet the residency requirements, but 18 percent stayed on the land from six to twenty-four years, and 22 percent remained on their land from 25 years to most of their lifetimes" (1996, 191).

The length of time homesteaders stayed on their land is not the only measure of their success. Lindgren found that women homesteaders benefited from their claims at various stages of ownership. Those who sold soon after proving up often used the profits to reach other goals such as advancing their education. Some, like Alice Newberry, who left her claim after proving up, retained ownership for many years, benefiting from the income that rental of the property provided. Others consolidated their property with that of a husband or family member. For others the land became an asset to fall back on in later years (Lindgren 1996).

◊ Who Were They?

Studies of age and ethnicity show that homesteading women came from varied backgrounds and life experiences. Research indicates that the majority were white women twenty-one to thirty years of age. Although most single women homesteaders had not been married previously, a small percentage were widows or abandoned wives (Bauman 1986). Emma Peterson, in her mid-fifties, childless, and widowed twice, moved from Omaha, Nebraska, to Wyoming to make a fresh start homesteading (Thorpe 1976). Glenda Riley provides two examples of divorced women homesteading: a woman who homesteaded on 360 acres in Montana with her four-year-old daughter, and a divorced woman with a four-month-old child who joined the Oklahoma Land Run. Jill Thorley Warnick notes that some Utah women who filed under maiden names were actually polygamous wives as in the case of Mary Ann Wilson, who had been the second wife of Henry Lunt for thirty-seven years at the time she filed for a homestead under her maiden name. Perhaps Wilson established a separate household because of estrangement from her husband or, since entries by polygamous women as head of a household were unlawful, because she wished to "circumvent the law to add to the husband's land holdings" (Warnick 1985, 69).

Elaine Lindgren found some ethnic diversity in North Dakota women homesteaders. She identifies five black women who filed on homestead land. In addition, 29 percent of the women homesteaders in North Dakota were immigrants, primarily from Scandinavian countries and Canada. Lindgren also notes that single women homesteaded as part of Lebanese and Jewish colonies in the state. Further evidence of immigrant women homesteaders appears in community histories such as *Wheels Across Montana's Prairies*, which includes the account of Cecelia Mattinsen, who came from Denmark to homestead in 1913, and Kate McMurray, who immigrated from Ireland with her family and later homesteaded alone (Prairie County Historical Society 1974).

Paula Bauman's study reveals that most Wyoming women homesteaders migrated from nearby states, such as Nebraska and Iowa, and were American-born. Her findings are corroborated by an article in the Riverton, Wyoming, newspaper published after land on the Wind River Reservation opened up for homesteading in 1920. This special issue of the *Riverton Chronicle* reported that nine of the first one hundred people to file were women. Four of them came from other parts of Wyoming and five were from states to the east: Nebraska, Illinois, Iowa, and Ohio (Chenery 1926). Similarly, Katherine Harris found that most women homesteaders in northeastern Colorado were white and American-born (1993). The reason for greater ethnic diversity in North Dakota and Montana has not been studied; however, a plausible explanation might be the degree to which railroad companies advertised homesteading opportunities in those regions abroad and within the United States.

A significant number of women homesteaders had some sort of professional training. Many were schoolteachers who found that teaching a rural school while homesteading was a good way to augment their income. Others were trained as physicians, nurses, accountants, or secretaries. Often the additional income they earned from these professions allowed the women to hire male workers to help them make improvements required on their homesteads. A 1915 *Denver Times* article reports that "Many teachers, nurses and stenographers take up claims and . . . express themselves as delighted with the restful atmosphere" ("Women Are Taking Up Much Land in Colorado" 1915, 1). However, the amount of education she had seems to have had little bearing on a woman's success as a homesteader, and experience with farming or ranching was also not a prerequisite for success. Instead, requirements for success seem to have more to do with one's nature. Cecelia Weiss calls it "pluck," and Elinore Pruitt Stewart explains it thusly in a letter to her former employer in Denver:

> To me, homesteading is the solution of all poverty's problems, but I realize that temperament has much to do with success in any undertaking,

and persons afraid of coyotes and work and loneliness had better let ranching alone. At the same time, any woman who can stand her own company, can see the beauty of the sunset, loves growing things, and is willing to put in as much time at careful labor as she does over the washtub, will certainly succeed; will have independence, plenty to eat all the time, and a home of her own in the end (1914, 215).

◊ A Goal of Marriage?

What are we to make of the fact that the very author of the above quote, Elinore Pruitt, married her employer Clyde Stewart eight weeks after she arrived in Wyoming and only one week after she filed on homestead land adjacent to his ranch (George 1992)? Could single women homesteaders have been motivated not so much out of a desire for autonomy as out of a desire for matrimony? In the American society of the early twentieth century, marriage was the culturally approved option for women and being married the most approved status. Popular literature of the day, domestic novels, and women's magazines assumed that most women aspired to marriage.

Given the cultural pressures to marry, is it possible that single women homesteaders were simply husband hunting? As there were more men than women in the West, perhaps a girl might think that her chance for finding a spouse would improve there. And if she also owned 160 acres of land, she might reason that such a dowry would make her a more attractive marriage partner.

Elinore Pruitt Stewart's biographer, Susanne George, explores the complicated motivations behind Elinore's seemingly hasty relinquishment of the freedom she professed to want. Perhaps Elinore was a realist who saw the impossibility of proving up on a homestead on her own while also working full-time at the housekeeping job she had been hired by Clyde to do. Perhaps she was a romantic who fell in love at first sight. Elinore's daughter, Jerrine, believes "that what began as a strictly business affair blossomed into love . . . because of mutual attraction and the need each had for the other" (George 1992, 13). Stewart herself delayed confession of her marriage to her former employer and correspondent Mrs. Coney, saying "It was such an inconsistent thing to do that I was ashamed to tell you" (Stewart 1914, 79–80).

The fact that Elinore chose to marry when she had the opportunity does not necessarily mean that marriage was the reason she moved west. Historian Susan Hallgarth remarks, "It might seem natural to assume that since women were scarce and marriage was the social norm, all women in the West either were married or soon would be. The facts, however, do not bear out that assumption" (1989, 26). Statistics on marriage patterns of single women homesteaders shed some light on whether marriage was a high priority for them. Bauman's study of single women homesteaders identifies fifty-two single women homesteaders in Natrona County, Wyoming, between 1890 and 1908. Of those women, seventeen had married between the time of filing and proving up, thirty-five (69.8 percent) remained single. Of twenty-one women homesteaders in Laramie County, Wyoming, five married, but sixteen did not (1986, 48).

Elaine Lindgren's study of North Dakota single women homesteaders notes that in a sample of 167 women, 57 percent did not marry between the time of filing and proving up while 43 percent did. Lindgren's study also demonstrates that if they did marry, women homesteaders were in no hurry to do so. The median age of marriage for women homesteaders was 27 years compared with a median age at first marriage of 22 years for the general population of the United States in the years 1890, 1900, and 1910 (1996, 112–113). These statistics show that it would be an error to assume that marriage was a major motivating factor for single women homesteaders. Among these women, however, some may have thought of future marriage to a western man as a possibility they did not oppose. If marriage happened, so much the better, but meanwhile these women were learning that they were capable of taking care of themselves.

◊ New Friends from the Past

Having learned, in general, who these single women homesteaders were and a bit about their rates of success, it's time to meet their spokespersons. The women whose voices you hear in this anthology are Elizabeth Abbey Everette, Metta Loomis, Cecelia Weiss, A. May Holaday, Zay Philbrook, Kate Heizer, Alice Newberry, Julia Erickson Stockton, Ida Gwynn Garvin, Dr. Bessie Efner Rehwinkle, Katherine Garetson, Alice Hildreth Zehm, Florence Blake Smith, Madge McHugh Funk, Mary Culbertson, Helen Coburn Howell, Mary Sheehan Steinbrech, Nellie Burgess, Esther Dollard, Geraldine Lucas, Emma Peterson, and the unnamed women quoted in the stories of journalists Mary Isabel Brush, Joanna Gleed Strange, and Mabel Lewis Stuart.

If it hadn't been for Elinore Pruitt Stewart, I would have never come to know these women. I became acquainted with Elinore through her book, *Letters of a Woman Homesteader* (1914), shortly after I moved to Wyoming in 1983. Reading Elinore's letters made me question the western history texts I read that proclaimed women were reluctant pioneers. That certainly didn't fit Elinore's experience or my own. Having made a recent move from a city with the same population as the entire state of Wyoming, I could identify with the West's pioneer women; having settled in southwest Wyoming as Elinore did, I could identify with her in particular.

I wondered whether other single women homesteaders had written about their experiences. First, I looked for women homesteaders in Wyoming and as they began to reveal themselves, I found links to single women who homesteaded in neighboring states. I owe as much to serendipity as to scholarship in finding these women's stories. People who knew of my interest might suggest a person they knew of or a book they had read. A footnote in a scholarly article might suggest a possible source. Even an Internet search for "single women homesteader" paid off as in my discovery of the Estes Park women homesteaders.

The more stories I read, the more my hunch was confirmed: numerous women were eager for and empowered by their homesteading experiences. By capturing in written words what it was like for a woman to stake a claim and prove it up on her own, my new friends from the past had created a time capsule, just waiting for a new era of readers.

neglected, and many congenial friends can be found among the settlers. To be sure, one does not have regular calling hours, for visits in the sagebrush are made by the day. One goes before breakfast, as it were, and stays until evening. Distances between the homes are too great to be taken lightly. But parties in the land of hope and thirst are just as much fun as they are in the city and many of them are made to serve useful purposes as well. If a homesteader has a big job on hand he invites all of his friends. After many hands have made light work of the task there are "eats" for which every one is more than ready, and thereafter the festivities begin. A potato picking party to which my sister and I were invited by a homesteader who lived several miles away proved almost to be our Waterloo.

On this occasion no one near us was going, so we decided to rent the horse and wagon of a neighbor. The horse, the wagon and the harness had been brought around and left the night before. When we were ready to start, a serious problem confronted us. Neither my sister nor I had ever harnessed a horse. The straps, buckles and hooks with which he was to be attached to the wagon completely mystified us. For long minutes we stood and looked at him, waiting for inspiration. As no inspiration came, we began to try first this and then that combination, but without results satisfactory to the horse. At last the power of advertising made itself felt. I remembered the harness catalogue I had sent for. With the aid of its pictures, working slowly and systematically, we finally had the animal all hitched and buckled up ready for action. Not particularly confident even at that, we decided to stop at the house of a friend who lived on the way, to have him look over the job. As usually happens in such cases, he was not at home when wanted, but we reached our destination without mishap and were much commended.

One has friends here as elsewhere and I dress as becomingly as I can. Why shouldn't one look pretty if one can? That isn't a crime, although a girl must be rather conservative in the sagebrush. Since, as before mentioned, the people do not have much diversion and therefore take a lively interest in each others' affairs, a young woman alone must be more than conventional to avoid being talked about. It is not sufficient that she avoid evil itself; she must avoid even the least appearance of evil. We young people, for example, like to get together for a chat now and then and the young men are disposed to call on the young women out here just as normal young men are everywhere. But when a young fellow from a distant farm rides over to call on me, I cannot ask him into my home. To be sure there is no other place except a hard wooden bench in the broiling sun on which to sit, but that is not the point. It is not proper to ask a man inside, for I have but one room and no chaperon. So we look for the soft side of the bench, try to find a few feet of shadow cast by the Piano Box and thoroughly enjoy ourselves in spite of everybody.

I have often been asked if it is not dangerous for a girl to live alone in a sparsely populated, isolated place. I have never been very much afraid, although there are

STATEMENT OF THE OWNERSHIP MANAGEMENT, ETC.
of SUNSET, The Pacific Monthly, published monthly at San Francisco, Cal., required by the Act of August 24, 1912

Name of   Post-Office Address
Publisher, Woodhead, Field & Company   San Francisco
Editor, Charles K. Field   San Francisco
Managing Editor, Walter V. Woehlke   San Francisco
General Manager, William Woodhead   San Francisco

Owners: (If a corporation, give its name and the names and addresses of stockholders holding 1 per cent or more of the total amount of stock.)

Woodhead, Field & Company;
William Woodhead, San Francisco   Willard M. Wilson, ...
Charles K. Field, San Francisco   ...-Park; N.Y.
Walter V. Woehlke, San Francisco   Graham C. Patterson, ...
Robert R. Anderson, San Francisco   ..., Ill.
Robert Green, San Francisco

Known bondholders, mortgagees, and other security holders holding 1 per cent or more of total amount of bonds, mortgages, or other securities:

William Woodhead, San Francisco
Isadore Zellerbach, San Francisco
William Haworth, Everett, Wash.
James R. Anderson, San Francisco
Lillie A. Anderson, San Francisco

Woodhead, Field & Company
per William Woodhead,
General Manager

Sworn to and subscribed before me this 24th day of April, ...

3. Heroines of the Popular Press: Homesteaders' Stories, 1911–1928

The first published accounts of single women homesteaders' experiences appeared in popular magazines. According to Frank Mott's *A History of American Magazines*, periodicals widely circulated in the early twentieth century exercised "an almost incalculable influence upon the moral and intellectual development of individuals, upon home life, and upon public opinion" (1957, 14). Another study estimates that in 1905 the average household subscribed to four magazines (Honey 1992, 3). *Collier's*, one of the magazines that published stories about single women homesteaders, had a circulation of almost a million readers in 1905 (Mott 1957, 59). The fact that at least thirty articles by or about single women homesteaders appeared in these periodicals between 1913 and 1928 suggests that stories with the theme of female independence appealed to readers of general interest magazines such as *Collier's*, *Atlantic Monthly*, *The Independent*, *Overland Monthly*, and *Sunset*.

Another factor influencing magazine publishers to print stories of single women homesteaders was a national interest in the back-to-the-land movement during the early part of the twentieth century (Layton 1988, 15). It is possible that women reading the stories of single women homesteaders in magazines may have been encouraged to try homesteading themselves.

Magazines printed stories with a promotional tone, as if trying to convince readers to take a chance on homesteading. For example *Sunset* magazine, owned and operated by the Southern Pacific Railroad from 1898 to 1916, promoted travel and settlement of the area it served (Star, online article). Thus it is not surprising that stories of successful women homesteaders appeared frequently in *Sunset*. Likewise, *Overland Monthly*, published in San Francisco, "was much given to promotion" of the West (Mott 1967, 409) and favored articles focused on western topics.

Written during the time the women were actually homesteading or shortly after they had proved up, these accounts are consistently optimistic, focusing on useful information about homesteading and glowing reports of its rewards. Whether written by the homesteader or by someone else, most of these articles combine the characteristics of instruction manual and testimonial, revealing how a young woman alone has gone about the business of homesteading and how she has improved her life by doing so.

◊ Telling Their Own Stories

The following accounts of homesteaders Elizabeth Abbey Everett, Metta M. Loomis, Cecelia Weiss, A. May Holaday, Zay Philbrook, and Kate L. Heizer appear in chronological order by date of original publication. With a humorous tone, contrasting with the earnest and straightforward narratives of most single women homesteaders, Elizabeth Abbey Everett speaks of government claims as gifts from her Uncle Sam, extending the personification throughout the piece. In accounting for both the costs and rewards of homesteading, Metta Loomis admits that as the daughter of an Iowa farmer, she has an advantage over other homesteaders; yet, she suggests the experience would go better for her if she had another woman homesteading nearby. A unique feature of Cecelia Weiss's story is her concern with the social aspects of homesteading, especially courting practices, and hers is one of the few narratives to discuss overtly the problems an unchaperoned woman faces. May Holaday's article celebrates the liberation from social constraints that women felt as a result of their westward moves, arguing that in the West a woman is allowed to redefine her identity and place in society. Zay Philbrook acquired her home in the West by making a "Timber and Stone" claim rather than a homestead claim, which, she explains, has the advantage of not requiring residency or improvement, although she had to buy the land outright from the government. Although Zay does not mention her profession, the fact that she spent only summers on the ranch suggests that she was a schoolteacher. Another teacher, Kate Heizer, offers advice in her article to all homesteaders, not just women, giving more attention to the stressful process of choosing the land than do other writers in this collection and discussing openly "why homesteader's fail." She also writes of quality of life issues, which women's homesteading stories do not typically address, observing that compared with repetitious jobs with little hope for advancement in urban areas, a homesteader's life with all its deprivation is compensated by variety of work, hope for the future, and a chance to play an important part in the community.

Elizabeth Abbey Everett — 1913
"Uncle's Gift"
The Independent, January 1913

The day I was twenty-one my Uncle Sam offered me a farm for a birthday present. I had not finished my education and I didn't think much about the gift then, especially as he said the offer would hold good until I married.

Uncle Sam is my uncle on my father's side. He has never shown much confidence in my mother's business management, nor, in fact, in any of us women folk.

After I had taught a few years, I got rather tired of the confinement of the schoolroom and began to realize, as most teachers do at some time or other, that though teaching looks, at a distance, very profitable, in reality it does not give much opportunity to secure a competence for one's later years. Then I began to think with interest of Uncle's offer.

He is generous in a way, but he has some frugal ideas. He always told us frankly that he was not giving us the land to speculate with, and he seemed afraid that we would not appreciate the value of the gift. So the chief condition he made was that we should live on the land for five years and improve it, before he would give us our deeds to it. I should have said before that he had made the same offer to all his nieces and nephews, except that he said nothing to the boys about withdrawing the offer when they married. But that is quite in accord with Uncle's ideas.

Sometimes Uncle is better than his word. When Cousin Jack came back after three years' service in the Philippines, he accepted Uncle's offer. But he had lived on the farm he selected only two years when he received a deed to it. Uncle likes to encourage patriotism, and he said that anyone who was brave and devoted enough to fight for his country ought to be encouraged. So he deducted the term of Jack's service from the five years he required of the rest of us. He offered to do the same for Cousin Jerry if he would serve in the navy, but Jerry preferred to stay on land.

It happened that brother and Cousin Caroline had chosen adjoining farms. They got pretty well acquainted, and thought a good deal of each other. Brother didn't enjoy doing his own housework, and Caroline didn't like to split kindling, so they decided to marry and continue improving their farms together. But when they spoke to Uncle Sam about it he said he was willing, only they would be one family then, and would need only one farm. They might choose either one they wished, but they could have only one. They decided to wait and not marry until they both had their farms, but they seemed to feel a little hurt and thought that Uncle Sam was rather parsimonious.

And really, you know, he does seem that way sometimes. He has let the people who work for him bamboozle him most shamefully, and some of his prosperous relatives have worked him to a finish. Every once in a while he seems to wake up to the fact that he is being tricked. That makes him suspicious of the others, and he imposes very hampering restrictions on some of his poor relations, often on those who are trying hardest to please him. I will say for Uncle Sam that I think he is better to his poor relations than anyone else I know of, and he is very generous about adopting anyone who asks, and he tries to give them all an equal chance, but he is too lenient, and lets selfish people abuse his generosity; then he turns severe, and it isn't always the guilty ones who suffer. He is fair-minded, tho, in this way: to those of us who did follow out the rules he laid down for us he gave the farms he had promised willingly, but you know it is a little irritating to have to conform to a lot of persnickety regulations when you see other people disregarding real essentials and getting the same benefits.

Of course these criticisms are all in the family. I notice that a good deal of the grumbling about Uncle Sam that is indulged in is just a sort of mild enjoyment of a family privilege. I must admit, tho, that it is rather bad manners.

Personally I've found Uncle a very pleasant old gentleman. I've got pretty well acquainted with him thru trying to understand what he wanted me to do. He is always interested in education, and very generous in helping it on. He is public-spirited, too, and he has given a good deal of land and money at different times to induce companies to build railroads into unsettled parts of the country. Sometimes, it is true, his benefactions have seemed rather ill-advised, but he meant them well.

He is very fond of trees, too, and has planted a good many in different parts of his estate, and works very hard to prevent fires among them. He is planning to do a lot more planting, and he told us when we choose our farms that if he decided to turn that part of the estate into woodland he wanted to reserve the right to do so; but, in that case, he would let us pick out a farm somewhere else in exchange for ours. There are some of his nephews who have used this generous offer really to swindle—well, I won't criticize, since it is all in the family. He used to be very free about making gifts of valuable timber lands, but I guess he is learning a thing or two.

He has always been very careful about giving away mining land, when he gives any of his relatives a present he always mentions that he is giving it to them to encourage an interest in farming, and if they find gold or any other mineral on it before he has actually given them the deed to it he expects them to tell him and give the land back. But that is fair enough.

In fact Uncle Sam is fair and generous; at least I have found him so. And, while we are talking about it, it occurs to me that my Uncle Sam is your Uncle Sam, too. Why don't you ask him for a farm?

Metta M. Loomis — 1916
"From Schoolroom to Montana Ranch"
Overland Monthly, January 1916

"I wish that we were safe on some good farm."

How often one hears the wish from those who are noting the advancing price of farm products and the shifting business values of war times. This condition produces a feeling of uncertainty that is serving to awaken a new interest in farming, and increase the number who are trying to find a way "back to the land."

It is an undertaking for a man to cut loose from the anchorage of a comfortable salary and stake his future on a homestead, but for a woman to venture such an undertaking requires more than ordinary fortitude. When a woman is successful in making one of Uncle Sam's farms pay her in money and health and happiness, the knowledge of her work becomes a source of inspiration and encouragement to those who are wishing for the security of a farm. It was in the hope of furnishing such encouragement that a woman who has converted one of Uncle Sam's homesteads into a flourishing farm has been persuaded to tell her story—to report her efforts, and furnish statistics of her work—to blase a trail of personal experience that may be some guide to others who may be trying to find a way "back to the land."

"My story starts on an Iowa farm," began the narrator as she looked with satisfaction over her own farm, so beautiful with spring's promise of autumn's harvest. "My farmer kin all enjoyed the rural life, but they all assured me that farming was drudgery, and congratulated me on my great good fortune in escaping from the labor of the farm for the easy work of teaching school.

"Some way, I don't seem to be made to live within doors, and the enthusiasm with which I began teaching very soon began to wane and was slowly but surely replaced by a longing for horizons instead of walls—a longing which must be felt by thousands who chafe against the ceaseless grind and close confinement of the school room, the office, the shop and the factory.

"I happened to be teaching in Montana at the time the bench lands near Ft. Benton were opened to settlement. My nerves were out of tune, and I felt that life was pretty much of a squeezed orange, but I had enough energy to

Metta Loomis, seated here in the doorway of the home she built on her homestead, worked hard to succeed at homesteading while continuing her teaching
career. (Overland Monthly, *January, 1916*)

react to the land fever excitement, and it was not long before I was planning
my return to farm life with all the eagerness that I had felt in leaving it.

"The lone man is much handicapped when he becomes a homesteader,
but the lone woman is almost incapacitated for homesteading, and her first
move towards entering a claim for a homestead should be to induce some
other woman to join her. Two women taking up adjoining claims can build
near enough together to utilize the same machinery and to save expense in
hiring help, and also to provide mutual protection—protection not so much
from physical danger as from that sense of loneliness that comes when one
lives without companionship amid the overpowering forces of nature, in the
rough, unsubdued by civilization.

"I broached my farm scheme to a kindergartner who assured me that she would just love to have a farm, because it was such fun picking flowers, and she loved fresh vegetables. I knew something about the work and care needed to make a success of a farm, and I decided it would be folly for me to try to make such blissful ignorance wise to the realities of the farm. Next I tried some of our older teachers, but they refused to commit themselves except to say: 'If I were only a man I would do it in a minute.'

"I felt that I had every qualification for farming that a man has except the brute strength, and I argued that that was the cheapest commodity to hire. As long as our Uncle Sam would allow teachers the privilege of proving up on a claim while continuing their school work, I proposed to work for a vine and fig tree of my own, rather than to content myself with the cheerless prospect of an old ladies' home or a teacher's pension.

"My enthusiasm finally became contagious enough to induce our drawing supervisor to join me in my plan to take up a homestead. She had health and one hundred dollars in the bank. I had a brother who was making good as a homesteader, and four hundred dollars in cash, besides we both had positions, good for fourteen hundred, and one thousand respectively. Thus equipped, we proposed to take up a claim, engage in dry farming, and use our salary to convert our three hundred and twenty acres of wild grassland into a prosperous farm. Our plan was to raise all the varieties of grain that are adapted to the climate, keep as much stock as we could feed, besides raising garden truck and poultry to supply our living, and to sell if there were a market for it.

"The filing of our application and the drawing of our land was quite as conventional as securing a teacher's certificate, but conventionality ceased September 27, 1909, at precisely five-fifteen in the afternoon, when the Great Northern train stopped at a lonely watering tank and two school teachers who would a-farming go, clambered to the ground. As the engine puffed the train into motion, and the teachers saw the coveted horizons, surrounding the grazing lands where were uncounted number of horses, sheep, cows and antelope, our undertaking suddenly looked terrifying. A loud 'hello!' soon broke this spell, and we were restored to enthusiastic ranchers by the greeting of our agent. 'You don't look very husky, for farmers, but you are getting the pick of some of the best bench land in the State. There is a big spring in that coolee yonder besides the immense reservoir belonging to the railroad, both of which show that you will be dead sure to strike water when you dig your wells. This bunch of grazing cattle proves there is moisture in the ground, and it only needs cultivating to raise good crops. You ladies are sure plucky, and here's good luck to the pair of you.'

"In half an hour we had set our stakes and were being driven back to Ft. Benton. We filed our claims the next morning, and returned to our work in the proud assurance of our new possessions.

"That winter we read the free documents furnished by the United States Agricultural Department for our diversion. We made sunbonnets and bedding rather than fancy work, and we bought lumber and nails instead of dresses and hats.

"Early the next March we sent the rancher brother to build our shacks, a mere box car of a house with two small windows. The cost was one hundred and ten dollars for each.

"March 28, 1910, we started for our first taste of real ranch life. Unfortunately, the only train that stopped at our watering tank would land us at our destination at 11:30 p.m. The night happened to be pitch dark, and our furniture, lying in heaps where it had been thrown from the freight car, caused many a groan and many a bruise as we groped our way to our shacks.

"As the light of the train disappeared in the distance I would have given my ranch, shack, sunbonnets and bank account for a large sized masculine shoulder and a scratchy coat, where I might have buried my head and wept comfortably, but such luxuries are not for the rancher novitiate. While each was protesting against the enthusiasm that had brought her to this desolate plight, our eyes accustomed themselves to the dark sufficiently to discover two black specks, which we knew must be our shacks. Gripping hands and tugging at our suitcases, we at last reached the nearest shack.

"For that first twenty-four hours it seemed a case of 'cheer up, for worse is yet to come.' By the sense of feeling we found the matches in our grips, and then it was an easy matter to locate our candle and to find some blankets, in which we wearily rolled ourselves up and lay down on the floor to await the daylight. In the dimness of the early morning we went to the spring for water and picked up bits of coal along the track. We soon had a fire and cooked one of the best breakfasts I ever ate.

"Fortunately, a Japanese section boss had left a rude push cart near the watering tank, and with that we managed to gather up our scattered 'lares and penates,'[1] and by a combination of shoves and pushes, groans and jokes, we succeeded in getting enough furniture into our shacks so we could luxuriate in chairs to sit on, a table to eat on, a stove to cook on, and before night-time a bed to sleep on. I assure you it was two tired farmers that [at] four o'clock quit work and went to bed.

"Every rancher and farmer remembers that summer of 1910 as the hottest, dryest ever known, and we shall always consider it as such. The buffalo grass withered and died. The sheep and cattle were driven northward for pasturage, but the two teacher-farmers were left in their little box car houses with the sun beating down at the unspeakable degree of 108 in the shade, for days at a time. We devised several methods of making life more bearable, one of the most successful being by baking lemon pies. I never think of that summer without being thankful that I knew how to make good lemon pies, and also for the correlated fact that two men liked lemon pies, and one of those men had charge of the refrigerators on the trains that stopped at our watering tank, and the other was the fireman on the same train. It is certain we never had occasion to complain of our ice man, and we never had to go far to find coal to bake our lemon pies.

"At last the summer was over, and we went back to another year of teaching school, saving money and planning for the next season on the farm.

"My fall shopping was mostly done at the hardware store. It is surprising how wire fencing and farm machinery will use up pay checks.

"Although the season had been so dry, I hired a man to break forty acres for me that fall, and early the next spring had it sown to flax, which yielded seven bushels to the acre and netted me one hundred dollars as my share, which was one-third of the profits.

"During the summer of 1911 we made vast improvements on our farms. Our shacks were transformed into homes. The price was just $150, and consisted in adding a bedroom, shingling, ceiling, and best of all, we built in a real cupboard, a closet and bookcase. A well was dug at a cost of $100. A garden had been planted in the early spring, and we raised an abundance of peas, beans, onions, cabbage, potatoes, etc. Oh, this summer was spent in the lap of luxury in comparison with the previous season.

"That fall I decided to have another forty acres broken. By this time, we could count sixty shacks in our valley, and there were plenty of farmers who were anxious to work on shares. The following spring I planted wheat and raised fifteen bushels to the acre.

"Our Uncle Sam is continually looking after the interests of the farmers, especially those who carry on dry farming. An appropriation was made by Congress in 1912 to secure and distribute the seeds adapted to the needs of those sections which have scant rain fall. We hope to have special types of sorghum, wheat, oats and grasses which the experimenters predict will increase our harvests and add greatly to the land value of all this region.

"It has cost me about ten dollars per acre for improvements and to prove up on my land. I have put about $3,000 on my place, and it has produced about $700, of which $400 was paid for help. At least $500 of my salary has gone to my ranch each year, and every penny which the place has produced has gone right back into improvements, and I have had to borrow $500.

"I proved up on May 22, 1915, under the five year act. At that time I owned my farm, which I value at $30 an acre. The land is all fenced and cross-fenced. I have 170 acres planted to wheat, twenty acres to oats, eight acres to alfalfa, and twenty acres to summer fallow. The prospect is that we will have record crops. I have four fine brood mares, a riding pony, a two year old colt, three one year old colts and two spring colts, a cow and a calf, besides some fifty chickens. I have a fine barn, a chicken coop and a root cellar. I also have a wagon, a carriage, harness, and farm implements. I am enjoying my home, and teaching our country school, which is half a mile from my house.

"Our watering tank is now surrounded by an enterprising little town, and look in any direction as far as the eye can see, the land has all been converted into thriving farms. Loss of position and fear of prolonged illness have lost all terrors for me. One couldn't be sick in this glorious air.

"I started in with the disadvantage of health none too good and nerves none too steady, and the advantage of such general knowledge as most farmers' daughters absorb, and a position worth $1,000 a year. Aside from these, I have had no special handicap and no special qualifications for my undertaking. I have done nothing but what any teacher could do. There are still homesteads to be had, and Uncle Sam allows the teacher to draw her checks while proving up on her land. The farms that Uncle Sam has to give away need very careful management in order to make them into paying propositions. They are merely opportunities, not certainties.

"I advise most teachers to stick to their job. Those who have a longing for the simple life can buy a few weeks of that kind, which consists of picking flowers and eating vegetables fresh from the garden, but for those who have the real farm hunger, there is a way 'back to the land.' As for myself, I know of no other way by which, in five years' time, I could have acquired such riotous health, secured much valuable property, experienced so much joy in living, and infused so much of hope and buoyancy into life, and no other way to provide such cheering prospects for my old age.

"Uncle Sam's farms are a land of promise, but the promises are fulfilled only to those who are willing to give hard work and continual study to those farm problems which confront every homesteader."

Cecelia Weiss—1916
"Homesteading Without a Chaperon: Being the Experiences of Cecelia Weiss in the Sagebrush of Southern Utah" as Told by Her to Amy Armstrong, *Sunset*, June 1916

In the first place my 320 acres do not support me—yet. I support them.

This spring I put in forty acres of rye and I have a little garden. I don't care much for a steady diet of rye bread, and the rabbits share the garden truck with me. If I had depended for my living on the produce of the land during the four years since I picked out the half section and filed on it, I would be worse off than the people in the country where I was born, on the border of Russia and Poland. There are no relief commissions for girl homesteaders, and the Red Cross pays no attention to them. So I had to go to the city every winter to earn enough money to keep myself and the homestead going in summer.

So far the homestead with its improvements has cost me about a thousand dollars. This fall I shall receive title to the land from the government. They say that an unimproved acre in my vicinity is worth about ten dollars, so I figure that, should I desire to sell and find a buyer, I will have a profit of $2200. But I don't want to sell. I would rather make a real farm out of the sagebrush tract.

My homestead is in Iron county in southwestern Utah, so close to the main line of the railroad that I can hear the puffing of the locomotive on still nights when the wind is in the right direction. There is not a tree on it; when I filed on the land in 1912 not a tree was in sight clear to the horizon. The gray-green sagebrush covered the flat valley like a shimmering Persian rug to the foot of the bare blue ranges on either side. The land lay as the Lord had made it. There was no water to irrigate it, and no one had thought it possible to raise crops without irrigation until dry-farming began to be talked about.

I did not know a thing of dry or any other kind of farming. Since I, a little girl then, came to Salt Lake City fifteen years ago, I had never done any kind of work except to clerk in my father's jewelry store. And I never would have thought of homesteading if my sister had not taken the lead. Five or six years ago everybody in Utah suddenly began to talk of dry-farming; lots of people came from California to take up land that nobody had wanted before and we caught the infection.

My sister was to take up half a section and prove up in her own name while her husband looked after his business in town and supplied the funds. I saw my chance and picked out 320 acres touching my sister's land at one point. Without my sister's companionship I think I would have deserted before the first season was half over.

There was nothing on the land except sagebrush, and sagebrush was all around it. Only here and there a homesteader had cleared a little space and built his shack. About eighteen and twenty claims had been filed in our district, but only two of the men had their wives with them. From the first we were known as "The Girls."

We could have enjoyed great popularity among the women-hungry men had it not been for two circumstances. My sister had a husband who was at their home taking care of his business and I was handicapped by the fear of gossip and scandal which, mushroom like, spring up overnight without provocation out here where folks have nothing to do for recreation but scan the empty miles and sit and think about their neighbor, until they light upon some choice morsel of gossip which will make good conversation at the occasional meetings. A young girl unprotected and without a chaperon is the best of material for such stories. The settlers are not at all unkind; they are only human, but a young woman must be very careful. More of this anon.

The first thing for me to do was to have a shelter built, for I could not manage the construction of that myself. So I hired my nearest neighbor, who lived three quarters of a mile away, to put up a little board structure for me at the cost of about $50 in all.

I was not allowed the privilege of naming my residence. It was no sooner up than a facetious homesteader passing by remarked: "The piano box is finished," and "The Piano Box" it is now called by everyone, the nickname having clung to it ever since. It is 8 X 10 feet, without lean-to or addition of any sort. Its equipment consists of the following articles: One cook stove; one single bed; one small table; one chair; one bench; one tiny looking glass, a dresser, home-constructed from a box and a couple of yards of chintz, and a clock. The latter is a most important adjunct in helping the hours to pass. My sister's shack is similar though of necessity a trifle larger; as she insisted upon bringing her piano, which has been a wonderful comfort to her. My "Piano Box" is not entirely weather-proof, but as it rarely rains in summer it affords sufficient protection.

I had to have a house of my own, as I could not obtain a patent unless I had my legal residence on the land for three consecutive years. The government insists on this requirement and if your homestead is worth having, there are always enough newcomers who will start a contest for the claim if they are given a chance. But the government grants the homesteader a furlough of five months every year during which time he or she can leave the

Cecelia Weiss in front of her homestead garden. She and her sister built the pictured fence themselves to save money and pass the time while meeting the residency requirement for claiming their homesteads. (Sunset, *June 1916*)

land. This furlough must not be extended, though, even for a week, as the homesteader is carefully watched by those who covet his land. Mere residence on the land, however, is not sufficient. The claimant must also cultivate at least twenty acres the second year and the third year forty acres must be in crop.

Of course I am not strong enough to drive two teams of horses dragging a railroad iron over the ground in order to clear it of sagebrush. For heavy work of this kind I have always paid cash. A neighbor brings over his team and his implements and does the plowing, seeding, hauling and other heavy work for $3.50 a day. The arrangement suits both of us, though it increases my cash outlay and, worst of all, adds to the hours of leisure at my disposal. So far as I can see, this overabundance of spare time is one of the worst features of homesteading. Unless one has the capital to improve the entire claim in two or three years, there are always long intervals when one can't find anything to do except to contemplate the scenery and watch the hands of the clock go 'round. I never knew how much time there is in the world, how it refuses to be prodded and hurried in its snaily crawl until I contracted with Uncle Sam to spend seven consecutive months in the sagebrush with the nearest neighbor almost out of sight and not sufficient work to make me forget the heat.

It is a little better today. When I first came into the Escalante valley, the store nearest to my homestead was at Lund, seventeen miles away. I did not have to go there for my furniture, though. Most of it was bought from other homesteaders who were either going away, disappointed, or replaced it with better articles. Today Beryl, a little over a mile away, merely a sidetrack three years ago, has a station, a hotel and a store. We were in the wilderness three years ago; we are in the suburbs now.

But the water problem is still with us.

As I mentioned before, the land in the Escalante valley was to be had free because no one wanted it, and the lack of desire was caused by the lack of water. There is no running water of any kind for miles and miles and miles. To survive one must drill a well and set up a pump, which is an expensive undertaking. Sister and I have no wells, but the neighbor who lives three-quarters of a mile away has installed water works. He became our source of supply. Until I had to walk a mile and a half and carry every drop I had no conception of the value of water, and I never knew how much of the precious fluid is wasted criminally when you only have to turn the faucet to wash your hands. Water conservation became a religion with me.

Since my sister was even farther from the well than I we kept house on the community plan. Each day we walked the three-quarters of a mile to the neighbor's for a bucket of water. One bucket we "banked on" to last out the day for drinking, cooking and washing purposes. At that time I was not at all accustomed to walking except for short distances on paved streets. Three-quarters of a mile over stubble and through high grass and brush was a good morning's exercise; the distance back, lugging a heavy bucket of water, seemed four times longer. You had to be thirsty those days to permit yourself even the luxury of a drink.

Looking back on the carting of that bucket of water I am reminded of the dry farmer who, on his first visit to the big city, stopped in the middle of the street and held his sides, laughing. A sprinkling wagon in full action was approaching, "Gee, won't that fool be mad when he gets home and looks into the tank," chuckled the dry-farmer.

It was so with us. The bucket was never a full bucket by the time we reached the shack. And this bucketful of water had to do double, sometimes triple duty. We watched over it as a miser over his hoard. We were in truth slaves of the bucket. I would wash the dishes in the morning and put the water carefully aside to save for washing the dinner and supper dishes. By the time night came it had just about outlived its usefulness. My sister and I took turns washing our faces in a small as basin of water as we could make effectual, then save the same water to wash our hands the rest of the day. When we felt extravagant and ventured a bath we would save the water to wash our clothes.

The water problem is not such a difficult one now. Though I have as yet no well on my own place of course, not having my title, the neighbor delivers a barrel of water each week; and with just a little thought, economy and sole leather wore out on special trips with the bucket this lasts fairly well.

Getting the land fenced is always one of the worst jobs of a homesteader. My sister and I determined to put up our own fences in order to save money and also to keep ourselves busy. The summer days are terrifically hot, the sun beating down for hours with nothing to break the intensity of the rays for there are yet no trees. There is only a short time early in the morning and about an hour in the evening between 7 and 8 o'clock before it gets dark, when a woman can do hard outdoor work. When we began to dig the post-holes and set the posts for our fences, one in the morning and one in the evening was all we could manage. It was our very best effort and that left us tired out and sore in every muscle. But before we had been at it very long we had increased our output to ten holes in the morning and ten in the evening. In all we set 600 posts, saving at least $75, the cash cost of the work if done by hired labor. But the land is not yet all fenced. It is important to get this done as it can then be taken better care of and cannot be tramped over by ranging cattle. I could have rented some of my land for cattle holds, but I did not care to as it takes too long to get the ground back in condition after the animals have been on it for a while.

But homesteading on a dry-land farm is not all thirst, desolation and dreariness. The social side of life is not neglected, and many congenial friends can be found among the settlers. To be sure, one does not have regular calling hours, for visits in the sagebrush are made by the day. One goes before breakfast, as it were, and stays until evening. Distances between the homes are too great to be taken lightly. But parties in the land of hope and thirst are just as much fun as they are in the city and many of them are made to serve useful purposes as well. If a homesteader has a big job on hand he invites all of his friends. After many hands have made light work of the task there are "eats" after which every one is more than ready, and thereafter the festivities begin. A potato picking party to which my sister and I were invited by a homesteader who lived several miles away proved almost to be our Waterloo.

On this occasion no one near us was going, so we decided to rent the horse and wagon of a neighbor. The horse, the wagon and the harness had been brought around and left the night before. When we were ready to start, a serious problem confronted us. Neither my sister nor I had ever harnessed a horse. The straps, buckles and hooks with which he was to be attached to the wagon completely mystified us. For long minutes we stood and looked at him, waiting for inspiration. As no inspiration came, we began to try first this and then that combination, but without results satisfactory to the horse. At last the power of advertising made itself felt. I remembered the harness catalogue I had sent for. With the aid of its pictures, working slowly and systematically we finally had the animal all hitched and buckled up ready for action. Not particularly confident even at that, we decided to stop at the house of a friend who lived on the way, to have him look over the job. As usually happens in such cases, he was not at home when wanted, but we reached our destination without mishap and were much commended.

One has friends here as elsewhere and I dress as becomingly as I can. Why shouldn't one look pretty if one can? That isn't a crime, although a girl must be rather conservative in the sagebrush. Since, as before mentioned, the people do not have much diversion and therefore take a lively interest in each others' affairs, a young woman alone must be more than conventional to avoid being talked about. It is not sufficient that she avoid evil itself; she must avoid even the least appearance of evil. We young people, for example, like to get together for a chat now and then and the young men are disposed to call on the young women out here just as normal young men are everywhere. But when a young fellow from a distant farm rides over to call on me, I cannot ask him into my home. To be sure there is no other place except a hard wooden bench in the broiling sun on which to sit, but that is not the point. It is not proper to ask a man inside, for I have but one room and no chaperon. So we look for the soft side of the bench, try to find a few feet of shadow cast by the Piano Box and thoroughly enjoy ourselves in spite of everybody.

I have often been asked if it is not dangerous for a girl to live alone in a sparsely populated, isolated place. I have never been very much afraid, although there are quite a number of hoboes along the railroad. I have a .22 rifle, but never shot anything except two rabbits with it. Nevertheless, my sister and I had an experience which scared us a little. Late one afternoon three exceedingly rough looking men asked for food and shelter at my sister's house where I happened to be. When we told them truthfully that we had nothing to spare, they loafed around for a while and finally sauntered off in the direction of my shack.

I remained with my sister as long as I could. After dark I started for home, as no matter what happened I always slept there in order to fulfil the homestead obligations. I entered the door with fear and trembling, reluctantly said goodnight to the neighbor who had walked home with me, nailed a board across the door on the inside, put my rifle across the bed near my hand and lay awake all night trembling at every sound. Nothing happened. The neighbor watched my place throughout the night as well as he could from his own distant home, ready to come at the slightest sign of trouble, but he did not dare stay near me and take any chances with the school for scandal as he had a wife and children back in Kansas.

My garden is a source of great delight to me. I get up early in the morning to dig, pull weeds, plant and coax the radishes, lettuce and other things to grow. The results are not what they should be, I must confess, because the arid soil is not yet in good condition and I am not a expert gardener. And there are the rabbits and gophers. They do not wait to be asked; they simply help themselves. But the few things I do manage to raise help out wonderfully. Since the store was opened at Beryl and people in the vicinity began to raise more and more, the food problem is being solved. I chop my own wood, which I get in rather large logs that have to be split into stove size. It is quite cold when I first go to the farm, usually in March, and it gets cold before the seven months are up, so I have to have a fire part of the time for heat as well as for cooking.

It has taken pluck to stick to the venture and see it through. There have been times when it has been very hard to stay, but I have never even thought of quitting, though scores of men in this vicinity have been unable to hold on. Most of those who stay seem to think that their problems are solved when they receive their patents. To my mind the real task has then only begun. It takes money, grit, perseverance and self-denial to develop a farm out of raw land, and a dry-farm is harder to make than an irrigated farm. But we have hopes that by-and-by a reliable supply of underground water will be developed and part of the land at least will be irrigated. But even without irrigation water the aspect of the country is rapidly changing. Substantial homes are here and there replacing the shacks of the homesteaders, the square green patches in the gray sagebrush are growing in number and size every spring, and though there are many disappointments and failures, the shimmering valley is gradually becoming filled with real houses.

Disregarding whatever pecuniary gain there may be, it is a real inspiration to be part of a modern pioneer colony conquering the wilderness. At least it is an inspiration in the retrospect.

A. May Holaday — 1917
"The Lure of the West for Women"
Sunset, March 1917

I like the place in the far West I choose to call "home" because it appeals to me in so many different ways. Chief among these is the "independent spirit of the West," of which you of the East have all heard and which one notices immediately on coming out here. In fact I began to feel it in the air while crossing the Rockies and straight away my former ideas of the importance of class distinction and the observance of social conventions seemed to fall from me like a heavy cloak, which had long been a burden—and I was free! Free to live my own life in my own way, unhampered by what Mrs. So and So did or what Mrs. Somebody or other expected me to do. It is a freedom which really must be experienced in order to be thoroughly appreciated and understood.

In the great West people are accepted for what they are and do, not for what they happen to have. As a rule, no one tries to out-do his neighbor in foolish display, but each has what he can afford. And no one feels that he is expected to do any certain thing unless he pleases to do so.

A little bride in an eastern state was "worn to a thread" trying to keep up appearances on her husband's very modest salary. Her two older sisters had married rich men and entertained lavishly—as was the custom in their town. Helen felt that she must do the same or be criticized. Her entire time was spent in vainly striving to live according to her sisters' standards. The family physician (wise man he was) recommended a change of climate to avoid a nervous breakdown. Helen and her husband sold everything and came west. Starting anew among strangers, Helen became a changed being. For the first time she really began to live and is now happy and contented in the glorious freedom of the West.

I like my little corner in the far West because any person is considered just as good as anyone else so long as he behaves himself. There is none of the "I am better than thou" attitude manifested in the churches here or in any place where people meet together.

In the East you hear:

"That's young Bill Moore. What! You don't know the Moores? Old Bill and his fathers before him owned the old Moore homestead and its section of land for generations. All kinds of money, too."

In the West you hear:

"There's Henry Mead, the clever young engineer who builds all our steel bridges. He'll make his mark in the world, believe me!"

The broad-minded spirit of cooperation and helpfulness manifested in the West enables us to do big things in a big way. And 'tis no wonder our country is full of boosters." The West deserves it.

Zay Philbrook — *1918*
"My Wyoming Timber Claim: A Woman Pioneer in the Big Horn Mountains"
Sunset, December 1918

If you have ever ridden up some mountain canyon when your trail led far above the aspen tops into the higher silence; if, when the cool air was filled with the spice of wet sage, you have loped your pony over huge crumpled hills in an open world that seemed so full of God and happiness that you wanted to laugh and sob with the joy of living, then I'm sure you understand why we who have been here must always come back.

Sometimes, to return seems almost impossible. Railroad fare must be considered, the item of board at a ranch, or horses and a camp outfit if the wide freedom of the mountains is desired. Many who are at liberty during the summer months find this expense a serious drawback. Perhaps it is with you as it was with me. I had only a small amount of capital to invest, and I could not well spare the time to homestead. But after a summer spent high up in the Big Horn mountains with a forest ranger's family I loved Wyoming so much that I determined in some way to start a Western home.

Early the following spring my sister and I went West, rented a tiny cabin on the edge of Ten Sleep town, and began the hunt for some bit of land within my means. It was not easy. One can always homestead, and there is room for countless claims all through the mountains. But such a claim demands your presence for seven consecutive months of the year for three years, and it demands a certain amount of annual improvements. Practically, you must have considerable capital, both of time and money to prove up on a homestead claim. I was discussing this one day with the ranger.

"Why don't you take up a 'Timber and Stone' claim?" he asked. "Then you can buy it outright and live on it only when you wish. There are some good places up on the mountainside, on what you'd call the 'open range'."

In buying a Timber and Stone claim one may apply for from forty to one hundred and sixty acres, paying for it the government's appraised value of the timber—or stone—and the land. You may make the land your home or you need not live on it one day; you may dispose of the timber and stone or keep the place wild and untouched. Once your patent is obtained the place is yours absolutely. Only you must buy the land in good faith, under no previous understanding with any corporation or person for its disposal. And the land must be chiefly valuable for timber or stone.

One early morning in April the ranger stopped at my door.

"I'm going up the mountains to hunt wolf tracks today," he told me. "If you're game for a long ride I'll show you some places that might suit you for a claim." It did not take long to saddle my pony and to put up a lunch.

Up and up we rode, until the Big Horn basin lay spread beneath us. Up and up, until, above the cedar slopes, we rode into the clouds. The ranger led the way in and out half-timbered draws, pausing now and then to note footprints of deer or coyote along the way. Then we rode through a strip of wet pines and came out on a valley's edge just as the sun cleared the clouds.

"There's a place for you if you want it," said the ranger.

It was a quiet, happy little valley. Fenced along one side by a ledge of red rimrock, it stretched on the other side up over a timbered butte. Between lay the valley floor, rolling sage-land opening to the southwest to give a wide view to the distant Rockies. Up at the head of the valley several springs spurted from the hillside, tumbling down under cover of willows to form a stream that swept the length of the land. There were eighty acres of tall pine trees, through which the deer for years had trodden dainty paths. On that April morning, while the ranger and I watered our horses at the springs, suddenly the opposite hillside seemed to move and full twenty deer stood watching us for the long instant before they went bounding over the slope. All day we rode the mountainside, seeing one possible place after another, but none measured up to the first. At dusk we came to the edge of the great Ten Sleep canyon. A thousand feet below us lay a white ranch house.

"There's supper at that place before we start home if you don't mind the drop," suggested the ranger—and down the cliff we went.

The next morning I stood at my cabin door looking up at the little dark triangle of trees on the mountainside—the timber claim I wanted. Once started, could I see the thing through to the end? Could I establish a self-supporting home where friends could come to rest and love the mountains?

Zay Philbrook in front of her homestead cabin. She decided raising horses was the best use of her timber claim in the Big Horn Mountains of Wyoming. (Sunset, *December, 1918*)

Could I pay all that it would cost, not in money alone? I knew the two things I would fear if I took a claim four miles from any neighbor: I had had my horse chased by a range stallion as I rode alone; I had met mountain storms and crept under a bush, watching the lightning stalking up the canyon, rattling close above me. Neither experience was much fun. I looked up at the mountain and measured the responsibility, then—"All the rest is gladness"— and I chose my claim.

We were spending a few days at the Ranger Station, ten miles above the claim, when word came that a surveyor could meet me. I was linesman for seven consecutive hours, riding when I could, up and down rocky gulches, over hills waist high in sage, dodging through the pine timber.

There's a mighty uneasy feeling about having your claim surveyed when the pole nears the first corner; will the land line out rightly, or will the spring lie just over the division in a rocky forty that you do not want? I was lucky; fair and true, the line edged along the valley ridge, giving me my springs, my little creek, my great pine butte. We piled the corners in sagebrush or stone, then turned wearily back for our long delayed lunch at the springs. The place was glorious, banks of wild roses walled the creek with pink blossoms, wild peppermint tinged the air, warblers flashed through the willows above us.

It was dark when we rode down the mountain, and we were tired. Yes, like any tenderfoot, we lost our way, but we reached the cabin somehow, late that night. As the surveyor had come a long distance I paid him $32 for time and work, but his being a land officer saved me a trip to town. The filing fee, sent with the application, was $10. The government specifies that at least $2.50 per acre must be paid for such a claim; in your application you are required to name separately your estimated value of the land as well as the timber average to the acre. My one hundred and sixty acres and timber came to $430.

You can not buy a timber claim outright; there must be a certain delay before you are granted your patent. Probably there could be no objection to living on the land beforehand, but it would not be wise to risk work or improvement until the patent is obtained. The government is allowed nine months after receiving your application in which to send a timber expert to examine your claim. He may come the first month; he may never come. If you receive notice of this appraisement, you are allowed one month in which to send the price of the claim to the registrar. In my case the land was not examined, so the day the nine months was up I sent my $430 purchase money and arranged to have the land advertised in the local Wyoming paper for sixty days.

When this was accomplished, on the day set by the land office, I made my final proof. If you are at all reticent concerning your history, past or present, do not apply for a timber claim, for before you are through you must testify almost more than you know about yourself. The actual cost of final proof was $2.50 fee sent to the office, $3 to the land agent. The newspaper advertisement cost $21.20.

The patent reaches you a bit later, when the President has had time to sign it. But there is one other thing to which you must attend if you wish the full value of your land—you must protect your water-right by filing on any available spring or stream which forms your water supply. In Wyoming and other western states any water not previously so claimed can be filed on by another who wishes to use it, even though it has its source on your land. When I learned this I had the surveyor map my springs and make out my applications to use the water for stock purposes and for irrigating two small patches of ground. The two water filings, notary fees and maps cost me $22. In addition to this I must, of course, have the irrigation done and pay my small yearly tax on the land. My title to the one hundred and sixty acres, with timber and water-right, has cost me $50.70 for required fees, surveying and purchase.

Few of us lovers of the West can afford to start such a place just for the pleasure there is in it; we must look for some return for our time and money. If ever I have to dispose of the claim, it could make a good "dude" ranch. Or, with its sheltered slopes threaded by running water and its early feed, it would make an ideal lambing ground or a horse ranch, with adjoining free range. So I consider improvements an investment.

Fencing, in such rocky land as mine, cost on an average $100 for a forty-acre square—less, of course, should you do the work yourself. You can build a fair one-room cabin for $25; you can have it done for perhaps $100.

In choosing my place I made sure that the springs ran the year round, for sometimes mountain springs go dry in August. I expect to practice what forestry methods I can, and I find the timber is of a fair grade, which can be marketed. The Land Office at Washington told me that there was "no objection to using the land for a home," and I plan to make it, in every way possible, a self-supporting ranch. My elevation is something over 6500 feet. If the land were more level for plowing I should plant it to grain, as timothy does well at the Ranger Station, over 1000 feet higher. But there are only five or six irrigable acres. These I am clearing of sage, seeding part for a small hay pasture in the future, putting the remainder in vegetables and small fruits, with a try at the more hardy trees—apple and plum. They ought to have a fair show, as the creek is lined with gooseberries and chokecherries.

Last year was my first summer on the claim, and the vegetables in the garden lasted well into November. But in our country the late spring frosts are more to be guarded against than those of fall. I purposely chose a sheltered valley, yet one where the snow does not lie too late in the spring, for I wanted early pasture. The best use to make of this, the bulk of my land, seems to be to buy what horses I can afford. Yearlings come at from $25 up, and much can be done for them with good feed and handling. Mares might pay better, could I winter them myself, but that would be impossible without hay at the claim. Many ranchers turn their horses out in the bad lands in winter to shift for themselves, but I have mine wintered in ranch pasture at from $1 to $1.50 a month, according to the winter's severity.

These are the things I find a woman can do to make a timber claim profitable. You must expect some strenuous days, but you will know that every day brings fresh happiness, as you help the claim to grow, as the mountains become more friendly. Yes, it is worth while.

Kate L. Heizer — 1921
"Via the Homesteading Route: A Woman's Experience in the Sagebrush of the Uintah Basin"
Sunset, March 1921

Sunset Editor's Note:

Last year there were eighty applicants for each farm unit opened for settlement by the Reclamation Service on the Shoshone project. More than a quarter million ex-soldiers have registered with the Interior Department for farms when land becomes available. Even though the farm owner works longer hours for smaller pay than any other class of men, the desire to become owner of a piece of soil is as strong as ever. The trials and triumphs of sagebrush pioneering are set forth in this article by Miss Heizer, who was lucky enough to draw a low number in the lottery through which the irrigable area of the Uintah Indian Reservation was disposed of. But unfortunately the amount of land that can be supplied with water by building a crude ditch is negligible.

I am one of those citizens who have "proved up on" a claim of Government land, a process upon which there exists a variety of misconceptions. One inquirer has an exaggerated idea of the difficulties and hardships. Another has a mistaken notion of taking a pleasant vacation while waiting till he receives title to a piece of property that will place him above financial anxiety for the rest of his life. Conditions under which Government land is obtained differ, owing to various causes. Moreover there is also a great difference as regards the expense and time required to reclaim land, "reclaiming" in reference to Western land meaning to put it under irrigation.

The land I secured is in north-eastern Utah in the former Uintah Indian Reservation. After the Indians had been allotted their lands in severalty, the rest of the reservation was opened to settlement. As usual the Government provided that the right of entry should be in the order of numbers drawn by lot. Thousands of persons registered and drew numbers; I drew No. 247, which was considered good.

A few days before time to begin filing our claims we who held numbers were permitted to enter the Reservation to look over the country. The time was too short for those with small numbers to take more than a hurried view and we were distrustful of those who offered, for a consideration, to give us information. It is safe to say that some of us learned more in those few days than we ever did before in our lives. Whether we secured a valuable quarter section of land or a worthless one depended upon our judgment in selecting and luck in securing our choice. Sagebrush became the most interesting shrub in the world; it indicated a soil free from alkali; shadscale was a bad sign. Was there an excess of clay in that piece? By all means we must not make a mistake and file upon that piece with the big sand knolls or on that strip of cobblerock! What would fence posts cost? Then there were coal and oil deposits in the region. What if there should be beds of it under our land!

But all these queries were subordinate to the great question, "How can this land be irrigated?" As for myself I listened with intense interest to explanations of irrigating schemes, the feasibility of which I was as little capable of judging as I am of discussing the canals on Mars. But one idea I clung to with assurance. It would be better for me to secure a claim within a large tract upon which many persons were settling. Land in such a location, I reasoned, was more likely to become valuable than a small isolated tract, and I felt that so many people being interested increased the probability that an adequate irrigation scheme would be worked out.

Arriving at Vernal, where the land office was located, we found the little town thronged with people. Every one was keenly alert for information, but suspicious of all he heard. Professional "locators," who for fifty dollars would insure you a good location, were much in evidence. They added to the tension of the entrymen and entrywomen by shouting out in the crowd each evening the alleged number of persons who had drawn rock piles that day because they had failed to get advice from the "Wasatch Land Company." When our turns came to present our selections at the office, each one had the opportunity of choosing from the map any quarter section not already filed upon. It was a breathless moment! Our knowledge of the country was not accurate. One quarter might be the very best of land and the adjoining one worthless. On the map they looked all alike, and the legal description might not apply to the land selected.

Luck was on my side, for I secured a better claim than many a one who had had an earlier choice. But my success was not altogether a matter of luck. I had questioned and listened to every man who could give me any information, and it required judgment to determine which were giving honest advice, and which either mistakenly thought they knew or had interested motives. To get a piece of land having good soil and for which water could be secured for irrigation was a concern of first importance, but we were extremely anxious also that the location should be favorable in reference to probable lines of railroads and townsites. Some persons had inside information on these matters, we believed, and would use it, of course, for their own benefit.

The First Summer. For better or for worse, my choice was made. I went to my stopping place and lay for a couple of hours in a state of complete relaxation. The filing was done during the last week in August and through the month of September. This brought the expiration of the six months allowed for establishing residence at an unfavorable time for the settlers to come on their land and the time was extended until the first of May. As I did not wish to leave my school work before the close of the school year I went out during the Christmas vacation and "resided" two days upon my claim in the little log cabin I had had built.

The first summer was a hard one. Some of the settlers were able to secure water and put a small piece of ground under cultivation, but the greater number were dependent upon ditches yet to be constructed. A co-operative ditch company had been organized during the winter and many of the settlers, some taking their families with them, went to work upon the big ditch. The ditch camp, pleasantly located in the foothills near the river, was the scene of cheerful activity. But many of us, unable either to work upon the ditch personally or to stay on our claims, were obliged to make use of the right the Government grants under such circumstances, that is, to absent ourselves temporarily. I was able to stay on my claim longer than some others, for I had chosen my land on a gulch in which the flow of water lasted until midsummer. This gulch was a valuable asset to me in the early days, for besides the advantage of even a limited supply of water, the trees on the banks furnished me with logs for my cabin and with fuel. During those times in which I made trips out to my claim and back, I had, I must confess, some lonely days and nights. When I made my first winter trip there were several men "holding down" claims in the near neighborhood. But the second winter every one within a radius of a couple of miles had departed to earn money for the spring work. The man I had hired to bring me over from the stage station fourteen miles away left me at my cabin just at dusk. As far as one could see in the gathering gloom, the plain was covered by an unbroken expanse of snow. A fire was built and two candles struggled against the darkness. The stillness was intense. But the quiet was soon broken by the near and ferocious howling of coyotes. Round and round the cabin they raced. They seemed determined to break through the walls. They must have known there was only a woman inside and that she had no gun. And it was Christmas Eve!

By thus staying on my land a part of the summer and coming in for a few days at Christmas, and having some plowing and fencing done, I was enabled to hold my claim for three years. By this time people were well established upon their land. Those who could not get water made frequent trips to their homesteads and made as much of a showing of improvements as they were able. Land was beginning to have value and those who absented themselves risked having their claims contested. A contest was filed against mine, but some of the citizens, with unmistakable Western emphasis, advised the contestant to drop it—and he did. However, concluding not to tempt fate any longer I moved out to my place and began the required fourteen months' continuous residence. At the end of that period, having shown that I had cultivated a reasonable portion of my land, and paid $1.25 per acre due the Indian fund, I received my patent.

Not all Roses. The first two or three years on a homestead are usually accompanied by privation and hardship. I am not now speaking of those persons who have sufficient means to tide over the lean beginning, nor of those fortunate enough to obtain land near a railroad where employment may be obtained at times, and where, at any rate, supplies may be purchased if one has money to buy. I am referring to the typical homesteader, limited in means, holding his land fifty or a hundred miles from a railroad. Supplies being "freighted in" are necessarily expensive, often lacking altogether. The little, hastily built shacks that serve as houses are hot in summer and cold in winter. Pests of various kinds destroy the small crops.

Our greatest torments were the rabbits and prairie dogs. The first spring I lived on my place, not yet having bought a team and farming outfit, I hired a few acres plowed and harrowed. My brother, who was now staying with me, sowed alfalfa seed on most of it, but reserved a large strip for a garden. He planned to raise a great crop of beans and haul a wagon load of them to the railroad in the fall. But rabbits came in the night, common rabbits and great jack rabbits, and devoured the young plants. Scarecrows, guns and poison were futile. If I remember correctly we bought beans for home consumption the next winter.

The impudent little prairie dogs were most exasperating. They not only ate a man's crop up but they barked at him defiantly, dodging into their holes just in time to save themselves. Thousands of them were killed, but they seemed to remain as numerous as ever. My neighbor Conners came across the gulch, sat down on a bench in front of my cabin, wiped his face and exclaimed: "It's no use to fight the little beasts any longer. All the prairie dogs between here and Saskatchewan have heard of this opening and have come to feed on our oats and alfalfa. I saw a dozen or so in my field with 'U.S.' branded on their backs. They've just come down from Yellowstone National Park."

Why Homesteaders Fail. The disappointments and the failures accompanying homesteading are due to two main causes. Persons who are not adapted to the life, who are not farmers by nature, undertake it, expecting to make a "stake" and leave the land in a short time; the other cause is insufficient means to get a start.

Assuming that a family is used to some hardship, that its members have good health and a little money to meet the outlay necessary to begin cultivating their land to advantage, is there really any compensation for the privations they must necessarily endure? I answer emphatically, "Yes."

I have lived where men worked for wages year after year, with little hope of advancement. I have watched them slowly climbing the hill in the morning, dinner pail in hand; I heard the jokes about shirking work; I observed the deadening influence of a lack of a worthy objective. The work these men did was so standardized and their chances of promotion were so slight that they lost all hope of ambition.

On the other hand, I have found the poor homesteader without ready money in his pocket, weirdly dressed in torn, nondescript garments, but his face alight and hope in his heart. What if his last year's crop has not been a complete success? He knows where the trouble lay and can remedy it this year. There are many experiments to be made in testing the productive qualities of new land. Different methods of cultivation are eagerly discussed. One neighbor has secured an unusual yield of alfalfa by a certain process; another has been particularly successful with his livestock; this man and that have made big returns upon sidelines, honey, potatoes, cheese or poultry. In spite of past failures the homesteader feels that there is another chance.

But variety of work and occasional successes are not enough to give contentment and interest. There is something that comes to a settler upon land more gratifying than the satisfaction of slowly and surely acquiring a competency. This something—I speak from personal knowledge—is the realization of being an important factor in the community, one whose voice has weight, a person to be consulted about matters of public interest.

But still the questions persists: "Does it pay in actual money value?" and the answer is: "It depends upon the individual." An incident will illustrate the type of men who succeed upon a homestead.

It was the Fourth of July. The settlers in a certain area had arranged to have a big picnic in the foothills. Some had gone up the night before and camped on the grounds, and most of the rest went early in the morning. Now the ditch system was not complete. The main ditches were too small and no dams had been built. As the season advanced the water supply was becoming inadequate for all needs; the settlers were assigned turns for using it. When at a specified hour a man's turn came to use water from a certain lateral, he turned all the water in the ditch on to his field for a given period of hours. Our friend Jennings sent his family ahead to the picnic promising to follow later on horseback after he had irrigated his alfalfa. But, on account of the celebration, the neighbors whose turn came earlier in the morning had neglected to use their share. Jennings found he had a flood of water and worked all day giving his field a good soaking.

Jennings is today one of the most prosperous and respected men in the community, holding positions of vice-president of a local bank, president of a cattlemen's association and a member of the board of county supervisors.

Their Very Own. The man who is alert and ready to seize opportunities, who holds to a purpose until it is accomplished, is the man most likely to succeed in any undertaking, and homesteading is no exception.

My original quarter section has shrunk to 110 acres. I had to sell 50 acres in order to be able to improve the balance. I have ninety acres in alfalfa now and I am studying agriculture. As soon as I have completed the course, I shall take personal charge of the ranch management.

At the present values in land, improved land can be bought at from $30 to $50 per acre, depending upon location; unimproved land for less. It is probable that, but for the war, one or more lines of railroad would have been completed through the reservation before this. All such work stopped, of course. Auto lines are the principal means for carrying traffic at present, but the people are not discouraged. They have plenty to eat. The war is over. The transportation problem must be solved sooner or later. So the settlers are holding on—to their very own.

◊ *Reporting from the Frontier*

In addition to articles written by the women homesteaders themselves, reporters published stories about the phenomena of women homesteaders in magazines and newspapers. Articles by those who observed homesteading women and recorded their stories are positive, filled with admiration for single women who dare to homestead. These reports generally include statistics and quotations to prove to readers that women in the West were indeed doing what had previously been undertaken primarily by men or family groups: staking claims, working on them, and successfully proving up—sometimes in rather unusual ways. In addition, some of the articles offer suggestions for readers who might want to join the growing numbers of women filing claims of their own in frontier regions.

The following articles appear in order of their publication. In the first, published in *Collier's* in 1911, reporter Mary Isabel Brush focuses on what motivated women to give up the amenities of city life for the "career of the pioneer" and concludes that the freedom these women experience is the greatest reward of homesteading. In a *Collier's* article published two years later, Joanna Gleed Strange may have returned to Tripp County, South Dakota, to check on the progress of the homesteaders Brush featured. Like Brush, Strange downplays the difficulties and emphasizes the rewards of homesteading, giving glowing descriptions of the landscape, climate, and agricultural possibilities. Mabel Lewis Stuart's article completed a series of three articles by and about single women homesteaders published in *The Independent* in 1913. (See the first, "Uncle's Gift," earlier in this chapter.). Her estimate that "more than one third" of homesteaders were women is unverifiable and probably high, although it might have been true in certain areas. Stuart seems intent on disproving any notions of presumed dangers and disadvantages of homesteading. A description of the varied activities available to homesteading girls reassured potential women homesteaders that they would not lack opportunities for social contact and community involvement.

"Woman on the Prairies: Pioneers Who Win Independence and Freedom in Their One-Room Homes"
Mary Isabel Brush, *Collier's*, January 28, 1911

A grass-widow is living in the Rosebud country of South Dakota in a house which is just the flat dimensions of the rug she used to have in her sitting-room back East.[2] It stands on 160 acres of her own land, and beyond that the unfenced, treeless undulations of Tripp County, recently opened to homesteaders, stretch as far as eye can span.

Rather a disproportionate allotment of front yard and floor space; of perpendicular rise of building and horizontal extent of unbroken, yellow land! Everything in that country seems out of keeping with the sweep of land, however, except the acreage of blue sky. As for the reason of the widow and her residence of one room on the Dakota prairie, she gave something of that, as she sat, fair and much under forty, in her oak rocking-chair, with its back to the window.

It always stands with its back to the window, except when she drags it down the narrow middle aisle of her residence two or three times a day, out into her ample yard, and turns it around. There is no such thing as changing its relative position to the other furniture. For in that cramped interior there is, besides the chair, a piano, a sewing-machine, a typewriter, a bureau, a table, a couch, a music rack, serving also as sideboard, and a stove.

Out in her garage, built with her own hands, the same rigid economy and order are observed; as well as in the piano-box, which sits along one side of her house and looks like an annex to it; in her feed bin, which is a dry-goods box with a hinged lid; and, most particularly, in her cave. This last is a combination of storehouse, cellar, and front porch. In its 8 by 4 by 6 boundaries it contains two trunks, endless jars of fruit and cans of vegetables, and a chair on which the widow sits on hot afternoons.

"Ah, well," said the mistress of the estate, as she rocked in her oak chair and stirred the yolks of thirteen eggs, all of which were to go into one flaky cake for herself and her hired man; "I used to think when I had my 10 by 12 rug and my sitting room, and—and the rest—that life contained nothing. Now I have my 10 by 12 house, my yellow land, and my freedom; and I think that life contains everything!"

Why does a soft-voiced, tenderly reared woman deliberately relinquish a world of Irish crochet dresses, afternoon teas, automobile races, and weekly first night performances? And, having turned her back on it, why does she choose the career of the pioneer, where the only spectacle is the stretch of unplowed country and of cloudless sky?

Why is she content to cook three square meals a day on a gasoline stove with two detachable ovens; to move the sewing-machine in front of the couch, in order that one may sit while dining; and to jab several holes in the violet-flowered wall-paper with the rocker in the attempt to move the chair to the opposite side of the sewing-machine for occupancy by the hired man, who is one's dinner companion?

Why stay when one's diversions are to wash the automobile and to manicure and rub down the horse; when one's work is to follow the plow for an hour or two, and pick up sticks and stones to help clear the fields?

Why do divorcees prefer to take a chance in a new country rather than a flyer in the matrimonial market again? Why do stenographers give up their private secretaryships, and the young girls from good homes west of the Mississippi, where nothing more is required of them than to wash a few dishes and make up a few beds every day—why do these prefer to go out to civilization's end and stake off for themselves an untractable piece of country, undefaced by even a piece of lumber with which to build a house?

In the cities you hear every once in a while that such and such a woman has gone West to take up a claim. When the land drawings are announced, you read perhaps that the first choice of locations has fallen to a woman, and that something like a third of the prizes have gone to her sex. Later you read of this one or that who has gone out to fulfil the requirements of the Government that she live on her claim for a time. Presently a letter is printed from her under the headlines: "Has Land; A Hubby Not Needed. Chicago Girl Who Drew First Choice in Homestead Drawing Spurns Offer of Marriage." In the course of weeks she comes home to visit, and her friends say that she looks fit—so sunburned, and the little lines from around her mouth and eyes all gone! Nobody has a very clear idea as to what makes up her life out in the void, which to the minds of many stands for the West. They think of her as an isolated and queer person who has taken up a tract of scenery somewhere beyond the Mississippi and passes her days sitting on a foot-hill overlooking a clear stream filled with mountain trout. Or perhaps as conducting a neatly appointed farm with a fence around it.

When you travel through the West, on the branch railroads, you see her in a different character. You see her on free, rolling stretches of fair prairie, plowing. You see her in the sage-brush deserts, irrigating. She is not—it comes over you in a flash of illumination—an isolated, queer character, working out her own unique destiny. She is two thousand strong—men who handle the statistics of the Land Office hazard the guess that she is present in that number, with many more to follow.

She comes to the Frontier Day celebrations in Cheyenne. She and her tough, amiable little mustang have crossed miles of parched country to get there. She rides like the soldier, the cowboy, and the Indian, sitting to the trot, with toes pointed out, calves gripping the pony's sides, and shoulders relaxed to the jar of the animal's movement. No fancy posting for her! When she arrives, she swings freely out of the saddle, fresh and eager for the activities of the day. Her hands are as brown as the leather wristlets she wears, and the flame color in her face does not pale beside the scarlet of her silk handkerchief, drawn loosely around her neck.

She talks knowingly about the disheartening season, tells you there won't be thirty per cent of a crop and that even those with first, second, and third irrigating rights are "up against it." She tells you how times she has to bring her dogs, cats, chickens, pigs and calves all into her house and her cave to protect them from the coyotes and the sand storms. It doesn't matter! They are good company! Would she go back? Well, she should guess not! No more little town life for her! And no more submitting to a dictating father and brother, who think they know it all. Of course they come and help her sometimes, and it's mighty fine to have their love and care. But it's better to have it under your own roof than theirs. When you live with them and haven't anything except what they give you, you simply have to do everything their way—that's all!

She is one of the pioneers. Eastern women didn't come much when she began. It's still a fad with them. Sometimes they drop their underlip a little when they first see their claims, but they're mighty game. And they're going to make a good thing out of ranching because they go about it scientifically. Western women don't think they are doing anything so unusual, and they go about it in a more or less haphazard way—as they have seen their fathers and their mothers do before them. The Western women who began scientifically ten years ago are the ones you read about in the papers now as going to Europe every year and stopping over in New York for a few days where they say things for the papers. They don't live much on their ranches now, but in the hotels of Los Angeles and Denver.

Out in the sage-brush country of Idaho, a Chicago girl tramps every day in the wake of a grubber. She carries in her left hand a torch of her own making, which consists of a broomstick surmounted by a piece of gas-pipe rolled in cotton and dipped in kerosene. In her other hand she carries a rake. She is slight and dark in coloring; dimples play around her mouth. She wears knickerbockers and a big, floppy hat. Every once in a while she stops in her march, lays down her torch and rakes the loose sage-brush into a heap. When she has stacked it, with the rabbit brush around the tough roots, she produces a match from her hip pocket, lights her torch and fires the stack. She watches it burn deep into the earth, and scatters the ashes. Then she takes up her march at double quick under the fierce sun until she overtakes the grubber.

She has been a dressmaker in Chicago, and has taken this quarter section in her own name, under the Carey act, for seven women of her city, all of who are now engaged in business.[3] They are going out to take up their residence on the claim within a year. They will build a community clubhouse with private sitting rooms and bedrooms and a common dining-room and kitchen. They will make their homes there until they marry, whereupon they will become disqualified. One expects to raise bees, another garden stuffs, another potatoes, and another small fruits. The youngest—she who is out there now doing the heavy work of the enterprise—will be manager and overseer, unless matrimony overtakes her before that time. She has already had the lateral irrigating ditch tapped and turned on her ground, making all of the negotiations herself, and now she personally irrigates her own section, managing as many as ten of the little rivulets. It requires expert work to keep them unobstructed and freely flowing.

But in the fair Rosebud country the woman homesteader lives in greater contentment than in the dry and mountain-bound regions farther west. You see her dark head framed in a window, which she has evidently hurried toward, when she heard the whir of your automobile a quarter of a mile away. She answers your careless wave of the hand eagerly, and you think of her, of the queer, lonely appeal of her strained attitude until you ask Mr. Ernest Jackson of Dallas, who is hurrying you through the Rosebud country in his machine, to take you back.

Will she tell her story? She'd love to. She looks a little like Tess of the D'Urbervilles, with that attractively imperfect upper lip. She stands straight and tall on her doorstep, and she seems as if she were fettered by nothing in that wide stretch of earth or sky.

What is that ugly, gray, infinitesimal shack flaunted right in her very front yard? (Her own dwelling is 12 by 14, is made of lumber, and is painted gaily in white with bright yellow trimmings.) Why, you know she is a squatter. Her father drove her out from Dallas—fourteen miles—on the 29th of last September, a few hours before midnight in the light of the moon, just as the law prescribed that squatters should do. The night was so light and the country was so unobstructed—so free from trees and ravines—that you could easily see there was no one on it. They had stayed until past midnight, just as the law required, and then the next day, when she went to file in Dallas, this man said he had squatted on the land, was there before she was, and had stayed until after midnight. So he had filed, too, and they were contesting the claim! If she lost, she was certainly going to appeal her case.

No word about thinking it queer that a man would contest a woman, although many masculine spectators of the little drama have said they would never have the heart to hold out against her. She, however, is preparing to take her medicine.

Was she sorry that she had come? Oh, no, indeed, unless, that is, she lost her land. And then she would start right in to get some more. Still, she was a poor girl, and her little house cost $200. She had to teach three years to save that, and it made her sick to think of teaching again. Teaching dried up the very soul! Her cave was all dug, too. Her father had dug it, of course;

but he had been at the greatest amount of trouble. One side fell in, and he had to dig it out and insert boards to make it secure. Her fire ditch was made, too, and although she had been at no expense for it, she would hate to have her father's work all go for nothing.

She invited you inside to sit down. No such signs of opulence were manifested here as in the widow's home. Much more furniture could be accommodated in this house. There was a couch and a stove and a screen with another couch behind it, on which her father slept in his frequent visits. There was a bit of a tennis net hung on the wall and strung with pictures of young men and girls bent with laughter and holding hands.

Neighbors, as she said, were not far away; not more than three miles and a half, as a crow flies. Quite a distance, one might think, at times, but, at any rate, the small, delicate-looking, blond mistress of the next estate said she warded off homesickness by watching the smoke from the white and yellow shack of the dark, sullen Tess of the D'Urbervilles pioneer. The only companions of this little blaster of untrodden paths were Trip, her spaniel, and Dan, her canary, both of which she had brought with her from her father's home in the rural districts of Illinois. They and her organ on which she played hymns, as she used to do on Sunday evenings at home, kept her in good spirits before she was acquainted.

As for going back to that life of dependence—she drew herself to every inch of her four feet nine—she should not think of it. Her father tried to dictate to her whom she should marry, and, what was more important, whom she should not. And she considered that was something to be decided in one's own heart. Besides, it was always that same sort of dependence; that giving way to her father, her brothers, to the deacons in the church, to the directors of the school! Ugh! She loathed it! She wished to be free—free! And she loved farming. She was never going to sell her claim. She liked to get out in the fields and work! Her brother had come out with her and they had driven from Dallas with the thermometer at zero to the site of her present home. There was not a stick of wood on the farm. They looked for a long time at the spot where the house now stands, and she did not feel discouraged.

As for the solitariness of it, let me quote directly from the homesteaders: "Loneliness is loneliness everywhere. You can feel more out of it sitting in the Hotel Ritz in Paris than sitting on a pile of lumber in front of the unfinished hotel in Jordon" (Jordon being a coming metropolis of Tripp County). "And as for society, it is nonsense to say there is none in a new country."

One function took place there recently for which twenty-five written invitations were sent through the mail, some of them to the remotest confines of the country, and twenty-five acceptances were received, every one complying with the requirement therein named that guests should bring their own chairs, knives, forks, and plates. There was a dance given in the new lumber mill at Jordon in which the participants numbered three hundred. And on the word of her who will be mistress of the hotel when it is finished, until recently a trained nurse in one of the fashionable homes in New York, you would scarcely see any place a better looking assemblage of young men and women. The girls were pretty and smart looking. The young men had nearly all of them been to college. Days later, in making the tour of the county, you saw dance programs dangling from bureau posts by red ribbons. It was by no means the affair of the year, however.

The assistant banker of the town of Winner had been there, a beautiful young girl, chic in her khaki, divided skirt, and her shirt-waist. She sat on her high stool in the new office building, and looked out through the plate-glass window at the street, which was indicated by a few wheel marks in the sod.

"Yes, I had a nice time at the dance," she smiled. "But those big dances are not nearly so attractive, I think, as the little parties we give in our own shacks. I have my sister and my brother visiting me from Kansas City. Last night when I got home I found that some of the men in the neighborhood had proposed to have dinner at my house. Some of them had sent chickens, others corn, and all sorts of things.

"I ride in here every day from my shack, which is over there off the main road eight miles, and then I ride home again in the evening. When I got there last night I found dinner in full blast. We have such jolly, informal times! And I do love my freedom so! I had a dreadful time to get away from home. My father and my mother and my brothers promised me anything if I would give up the scheme, but they couldn't give me the only thing I wanted, which was this wonderful independence and freedom. All the girls I know in Kansas City are wild about it."

And by way of corroboration of this truth, in walked a newly enrolled resident of the community. She was small and slight. She wore a one-piece frock, with a long waist-line, and a flounce of a skirt, all of which had been created by the hand of an amateur. She had come up from Kansas City for two weeks, and then decided to remain permanently. The letter of her former employer, accepting her resignation, was in one hand and a newspaper in the other. This was the first day in seven years that she had not felt the restraining influence of those employers, the slavery of having to get somebody else's thoughts on to paper without altering their form and to do it within a certain length of time. Now she felt free! The newspaper in her hand contained extracts from a letter she had written home telling of the splendid young quarter-breed Indians of the country, who were so fine, so handsome, so rich! The headline on her letter read: "Kansas City Girl Tells of Quarter-Breed Beaux!"

A glamour and a rapture seem to play about the lives of all those who enter this land of golden sunshine and golden crops. The postmistress, far up in the northern part of the county, feels it as she performs her daily tasks. When she discovers some passing countryman whom she can induce to stop at every home along his route and deliver mail, she is frankly pleased to have accomplished so much for the Government without expense. When she fails, she is no less pleased to harness her own private cayuse and distribute it, free of all charge, to recipient and to Government alike. On such occasions she leaves a card on her door stating that in the absence of volunteers, she has gone to deliver the mail in person, and the hours at the post-office are necessarily, abandoned until this is done.

She acquired her position through the cooperation of all the residents of her section of the county, who signed a petition in her behalf. When she got it, she partitioned her 10 by 12 residence into two rooms, one of which she devotes to Governmental purposes. Now she has the happiness of earning a salary while she is acquiring a quarter section of land, and she works for a taskmaster whose one demand is efficient service, in the rendering of which she is undisturbed by petty naggings or jealousies of rival employees. Sometimes, she says, she fears it can not be true, and that she will wake to find herself back in that old schoolroom, the thought of which puts a look of care into her face.

Of all the women—young and not so young, frivolous and demure—who discussed their reasons for taking up a new life in a new country, not one said anything about hoping to make a large sum of money. The grass widow said she expected her land to be her meal ticket for her old age, that she was putting her $300 into it instead of into a home for the feeble, and this was the only instance of the mention of financial returns. You asked them if they did not rather begrudge putting their hard-earned money into a rake, a harrow, and a plow, but you scarcely caught their attention with the question. You asked them if it was not disheartening to find the yield so light in one's first year and to be at expense of a hired man when the men homesteaders could do everything for themselves? But they answered: "Oh, no!" and pointed out the excellent results in this dry year throughout the neighboring country of Gregory, where women, who two years ago were homesteaders like themselves, now have fifty bushels of corn to the acre.

When you are automobiling through the country of an evening, you see them with the young men homesteaders in couples, riding horseback over the roadless land. You see them walking, miles from home, with springing step across the yellow sod. Hours later, in your rambling course, you see them pull up at their own shack, dismount, and unsaddle. You see them drag a key from their belt, thrust it into the lock, swing open the door of the little dark dwelling, and, with buoyant self-reliance, cross the threshold of a home 10 by 12 by 8 that is all their own. Presently a lamp sheds its starry light a little way across the darkness, and you realize their satisfaction of possession. Out there at civilization's end, they have something which is all their own, which they will mold and manage and make support them; and they are free!

"The Last Homesteads"
Joanna Gleed Strange, *Collier's,* January 1913

The period in American history which comprises the conquest of the wilderness approaches its close with the opening up of the last Government lands for settlement. In April, 1912, three thousand farms were opened to homesteaders on Indian land in Bennett and Mellette Counties in South Dakota. The October before, fifty-two thousand people registered for chances on these farms, and those drawing lucky numbers had the opportunity in the spring of picking out sites for homesteads.

The farms are scattered among those of the Indians, for these counties are in the Rosebud and Pine Ridge Indian Reservations. The prices paid to the Government range from 50 cents to $6 per acre, and the land is so valuable for farming and grazing purposes that those who locate themselves here and stay the allotted time will have farms of 160 acres each, ranging in value from $2500 to as high as $10,000 by the time their titles are clear.

It is no wonder, then, that the little town of White River, one year old last spring, situated in the center of Mellette County, has been a busy and wide-awake place since early last spring. Here by the middle of April the selection of land began and continued until the last of May. The woman who drew No. 1 in the fall had first choice of all the land which was open. The man who got No. 2 had second choice, and the rest followed in order. Fifty numbers were called each day during the first week, and after that one hundred numbers a day until four thousand numbers were called and the three thousand farms were taken.

The experience of former land opening shows that about one-third of those qualified to select land drop out, pushing the other numbers ahead and leaving places at the end of the line for others. Those who are withdrawing now are people for the most part who registered in 1911 "just to see what would happen," with no intention of homesteading. Some few "landed" in White River several days before the drawing, when the little town was drenched with the worst rain of the season, and the prospects were so disheartening, with no sunlight to touch off the glorious country, that they left before the drawing commenced.

These people were shortsighted if they wanted farms, for good Government land is very scarce, and so valuable is this Dakota land and so ardent were the people to secure numbers that they came from practically every State in the Union to register. Four registration places were opened October 2, 1911, in South Dakota—one in Rapid City, one at Chamberlain, one at Dallas, and another at Gregory—and for each of these three thousand claims there were seventeen people registered. South Dakota, of course, had the greatest number of registrations, and the near-by States, such as Iowa, Nebraska, Colorado, Minnesota, Oklahoma, Kansas, and Arkansas, were represented by big delegations, but people also registered and drew numbers from West Virginia, Pennsylvania, Washington, California, New York, Montana, New Jersey, Texas, and even Honolulu. The registration lasted three weeks, and then the names on cards, enclosed in sealed envelopes, were all collected at Gregory, put into a large receptacle, mixed up with a pitchfork, and the preliminary drawing began.

The first name that was taken out was that of Mrs. Mary J. Kendall from Rapid City, and it is a satisfaction to know that the right thing reached the right person when Mrs. Kendall drew No. 1, for her husband has been an invalid for years, and Mrs. Kendall has had a struggle to support her family. She, of course, had the first choice of the land at the drawing, and she chose a quarter section in the southeastern part of Mellette County, seventeen miles from the little town of Wood, which as yet is so new it will not be found on any but the new county maps. In a few months the railroad will pass near by, and by the time she has "proved up" on her claim, which means that she has lived on it for a least fourteen months and has made the improvements required by the Government, her farm will be worth a good sum even if she desires to sell it as soon as the title is hers.

In opening these two counties the Government first surveyed the land and divided it into sections and quarter sections. To every Indian at the head of a family there was allotted a half section of land, and to every Indian child a quarter section.[4] The Indians were given the first choice and have the best land, but a great deal of the land which was left is first class. Values were placed on each tract and maps were distributed showing this survey, together with the lands taken out for school purposes.

Many of the people go over the land before they file, and make their own selections without help. Those who are unfamiliar with the South Dakota country find it more satisfactory to leave their selections to locators whose business it is to know the land and who, for a fee of from ten to twenty-five dollars, select as nearly as possible the kind of farms best suited to the needs of their clients. Of course there are all kinds of locators, some of them honest and others grafters, but the legitimate firms have men working for them who know every inch of the ground and can give valuable advice to homesteaders.

The best of the land is in Mellette County, the Bennett County land being mostly grazing land at a distance from any town. White River, the county seat of Mellette County, is situated on a beautiful level plateau overlooking the Little White River and surrounded by wonderfully rich territory of farm land. It is the trading point for nearly all the Indians in the central and western parts of Todd and Mellette Counties, and it is also the point to which the railroad will doubtless come within the year. At present it is reached by stage or automobile, thirty-two miles from Murdo Mackenzie on the north and sixty miles from Winner on the southeast.

During the choosing of the land this little town, so new that the paint was scarcely dry on its first buildings, accommodated a thousand people in a space hardly adequate for two hundred. People came and went each day. Some of them located as soon as they had chosen their land, started out with their sod or wooden houses, and began life as homesteaders. Others went back home to come out again later, for Uncle Sam gives each home- steader six months before he must be on his land. But during all this coming and going, in spite of the lack of accommodations every where, there never was a better natured nor a happier crowd than the one at White River. Everyone knew everyone else with the true pioneer spirit, and such introduc- tions as these were heard on every side dozens of times a day: "Got a num- ber?" "When do you file?" "Well, I hope you'll have good luck." "Perhaps we'll be neighbors. Let me see now, where are you from?" "Oh, yes; well, my name is," etc.

The town was surveyed about two years ago and the first few houses built in July, 1911, but it grew to its present size within a few months. To those of us who came out from the East, where towns are nothing if not a hundred to a hundred and fifty years old, this building of a town overnight fairly took our breath away. When the filing began, White River boasted a dozen locators' offices, half a dozen hotels and boarding houses, three stores selling general merchandise, a schoolhouse, a drug store, a livery barn, and a moving-picture show, and it had grown to this extent in one short month. Before the filing was half over, the number of stores had been doubled. Houses were popping up on every side. As one woman said, "It is nothing to go to my door at supper time and find that two new neighbors have settled in my vicinity since noon," so fast did things progress. Soon a telephone line was through and telegraph connections made. With mail each day by stage from three directions, White River found itself a real town, with the hustle and bustle and liveness characteristic of every new Western settlement.

So the country is being settled; and such country as it is! Rolling tree-less prairies, with lights and shades constantly varying on their green-brown surfaces; many deep ravines; springs and creeks with some timber along the banks; sunshine and a expanse of blue sky quite unknown anywhere but in prairie counties and in mid-ocean. Parts of it comprise the Bad Lands, which make up for their lack of fertility by their wonderful pic-turesqueness. There are buttes, rough white clay buttes, rising to good heights in the most grotesque shapes—pyramids and columns, cones and jagged peaks—looking in the distance like the sky line of some Eastern city, without the cloud of smoke above them which the cities have. The air is like wine, and everyone who has arrived is enthusiastic over the country. The winters are cold, but it is a dry cold, less penetrating than the higher temperatures farther east. The summers are hot in the daytime but there is always a breeze and the nights are cool.

Of course when one comes to a new country one expects to put up with many disadvantages. Modern conveniences are few, and pioneer life does not include opera, the theatre, and public libraries. But one is sure of good health, even if there is no bathtub for fifty miles. And for fun—good, whole-some, genuine fun—the new town on the prairie will furnish more than any city at home or abroad can boast of.

"Like it?" repeated a girl from Omaha, who filed on a claim in Tripp County in the southern part of the State three years ago. "Like it? Why, nothing could make me go back to Omaha to live. I love it. I have my little shack fixed up with my own things, and last year I raised twelve different kinds of vegetables and the best hay in the county. I have my own saddle horse, and soon I am going to have an automobile. Like it? Well, you just come out and try it. I have yet to see anyone who doesn't like it after he's been here for six weeks."

And this is true. Everyone who has homesteaded is more than enthusias-tic. Any number of young women are living alone on their claims during the fourteen months necessary to prove up. Some of them are even taking five years for their homesteading, and in this way they have a longer time to make their payments to the Government. The five years have just been shortened to three years, and doubtless many of those who have filed will take advantage of this and live in their claim shanties three years instead of fourteen months. This country is excellent farm land. Corn and small grains of all kinds may be grown, and stories told of the melons "raised on sod" are marvelous indeed. There is excellent range land, and stock raising will be an important industry of the new country.

"The Lady Honyocker:
How Girls Take Up Claims of Their Own on the Prairie[5] "
Mabel Lewis Stuart, *The Independent*, July 1913

The Independent Editor's Note:

When we see the multitude of able-bodied young men hanging around Broadway hunting for somebody who will give them some sort of a job and the still greater number of young women laboring away in offices or idly waiting for some one to come along and marry them, our admiration goes out to the girls of the West who have the courage and enterprise to carve out their own fortunes and make their own homes. You may find them on Wyoming ranches, in Idaho forests or on Dakota plains; independent, energetic and cheerful; good stuff out of which to build a future commonwealth. In our issue of January 9 Miss Everett told how she had taken advantage of "Uncle's Gift." In our Vacation Number of June 5 Miss McCutchen gave us a[n] attractive picture of her experience as a honyocker. And here Miss Stuart explains more in detail what life on the prairies means to those who are living it.

In the western parts of North and South Dakota and in Wyoming and Montana are vast stretches of country formerly inhabited only by the occasional cattle and sheep outfit, and the attendant cowboy and herder, but now becoming thickly peopled by a variety of the genus homo known as the "Honyocker"or homesteader. It is probable that in the mind of the average Easterner the homesteader is a slouchy individual of the lonely bachelor type who smokes a stub pipe, lives on pancakes and bacon, and whose occupation of "holding down a claim" is never allowed to become irksome by the introduction of hard work. It is undoubtedly true that such individuals do exist on claims, but they do not by any means form the entire population of the claim country. On the contrary a large percentage of these pioneers of Uncle Sam's are not even of the masculine sex. More than one-third of them are women who are taking an active part in the up-building of a new country and incidentally acquiring one hundred and sixty acres of Uncle Sam's land. So it is evident that the "typical homesteader" may as fairly be considered feminine as masculine and the "Lady Honyocker" as fair a representative of the claim country as the man. Certain it is that she is taking her part with zest and courage in the development of those vast stretches of country which until a few years or even months ago were a part of the still "uncivilized" West.

To the girl on the claim life presents as varied an aspect—altho in a different way—as to the fashionable young lady in New York City. But there are features of the claim life of which the city young lady never dreams, or the result of which, if she did, would probably be the nightmare. To her the thought of being alone sixty miles from the railroad, in a 10 x 12 shanty on the wide prairie, would have only terror. Not so to the girl of the claim. Alone in her little shack, a mile from the nearest neighbor, she never thinks of being afraid. Why should she be? The fact of the great distance from the railroad insures safety from tramps. Distance from a saloon, from drunken men. Of what else should she be afraid? Coyotes? Well, to be sure, she sometimes hears them howling around at night, but they seldom approach nearer than a few yards, and are easily frightened away by shouting or singing. Rattlesnakes? Perhaps. She sometimes hears and sees them. Should a rattler coil to attack, which he never does unless disturbed, she can easily run away, but will usually return with stick or gun to slay the monster. No, fear has no part in the life of the girl on the claim.

Claim life is a decided change for most girls from the mode of living in settled parts of the country. The independence and freedom, together with the added responsibility of managing one's own affairs, are irresistibly and healthfully enthralling. Girls who come out to the claim broken down in health find they can do things which before they would have thought impossible. Some girls go fifty, even sixty or seventy miles for provisions, and many of them sod up their own shacks for the winter. If you wish to form an idea of what this little exercise means, go out to a piece of ground just freshly turned over with the breaking plow, take a spade, cut a piece of the sod about eighteen inches long and carry it a short distance. Remember that it takes hundreds of such pieces to sod up a shack, and you will understand the kind of work that some of these claim girls are capable of doing. Her fearlessness, her courage, and sprightly independence are winning for the pioneer girl the applause of the truest modern chivalry and have made her the subject of at least one real "claim ballad," "The Girl on the Claim," by Arthur Chapman. We cannot forbear quoting entire this little bit of western minstrelsy.

> 'Tis a shack in the open—the girl calls it home,
> And the winds of the prairie all murmur the name—
> She has driven her stakes and has furrowed the loam,
> And high is the head of the girl on the claim.
> She fears not the night, nor the storm in its wrath—
> She is proud of her day when the sun sets like flame;
> No prison-like shop casts its shade o'er her path—
> There is hope in the face of the girl on the claim.
> She is winning each day, toward the coveted prize—
> She is beating adversity's heart-breaking game;
> There is courage sublime shining out of her eyes—
> Hats off to the girl who has staked out a claim!

The castle of the Lady Honyocker is usually a shack 10 x 12, 14 x 16 or perhaps 16 x 20 feet in dimensions. It is built of rough pine boards green from a lumber mill near some pine forest with which these states are dotted. Outside of the boards, black tarred paper is fastened securely with large-headed tacks. The house is then sodded up to afford greater warmth in winter and coolness in summer.

Within, the little house is just what the individual girl makes it. She has her books, pictures, magazines, guitar, and perhaps even her piano and hand painted china. The little home may have the individuality and originality, tho perhaps not the luxury, of a Bryn Mawr or Vassar girl's room. In fact, many claim holders are college girls and their collection of many colored pennants and other college trophies grace the walls of the prairie shack.

The fact that the tiny domicile must be kitchen, sitting room, dining room, library, and bed room all in one—with usually 120 to 168 square feet of floor space—makes the disposition of furniture and supplies a serious study, the ingenuity displayed in the interior arrangement of these small dwellings would do credit to a modern house boat or a English pleasure-caravan. A folding sanitary couch serves as bed by night and sofa by day. The stoves, number O's, are tiny affairs but complete with four griddles and an oven. Most of the other furniture is home made, probably dry goods boxes. A corner cupboard reaching to the ceiling, or rather the rafters, is sometimes seen. This is a very convenient affair—serving as pantry and larder, dish cupboard, linen press and store room.

Varying interests claim the time and attention of the homestead girl. The Musician practices three hours a day on her piano, does her housework, drills the choir, tends her poultry and garden and has some time left for her favorite pastime of target shooting.

Household duties are more or less exacting on the claim, and girls who come out with the idea that life will be one long holiday are surprised to find how busy they are. If one is to live and if the frequent visitors (one girl counted fifteen in one week) are to be properly fed, bread must be made, the cookie jar kept filled, and other important details attended to. Before the cooking can be done there is also wood to be chopped from the huge pile before the door—it is possible for a girl to become a very good woodchopper.

The idea that the girl on the claim leads a lonely life is one not always easily disproven in the minds of anxious eastern friends. But a short stay in one of these busy claim communities would surely convince the most solicitous. Many times three or four girls take claims near together, building their shacks only a few rods apart. The writer knows one such little settlement in Butte County, South Dakota. Two sisters and their brother took up adjoining claims and the three houses are within a stone's throw of each other. Another pair of sisters, friends of the first two, took adjoining quarters and built their houses close together, and as near to the others as possible. This would be a half mile, the length of a quarter section. The houses were connected by telephone so that the two groups could communicate at any hour of the day or night.

Aside from this pleasant social life with the nearer neighbors there is a great deal to take away any tendency to "lonesomeness" on the claim in various social organizations. In the community of Redig, Harding County, South Dakota, a little church has been started, meeting at first in the shacks. As the interest grew a neat and commodious building was put up. During the winter a series of socials, parties and literary and musical entertainment kept the community humming. In the same settlement a young people's branch of the Woman's Christian Temperance Union was organized, and held several oratorical contests, receptions and other social affairs. Somerset parties were also very much the rage in this particular settlement while at a neighboring "town" (store and dance hall) the more gaily inclined found a chance to cultivate the "light fantastic."

It is not to be thought that the talents of the brilliant girl are wasted or buried in a napkin during her residence on the claim. Opportunities for social service are nowhere greater than in the claim country of the West. One does not need to live in Hull House or in a Frances Willard settlement in order to serve humanity. In a certain community called "Harmony Settlement" of western South Dakota some young women had come out amid the signs and lamentations of friends that they were going "out West to that awful uncivilized claim country." But the young women themselves viewed the situation in an entirely different light. In the midst of the most primitive pioneer life—not without privation—a phrase often upon their lips was "We'll make our civilization." The west needs forming as much as the city needs reforming. There are children brought up on the ranges of South Dakota who do not know that they live in South Dakota or the United States of America! Surely the Honyocker school teacher who rides sixteen miles to and from her school each day may feel that she is doing a work as important as ever Mamie Rose did for Owen Kildare.[6]

What think ye? Is it harder to ride in a street car in New York City to a mission in the slums to teach a Sunday School class of street gamins, or to walk seven miles in the burning sun, over cactus and sage brush and thru deep draws to take part in a temperance meeting in the West?

We are personally acquainted with one young woman who supplied two pulpits on Sunday, driving several miles between appointments. A gifted elocutionist who had delighted audiences in many states invited "all children under ninety-nine years of age" to a "safe and sane Fourth" providing with a friend refreshment and entertainment. A trained nurse who commanded a large salary in the city kept what was almost in reality a free dispensary, so lavishly did she give from her medicine chest in time of sickness. As healing as the medicine was the outpouring of sympathy from her full heart for her fellow creatures. Many a mile has she walked in the heat or cold to minister to a suffering neighbor, and it is probable that many a life has been saved by her efficient aid. The Bible class teacher in the Sunday School at Redig had expected to become a foreign missionary. But she took a claim and became a home missionary, delighting us Sunday after Sunday with her vivacious presentation of Jewish history.

Our Musician studied in a Chicago conservatory and was offered a college position, but she too came west and took up land. She also took hold of the music in the little new church, directing the choir, training the children, and making the old reed instrument thunder and peal like a grand pipe organ.

Instances might be multiplied of the ennobling work of our young women in the new West, and of their fine courage and determination. Surely they are to be congratulated upon the opportunity thus wisely seized upon—to become stable factors in the economic life of the nation—and upon their adaptability, energy and perseverance in triumphing over the trying conditions of pioneer life. But no less is our Uncle Samuel to be congratulated that his pioneer country has so large a representation of that class of true nobility and sterling worth, the "Lady Honyocker."

4. Please Answer Soon: Letters of Single Women Homesteaders

. . . .

The articles women homesteaders wrote for the popular press were, in most cases, written after the woman had proved up, an experience that qualified her to speak of homesteading with authority. Letters, however, were written while the women homesteaders were in the process of gaining that experience. Thus, their letters express the hope of success rather than the certainty of it, focusing on the homesteaders' immediate concerns and daily activities. As public documents, the popular press articles may have idealized the homesteaders' experiences to fit the expectations of editors promoting the back-to-the-land movement. The letters, intended for a private audience, provide a more candid portrait of the homesteaders' experiences.

Without long-distance phone calls and e-mail to connect people separated by long distances, letter writing played an essential role in early twentieth century American life. It was a way for a solitary woman to alleviate the loneliness that isolation on her claim may have imposed and a way to converse intimately with people who cared about her hopes and fears, her successes and failures. While writing a weekly letter home would have been common practice for any homesteading woman far from her family and friends, for a woman homesteading alone, letter-writing also seems to have substituted for the kind of conversation she would have had with a companion: discussing unusual incidents, remarking on the weather, making observations about people and landscape, making plans for the future, expressing her worries. The letters created a snapshot of the single woman homesteader's life for family and friends. Sharing the new life she was living in her letters may have been a way of reassuring her readers that she was doing just fine.

Being a good letter writer was a useful skill and something of an art. Thus, some writers not only conveyed information and feelings but included carefully composed and detailed descriptions of landscapes, people, and events. Alone in her cabin at night, with no radio or television and few books, a woman might spend hours creating a letter, imagining her reader before her. At other times, needing simply to convey information, she might scribble a hasty note. The letters included here illustrate both the hastily written and the carefully created as well as many variations in between. One might speculate on the effect of these letters on their recipients. A letter meant connection. The paper on which it was written bore the invisible touch of the writer; the words on the page depicted the characteristics of the writer's speech and personality.

People saved and reread letters, savoring the sense of the writer's presence conveyed in them. Did they think these letters might someday be read as historical documents? Perhaps so since, fortunately, some people saved letters over the course of a lifetime, passing them down to succeeding generations within their families or donating them to historical archives. These surviving letters are invaluable links to the past in which the voices of those who actually lived history can be heard.

More than any other genre in which single women homesteaders wrote, these letters allow today's reader to get to know the writers in a personal way, just as the original recipients did. Sometimes the letters reveal such private thoughts that you may feel you have intruded into a personal diary. The women reveal themselves in their accounts of what they are doing and in the way they respond to the challenges of homestead life. Alice Newberry confides insecurities about balancing homesteading and her teaching career. Julia Erickson worries that her increasing gray hairs mean diminishing prospects of marriage. Ida Garvin reports her declining health without a hint of self-pity. Each woman tells of at least one harrowing encounter with a snake, that biblical nemesis of women. Symbolic of any evil that might banish them from the "garden" of their homestead dreams, the snake is no match for these brave and determined women.

Their letters show the same themes present in other genres of women homesteader literature: the hope of improved economic and social status through homesteading, the dilemma of whether to marry, the delight in living close to nature.

One can sense their growing independence and confidence as they discarded Victorian expectations and took on whatever kinds of work needed to be done to support their claims. Single women homesteaders' letters show that they were shaping in words the new identities they were living out in their daily lives, and they were experimenting with bold observations they might not make in public.[1] Thus, Julia writes her friend Anna what she really thinks of her "man-crazy" acquaintance Bessie and Alice writes "Mama" that she has decided not to marry because she can't stand the idea of cooking three meals a day for a man. These women are not only writing letters, they are writing new scripts for their lives.

The following letters appear in chronological order by date when the women homesteaded. The letters of Alice Newberry, Julia Erickson, and Ida Garvin have been transcribed from handwritten documents, which sometimes required that I make decisions about unclear penmanship, incorrect word usage, and errors in punctuation and spelling. In the case of unclear penmanship, when possible, I made educated guesses about the word by considering its context and placed such words inside brackets [ ]. When it was impossible to determine the word or name, I left a blank space (_____) to indicate my omission. The manuscript retains errors in spelling and punctuation unless I believed they would interfere with the readers' understanding of the letter. In the Newberry and Garvin letters, I omitted lengthy passages with no direct relevance to the women's homesteading lives. I have indicated where these omissions occur with an ellipsis (. . .). In some cases, when an omitted passage relates indirectly to their homesteading lives, I have summarized the missing information in italics.

Alice Newberry, Colorado — 1903

Alice Newberry's letters to her family, written from her claim in eastern Colorado, provide insight into a single woman's reasons for homesteading and show how she managed the daily challenges of living alone on her claim. Alice's experiences illustrate several recurring themes in the collected writing of single women homesteaders. First, she was a second generation homesteader, the daughter of parents who homesteaded in eastern Colorado but gave up their claim after their marriage failed. Second, Alice continued with her career as a schoolteacher while she proved up, a combination that worked well for many women homesteaders. Third, Alice's letters illustrate how a homesteading venture that began with an entrepreneurial motivation ultimately became the source of as much emotional gratification as it did economic benefit.

Katherine Harris, who devotes a chapter to Newberry in *Long Vistas: Women and Families on Colorado Homesteads* (1993), explains that Alice had been teaching in Kit Carson County, Colorado, for several years when, at twenty-five years of age, she was convinced by a family friend, Mr. Well-born, that taking out a claim would be advantageous for her. Harris notes that Alice's letters illustrate how her somewhat reluctant attitude about her homestead gradually gave way to optimism about its prospects as she invested more and more of her time and money in it. Her experiences with managing the land and the men she hired to work it seem to have helped her find a direction for her life. Her ability to overcome primitive living conditions and unwanted varmints as well as unpredictable weather seems to have bolstered Alice's confidence in herself. So in 1909, having proved up and lived on the claim, off and on, since 1903, Alice gathered the courage to take the teacher's examination that would qualify her to teach in Denver. After passing the exam she moved to Denver where she was eventually able to build a home with the combined income from teaching and from leasing her homestead land for agricultural use. Alice's papers and letters show that she held on to her homestead land all her life, willing it to her nieces and nephews upon her death.

Comparing and contrasting Alice's letters with those of others in this collection reveals the significance of what she did not write as well as what she did. Like Ida Garvin's letters to her mother, Alice's letters to "Mama" seem written to assure her mother that she is doing fine, sharing with her mother her misgivings as well as her successes. The reader senses that the letters provided a way for Alice to talk through the various decisions she needs to make about managing the homestead, her teaching career, and her personal life. Alice wrote a different type of letter to her brother Eldon. In writing to him, she adopts a light, sometimes humorous tone, rarely revealing her inner thoughts and giving him instead practical information about her land and its value, perhaps in an attempt to assure him of her ability to succeed in her homesteading venture.

Unlike the letters of Julia Erickson, Alice's letters lack details of any romantic alliances she may have formed. Whether she had none or whether she simply decided not to confide them to her mother is unclear. She did admit to her mother that she would consider marriage if "I could find any-one who would have me." Alice's unmarried status may have been a choice influenced by the increased independence she felt after homesteading. She seems to have been a practical woman who would have preferred spinster-hood if she could not find a marriage partner who suited her.

The following letters are representative, not inclusive, of the collection of Alice Newberry's correspondence, which is preserved in The Colorado History Museum.

⚹　⚹　⚹　⚹　⚹　⚹

The following letter consists of excerpts from one written to her brother Eldon.

Flagler, Colorado
Sept. 20, 1906

Dear Eldon:–

. . . I spent several weeks this summer on the claim. I went down there the thirteenth of July. No adventures except snakes, and there were no rattlers among them. I killed two outside, one in the house, and let two get away.

I had always had a dread of finding a snake in the house when I went in for there was no threshold beneath the door. I had just heard a sermon on "Fear" and how it was a travesty on Christian faith for us to be afraid of anything for it showed a lack of trust in God. . . . So I resolved not to fear centipedes nor snakes. And I went into my little dugout. I had just hung up my bonnet and was congratulating myself on having so cool and quiet a place to rest in after my warm walk, when glancing toward my trunk, I saw several inches of snake disappear behind it. I went out of that place with a yell and a run. Of course I went back with a hoe before long and killed the "varmint." It was only two feet long, and fought at me only with its tongue. I was too wrought up to use mine. Most of the time I enjoyed very much. I have never felt so rested to go to school. . . .

I am studying evenings for I hope to enter Colorado College next year. That is in Colorado Springs. So I shall spend next summer on the claim, and the spring following the land will be mine "to have and to hold."

It is worth about ten dollars an acre, and will be worth more, I hope. That doesn't seem worth while to one who is used to land at one hundred dollars per acre. But it is constant by increasing in value, and there has not been a failure for five years past. Fine crops, this year, especially good, and no grasshoppers. I must try to improve the land as I can.

Thank you for the souvenir post cards. They help my collection out a good deal. It is after nine and I must go to bed. I am lazy or tired, one tonight; and I am afraid this letter will hardly prove interesting. But I wanted to thank you right away for the photograph.

Goodnight, with love,
Alice

⚹　⚹　⚹　⚹　⚹　⚹

Flagler, Colorado
April 21, 1907

Dear Mama:–

Your letter came this last week with the samples of roofing. I shall not bother to have a house built for myself. I prefer a dugout. It is so much cooler in the summer, and warmer in winter than anything I can afford to put up. . . .

After this year I shall have to go to work at something again, but I hope I can manage to stay with the claim until I get title to it.

ᶔ   *ᶔ*   *ᶔ*   *ᶔ*   *ᶔ*   *ᶔ*

Stratton, CO
June 4, 1907

Dear Mama:–

When I wrote you about a month ago, I did not tell you that I have a boarder. I didn't have him then, I believe. He is putting in the crop on my farm. Mr. Wellman furnishes the team and man and the seed and farming implements and is farming my land. I have to have so much land tilled in order to prove up. Breaking Costs $2.00 for every acre broken. This way it costs me nothing but the month's board and bother of having the man. He is a very good, mild, meek, patient, respectable married man from North Dakota.

There was no one else to board him because by the time he drove the team back and forth from Wellman's here—ten miles—the remainder of the day would not count for much, and any way he is so slow. Then it would be hard on the horses, and breaking the sod seems to tire them very much as it is. Mr. Wellman will have the crop. This is the way they always bargain in new land the first year. I am glad to get the work done in this way. I hope Mr. W. won't be hailed out as he was on his own place last year.

I am sure there never was a man who ate so much as Henry. He is very nice to cook for because he eats all of my experiments without a murmur. But there is usually very little left over to warm up in the way of potatoes. He will get through this week, and I know its wicked, but I want to say, "Praise the Lord." I wouldn't be married for anything, not to a man who eats so much. It takes all my time to cook.

When he is so slow I feel like throwing things and I have all I can do sometimes not to say things, sometimes. Our conversation is limited to my asking him if he will have some of this or that, and to him saying "please" or merely taking a dish without saying anything. After his hunger is pretty satisfied he may talk about corn or rain . . .

ᶔ   *ᶔ*   *ᶔ*   *ᶔ*   *ᶔ*   *ᶔ*

Stratton, CO
June 30, 1907

Dear Mama:–

. . . I was talking with a newcomer the other day. He said "Miss Newberry, you have a fine piece of land, but I mustn't tell you that for when you prove up I want to buy it." I told him I wouldn't sell. You know if you make any negotiations toward selling and anyone wants to take the matter up against you [by contesting the claim as land speculation], he can make you lose your right to the quarter . . . I always tell people I mean to live here always and be buried here. When I took the claim I thought it all foolishness and only did so because Mr. Wellman insisted that I use my right while I had a chance to get good land near town. Four miles seems near where so many are twenty miles from railroad for land. I have sixty acres broken. There are a hundred acres of bottom land, and the rest is slightly rolling—not as much so as our old claim near Clearmont. I would have taken that if I had had a chance, but never did. Mine is better land, not so sandy, though farther from town. . . .

After feeding Henry, her boarder, for a month, she writes the following:

. . . I have decided not to marry. Three warm meals a day, three-hundred-sixty-five days in the year for the term of my natural life is more than I can face. I have decided to study up a little and try to fit myself for a higher calling.

In the last four pages of this letter, she writes of the home she hopes to build one day to replace the dugout she currently lives in and her wish to bring her mother to live with her on the homestead.

. . . I am afraid I'll have to earn and save money faster than I ever have, if it is built in our lifetime, however. Lumber is so high I will build it of cement block for which I have plenty of sand down in the creek. Just wait till all this land on the flat produces three crops of alfalfa a year at fifteen dollars a ton. Howsomever, it will need lots of preparation before it can bring in any returns. Now laugh at me and call me visionary.

I hope Eldon can come home for a real vacation this summer, one longer than twenty-four hours.

Elda Blake was married last Thursday to Arthur Conly of So. Dakota, a new comer. I was invited and so were Wellman's. I did not go but Wellman's did. They had a very pretty small wedding—just a few old friends and relations—the nicest kind of a marriage, I think. All the cousins of ours are getting married. Some one in our family ought to begin. I would if I could find anybody who would have me. . . .

I met a minister from Berthoud last Sunday. He thinks me very plucky to stay alone on my claim. It doesn't take so much pluck to stay alone as it

Alice Newberry in her Denver classroom. (*Colorado Historical Society*)

does to mix with a crowd, sometimes. He has a claim 85 miles from here and will move his family there next fall. He would rather be on a claim than to have a steady charge. I think that's queer for a minister.

　　Well goodbye,
　　With love to all,
　　Alice

✳ 　 ✳ 　 ✳ 　 ✳ 　 ✳ 　 ✳

"The Burrow," Stratton, Colorado
Aug. 8, 07

Dear Mama:–

Since I wrote last I have been in Burlington attending Institute for two weeks. Then last week I was busy papering and cleaning. I did not mean to paper now that I know I am going to Burlington. During May and part of June I could not do so because the "man" was here. Then came the work on the medal contest and I was away so much that I could not get anything much done toward the cleaning. The medal contest came July 13. The 14th I went to Burlington, and did not come back until July 26.

I came to the claim immediately and had been here only a day or so when I saw a "brown worm with legs" glide across the wall above my bed and disappear in a crevice in the plastering just beneath the roof. I was as bad as Mr. Newbern for I watched it, fascinated, wondering that a caterpillar of that size should be in the house. You see it was after lamplight, and the wall was somewhat in the shadow. I wondered at its seeming so much more brushy at the ends than at the other diameters of its body. Then too it was moving slowly, and all the centipedes I have ever seen move quickly. I got a little more light on the subject by holding the lamp nearer the wall, and seeing what the thing was, started for the fire shovel. But it was too quick for me, and got away. I was undressing when I saw it and although the bane of my life is, and has always been, going to bed at night, and getting up in the morning, I certainly have never dreaded getting into bed as I did that night. I thought I would sit up until morning. But the novelty wore off after a while, and I went to bed, thinking that if I must be stung I probably would not mind it so much if I were dozing as if I were broad awake.

Next morning, I commenced papering. This I am telling you to explain why I am cleaning house in July and August when I know that school begins the first Tuesday in September, and that I must be away for so much of the time. I am not through cleaning yet, because I ran out of cheesecloth and old muslin. I have to put cloth on the wall first; otherwise the paper will not stick. I have been taking the cloth to the roof edge and to the baseboard. Then I paste the cloth to the wall, and after putting paste on the paper, stick that to the cloth. It makes three times the work, but the paper sticks well and the rough wall becomes firm as adamant, almost. You see this house has never been plastered but once, and that upon the sod and excavated wall. Native lime was used too and when I tried to put the paper on the wall itself, the grains of sand would stick to the paper and then drop out of the plaster bringing the paper also. The cheesecloth and paper together close the crevices, and it (the wall) ought to be proof against centipedes, snakes, [also worms].

Last week it rained every day but one. It is doing nearly as well this week. And oh, so hot! The thermometer was up to a hundred in the shade yesterday afternoon. It is 3 minutes after ten now, and the thermometer is at 90 in the shade. Once in a while I forget and look at the thermometer to see what time it is. That has not happened for quite a while so you see I am not so absent minded as I was when I got the thermometer. This is proof that a thermometer is a means of overcoming absentmindedness.

The "burrow" is very cool unless I have to have a fire. Then it is like a furnace and does not cool off until night. Therefore my mid day meal consists of roots and herbs, and cold "leftovers." I have had a great many radishes, and a little lettuce. I have planted four packages of radishes. The last ones planted will be ready to be devoured in a week or so. The lettuce seed I have put in has not come well. It cannot be good. I am putting in some more, and these nice rains ought to help it if there is any good in it.

The potatoes and corn are late, because of the cold spring. The cantaloupes and melons worry me greatly because they are not going to be ready to eat until after I go to Burlington. I go down and look at them very often; but they are not hurrying it seems to me. We had such a drouth late in June and all through July until the 26th so I suppose things are doing as well as they can. I have some little trees growing. I hope for the sake of Mr. Frank Howard and the tree's sake, too, that I will be able to raise them so that they will be a credit to the neighborhood and to me. There were seventeen when I counted them last. I want to plant some more, as soon as I can.

I noticed in the "Gazette" that Eldon is at home. I hope he can stay long enough so that he can get a real rest. I would have liked very much to come home this summer, but I can't of course.

I enclose a letter from Miss Chiph. Board is high in Burlington as you will see. But I think I will have to go to Spark's. I am afraid my money will, also. There won't be as much made by me as there was last year. I have met Miss Morris. She is one of Mrs. Fuller's favorites. I am another, I am told. But perhaps she would not care to do as Miss Chiph suggests. Every one in Burlington worships her and this last year has been the most profitable year in school work that they have ever had. Miss Morris introduced water color and drawing into her room last year. She told me that this year we would have it all through the school. During Institute, Miss Jandt from Sioux City, a friend of Mrs. Jane Adams Selders, whom Eldon has heard about, gave us lessons. She is fine, but my paintings aren't. After we put on the water wash, we painted sky and grass into our landscapes and then we put in trees where we thought they belonged. Then Miss Jandt told us to turn our wet paintings upside down, "to let the trees grow" she explained merrily, and of course if your work was all right this would cause sky and tree tops to blend nicely, and give an effect of distance.

[Page missing]

. . . picture is as it was, and was as it is. I am scared when I think of having to create any such sunsets before a class of 6th and 7th graders. I bought a box of colors and am trying to learn. I was going to show you the patch of corn on my claim and the hills beyond by means of my brush. But I have decided to call the composition "Spring" instead. The hills I changed to trees. Some of the bird's wings are unjointed, as you can easily see. That tender yellowish green in the foreground is the very tint of the young leaves of trees in the spring. Ever notice it? I never knew any pond to be so over-grown with green slime in early spring, as is the one in the foreground, right lower corner (I locate it so that you may be able to tell what it is.) But this might be so in a very warm climate. Indeed, I think it extremely probable.

I am sure I shall find the work very valuable this year, but I fear the pupils will not. It has helped me to cultivate my imagination and to see things I never could see before, and that no one else can ever see. But confidentially, I'd have refused the school if I had known when I signed the contract that I must try to do this. All that keeps me from it now is my great sense of honor, and the feeling that resignation would be prompted by the spirit of the quitter. But when I look at some of my productions I feel that duty and honor both demand that I hand in my resignation before I begin on the pupils. I send this as some slight consolation to Edna because of her lemon pie. Tell her if she will teach that painting class I'll make her three lemon pies a week. When you get through studying this work of art, please cut out the little sketch on the back called "On the Bridge" and send it (the "On the Bridge") back. I think I want to use it in school.

Is Aunt Josie still in LaMoille, and does she feel any better? How are Grandma and Aunt Alice? Where did Uncle Clem and Aunt Edie go this year for their vacation? Where is Florence? I wrote to her quite a while ago, but I presume she is busy. Is Eldon still at home? I suppose Edna's school begins the same day that mine does. I met Miss Docia Dodd. She seems younger and more girlish. How are you and how do you stand the hot weather? I must close. With love to all.

Alice

✷   ✷   ✷   ✷   ✷   ✷

"The Burrow" Stratton, Colorado

July 23, 1908

Dear Mama:—

My birthday again, though I presume it is not necessary to tell you which one. But serious as this is coming to be to me; it isn't the matter I am writing you about today. Mr. Wellman told me this morning before I came to the claim that a Mr. Mirium (a man with a family) north of me, wishes to rent my land, for farming because of the well and the fence. I can not charge him a cash rent because crops are too uncertain here, but if he furnishes everything I am entitled according to the custom here to one fourth of the crop. Some years that might mean quite a little — some years nothing. This year it's apt to mean the latter. Of course, if I rent to some one else besides letting Mr. Wellman have it I ought to settle up with him (W.) and have things entirely my own "to have and to hold". I owe him $96.37 and that absolves me from all indebtedness when it is paid. Now of course I could finish paying for the well, and let Mr. Wellman take the fence which he is willing to do — in that event, however, I'd be unable to rent the land at all because a fenced piece is more desirable, and since the fence is here and could strengthen my proof next May to have it, I wish to keep it.

Another thing, Wellmans hope to go to Arkansas as soon as possible. He did say he would not go until they sold everything outright, but now he has a chance to rent his place, and sell the stock, and they will probably close the bargain soon. So I wish to pay him up in full. So I have written Uncle Clem just now asking for a loan of one hundred dollars. I probably may not be able to get it. I thought I would rather ask him than Uncle John whom I have never seen. Though perhaps it would have been better to ask Uncle John. I do not know. I am very sorry to have to go into debt at all, (and yet I see no other way out of it) especially because I have no school as yet. Bethume has hired — hired the week before I went down. Mrs. Blake was and is, one of the directors and she seemed anxious for me to take the school, and spoke to me again when I was there, saying she wished I had taken it when she asked me last spring. It is eight months at $50. I wish I had taken it too, now. I have not heard from the Stratton board, yet, but if they turn me down, I won't be at all surprised. I would rather have this if I can get it for there's more in it than in a longer term at sixty — if they only have seven month's as they say they will.

Oh, Mr. Wellman says Mr. Mirium is a fine farmer, and that the place would have good care in his hands should I leave it after proving up next spring. Now I know you will be very [*from this point on the letter is written in the margins of the pages previously written.]* sorry to get this about my borrowing and I am sorry to have to write it, but I thought I ought to let you know what I have done. Of course, Uncle Clem may not care or may not feel that he can let me have the money. In that case, I'll have to ask Uncle John I suppose.

Fine rains again. Everything is growing fine now but it is so late. Mr. Mirium won't want the land until spring. I suppose, he would want to break out more of the bottom land, and that, of course, I wish done, if it can be kept under good cultivation. I know I should have hustled around and got a school sooner than I have begun to, but I really felt, and do yet, that I wished I might never see the inside of a grade schoolroom again. I presume now this is a sort of punishment—if I do not get a school. Every one looks at me and tells me I should take a rest from teaching. "If I only could." I wish I were a man, and I would.

Florence says in a letter I had from her the other day, that every thing points now to her going by way of the Atlantic to join others of the party in England. So she won't be here and in the light of what has turned up today, I can't see how I can come home. Sometime I think I don't want to have to see her go, and have to say "Goodbye." And if I can't come home, that will be the better way to look at it, undoubtedly. N_____ Tiffany is very anxious to have me make her a visit in Kansas City. Of course, from here Kansas City and Omaha are common points, and there is no difference, as she urges in the fare to Chicago, via Kansas City, than via Omaha. But I can't come. If I _____ it, and if I have no school I am sure of it.

I hope you can straighten this out. I have written so haphazardly.

Lovingly,

Alice

* * * * * *

Stratton, Colorado, May 6, 1909

Dear Eldon:–

Your letter came Monday, and I am returning the letter that belongs to you. I meant to write yesterday, but I have been busy washing, papering and cleaning this dirty little dug-out the paper was some I had left from a previous fracas of this kind, and so there was not nearly enough. I have eked out with newspapers, however, and the effect is wholesome in its cleanliness, though the style is new (perhaps) and unique. It is also a source of information and speculation. I can sit quietly in my chair and read about "Binks in Africa," the Small Ad and Real Estate section, and latest advertisements from Burlington. This method of papering is also valuable because it excites and cultivates the imagination. For instance there is a most absorbing (presumably) chapter about "The Loves of the Lady Arabella." I haven't read it, but some day when I have nothing better to do—I hope that time never comes—I'll probably find a good half dozen of these loves have been glued to the wall, and have so become invisible and unreachable. Anyway it's clean after the smoke and grime of last winter.

It's getting quite dry and dusty. No moisture of any kind has fallen for about two weeks.

About the money, Eldon, I think you are doing all you can, and more than you ought to do. You have sent mama all you can spare, and are shingling the house, besides. I will try to borrow what I need of Uncle John, and I am writing to you for his address. Please send it to me at once if you can give it. If I have half a crop, I ought to be able to pay him and Uncle Clem too this fall. Otherwise, I'll have to teach it out! as usual.

I hope to go home about June 7, if things work out.

Spring seems to be here at last. All sort of tiny lovely spring flowers—lilies, violets, buffalo peas—and hosts of others are here. The cactus has not yet blossomed. Such a long hard winter makes me appreciate spring as never before, and I am always anxious enough to be sure that winter is over.

Mr. Tate is putting in the barley. The wheat—about thirty-five acres is all in. It is a beautiful day. I am cooking onions for dinner. Can you smell them? Not that this has anything to do with the day.

Lovingly yours,
Alice N.

* * * * * *

"The Burrow," Stratton, Colorado,
May 10, 1909

Dear Mama:–

This is Monday morning, blustery and cool. I am not going to wash today. But instead I'll refoot some stockings which have been needing my attention for a long time, and clean out the safe drawer. I spent a great part of yesterday burning old letters from you all. I had saved them until now and carried them about, but letters from friends, even though I may not have many, do accumulate so in four years. So I reread them all and disposed of them. It took almost all of my day. I could not go to church because of great yawning gaps in the sides of my shoes and the new ones I had sent for had not yet come from Denver. I have been unusually hard on shoes this year. This makes my fourth pair since August, and that is the worst record I've ever made. I've had them wet so many times in spite of "overboots" as little Frankie Blankenship says, that the leather seemed to lose all life. I rubbed them with vaseline too, but I think I must have dried them too quickly, usually, because they break out so across the vamp. Yesterday was, in spite of old shoes a very nice day. It was so beautiful that after breakfast I walked across to the east side to look at the wheat which is now coming up. Mr. Tate has put in so well. Parts of my ground he has gone over five times already to be sure to rid it of thistles. He is one of the best and most thorough farmers here, and if I do not have a good crop it will not be his fault. He says that with three good rains when they are needed and with no hail, I should have two thousand bushels of wheat and barley. Of course, half of it will be his. But even then, if it is any price at all, I should make something—good interest off the nearly seventy dollars so far that I've spent on it. We need rain. We had a little Saturday, but we need more. He says my land is fine. But every one says so—if it had moisture. It is nearly all low land—a little sandy and it does not dry out so fast as the uplands. It is not as sandy as the piece northeast of Claremont where we used to be. But this is a farm bulletin, and what I want to tell you is about my day yesterday.

The day was so perfect as to weather, and I am always idiotic in my anxiety for spring. It seemed a joy just to be alive. The little yellow violets have scarcely lifted their faces above ground. I can't blame the modest little things for being shocked for "winter is lingering in the lap of spring" a scandalously long time this year. And the sand lilies! There have never been so many before; and they are dotting the land with their purity as the dandelions have strewed it with gold. So you can see that the air was filled with sweetness and perfume even when the meadow larks weren't brimming it over with liquid melody. It was better than being in church and not a bit hard to keep your mind on the text—"that surely the earth is full of the goodness of God." Some of the little blossoms that usually have no fragrance are daintily sweet this year. It may be because I've had no dreadful colds this year and because my olfactory nerves are in better condition than they usually are at this season, that I am able to detect all this delightful perfume. That's probably the reason. But it's a prosaic one. I prefer to believe that this terrible winter has brought the flowers up to their best a sort of "Sweet are the uses of adversity" and I managed to get a little preachment from the thought.

I came back to make my bed and burn letters. It could have been a little gloomy because the wind was getting boisterous by this time, and it is not a supposably pleasant task to bring up from their graves old ghosts. But there were no ghosts. I laughed over many of Edna's letters, especially the Benedict party in honor of Miss Henrietta. How nice Mrs. Benedict has always been to us! She, like Janet Norris and some other lovely people, I have known, seem never to have been able to see a vast difference in the rich upper soil where the Hoppes-Norris scions flourish and the impoverished sub soil where the Newberry's strive for existence. She even seems to think that subsoiling helps both layers! It at least gives the Newberry plants a chance for a little more sunlight and cultivation and air, and in that party of which Edna writes, perhaps one of the Hopps got a little stirring about the roots which was needed. But Carrie was never like that, and could never have acted as Grace did, over a matter of a little cultivation which it seems was not culture.

In the evening I went to Mrs. Tate's for the milk. She kept me all evening, and played for me. She played some of the things I love best. I think I have told you that she is a Denverite, a Catholic, and a whole-souled generous woman. She doesn't seem to think that because I am not of her faith that I am headed straight for purgatory—a state of existence from which it will be impossible to extricate me. There is one Catholic family here who seems to entertain that belief about all who are not of their creed. Mrs. Tate was educated in a convent. Such beautiful needlework as she can do—and musically illiterate as I am I know she plays well. She played so nicely, and I enjoyed the evening so much that I am afraid I stayed later than I ought. It was quite dark—no light but the stars, and they proved somewhat fickle for I was lost and had difficulty getting home. I thought I was going right until I saw that the constellation "Scorpion" did not seem to be where it ought to be. I have learned that the North Star is suppposably north, and looking for the Big Dipper I could make it seem nowhere—the Pole Star I mean now except in the _____ _____ _____ knew I was lost. I should have gone southeast from Tate's and I went straight south instead. So I located myself and got home at ten. I wasn't lost long. But after this when I call on Mrs. Tate and her piano Sunday evenings I'll come home earlier.

With love to all,
Alice C. Newberry

✳   ✳   ✳   ✳   ✳

"The Burrow," Stratton, Colorado
May 21, 1909

Dear Mama:–

I made up my mind fully this morning to try the Denver examinations. In that case, I can not start for home until after June 22 for the tests last three days, June 17–18 and 21. . . .

Now with me the case is like this. I like Colorado and I wish to stay here. I like Denver and I am sure I can do the work if they will give me a chance. I do not wish to stay in Kit Carson County any longer as a teacher, though I fully mean to build that house I've planned here on the claim, and live here with you some day when things "work out." If I can get a place in Denver schools perhaps you and I can do "light-housekeeping" together there and be together, if Denver is not too "high" in prices and altitude. . . .

Alice goes on to list advantages of living in Denver such as music and the ability to take courses at Denver University.

Summers we can spend here on the claim. If the claim does anything in the way of crops it will help and if it won't we'll have a few acres irrigated for garden and fruit and let the rest "go to grass" and pasture. I suppose Eldon will say this is "one of Alice's visionary schemes. . . ."

Of course all these plans, as yet, are "the stuff dreams are made of." But this is my scheme, as it has been for a long time. Only today, I feel daring enough to try to carry it out, if things go right.

Lovingly,
Alice N.

On June 18, 1909, Alice wrote a postcard to her mother saying she had taken the teacher's exam in Denver. Sometime before the fall school term began, she moved to Denver. Eventually Alice's mother went to live with her there, remaining until her death on December 18, 1920. Alice lived in Denver until her death in 1954 at aged seventy-five.

Julia Erickson Stockton, Montana — 1911

Julia Erickson's letters provide an especially intimate view of the thoughts of a single woman homesteader. Writing to her friend Anna Kittelson in Aberdeen, South Dakota, during her homesteading years, Julia shares her joys as well as her doubts as she establishes her homestead, makes friends in the community, and enjoys the attentions of young men in the area. Perhaps because Anna was also unmarried, Julia often wrote to Anna about romantic experiences, especially her courtship by "Tex," the man Julia eventually married.

Another theme in Julia's letters to Anna is her desire for Anna to join her in taking advantage of the opportunity to homestead. The correspondence indicates that Anna visited only once and that she never homesteaded, although one document suggests that she made an unsuccessful attempt to contest an existing claim.

Julia wrote her letters to Anna between July 1911, shortly after her arrival in Montana at aged twenty-nine, and March 1917, after six years in Montana had changed her circumstances considerably. Julia had proved up on her homestead and filed on more land; she had found a husband; she had two children. Reading the letters, one can see Julia mature from a fun-loving but determined young woman into a realistic, hardworking wife and mother. Throughout the correspondence, Julia's enthusiasm for homesteading and her belief that the land would bring prosperity is unwavering.

The nine letters included here focus on Julia's homesteading experiences from 1911 when she filed her claim up to the time of her marriage in 1913. All but a few of Julia's handwritten letters are clearly dated and indicate her location. Thus readers can track Julia's whereabouts during her homesteading years, whether she is writing from her claim near Flat Willow, Montana, which she named "Breezy Point," or from Minneapolis where she worked for the telephone company in the winter of 1912. She also wrote from Livingston, Montana, where she worked as a telephone operator in the winter of 1913 as well as from various nearby towns in Montana where she spent time. When Julia's father died, her mother came out to stake a claim on a homestead of her own near Winnett, Montana, and Julia lived there for a time to help her mother. She also wrote when visiting Tex, staying with friends near the "camps" where he worked as a civil engineer surveying the railroad line into Grass Range, Montana.

The story of how Julia's letters were preserved is as interesting as the letters themselves. The 1890s home where Anna's boss, immigration agent John Firey, lived in Aberdeen, South Dakota, was purchased in the 1980s by the Graf family. When the Grafs hired a workman to insulate the attic, bins of Mr. Firey's business correspondence were discovered in the attic crawlspace. Instead of destroying the dusty documents, Rene Graf saved as many of them as she could and eventually began sorting through the letters, old magazines, and business records. Among them she discovered

Julia Stockton's letters to Anna. These personal letters to his secretary had apparently become mixed in with Mr. Firey's business papers. Realizing their historical significance, Rene painstakingly typed Julia's handwritten letters and contacted Julia's children who were still living in Montana near the place where Julia homesteaded. The existence of the letters was a revelation to Julia's living children, Bill Stockton and Patience Hillius. After reading the letters they learned more of the father they had barely known and were reminded of stories their mother had told them of her homesteading life.[2] Unpublished until now, Julia Erickson's letters reveal a young woman's most personal thoughts as she struggles to build a new life for herself on her Montana homestead.[3]

* * * * * *

August 27, 1911
Winnett, Montana

My dear Anna:

Yours received last eve and of course it was the next best thing to seeing you. Oh dear: we had planned so much on you coming to see us and hurried to get every thing fixed before you came. You did miss it in not starting out with us. It is so much fun doing things. We have laughed some times till our sides ache. One of the Flatwillow boys has been so good to us. He moved us out here free of charge. Mr. Millsap donated the service of his horse. Then he put up our stoves, cut the chimney holes made our tables, put up some of our shelves, fixed our couches, hauled wood. Oh there were a millions things he did for us—that had we hired a man it would have cost us quite a good deal. We are only 3/4 miles from the Ministers family. They all have claims. Beers is their name (great name for a Methodist Minister). There are three grown daughters (2 teachers) one grown son and one little fellow. Then there is a young man staying with them who expects to marry the oldest daughter as soon as they _____. Really Mrs. Beers is one of the grandest women I have ever met. [G]ood hearted is no name for it. If she can't give us anything else she will have us take some drinking water home so as not have to make an extra trip down to the spring. They are all as nice as they can be my, we will never be able to repay them for their kindness.

Dear me how mean it was that you had to hurry back so it surely must have been an awful disappointment to you as well as us. But glad you got to go out west any way. Wish you could take a little run down to see mother when you go to see Haugen. But suppose you are a little sick of traveling.

Elmer was home six weeks this summer and just think Anna, he only gave mother $5.00 all the time he was at home and worked all the time he was there. Now when he has the heart to sponge on a poor woman like Carrie. For she is the one that buys the groceries and many other things I guess —and have poor old Mother 72 years old wait on him 6 weeks and only give her $5.00. My I get so angry when I think about it I simply boil. The grocery bill is three and four times as much when he is at home. For he has to have meat three times a day. I'm going home this winter for a couple of months to see how things are and if he hangs around there I'll read the riot act to him proper.

Well about how we spent our summer. The weeks after the 4th we went up in the mountains. Guess there was about 20 in the party. We surely had some grand time. We slept right out on the ground and my such a restful sleep. Its simply grand to do that. Then oh the mountains were just grand. I just love them.

Anna I can't begin to tell all the things I did. Only _____ the before they broke up camp Tex (the man in the case) had to go far away on a job. His is a civil engineer and also the man that located us. Well he went to Lewistown on Monday, came back Tuesday night in an auto. Took on Wednesday me along to Flatwillow then back to Mountains and in to Lewistown the same day. Stayed in L. till Friday midnight and took the train back to Musselshell and back to Flatwillow Saturday.

Bessie went back with Harry for he was her beau in the mountains and he is also the fellow that has helped us so much out on the ranch. On Friday before I came home Mr. Millsap and the store keeper got _____ a joke on Bess. Mr. Davis called Mr. M. to the phone and said Lewistown wanted him. Then Mr. M. Went to the phone and pretended he was talking to the clerk at Lewistown. Bess was in store at time. Anyway when Mr. M. hung up the receiver he told every body [that] Tex and I were married. Bess felt awful and wanted to sell her relinquishment and [of] all the talking she did you see she has not made much of hit out here. She feels as if the people are not good enough for her. And she as much as told them so. Millsaps said they would do a lot of things for me if it wasn't for Bessie. Oh you can't imagine what a time I've had with her but guess she is taking a tumble?? for she has been a different girl since she has been out here on the claim. And she is treating the Beers all right. She does not like Tex or any other fellow out here so don't say anything about him to her. Harry is supposed to be her fellow but he almost hates her for he knows she feels herself above him for he told me so. Now when he took us in to town Friday to the dance, he took me to supper and got another fellow to take her.

Minneapolis telephone operator-turned-homesteader Julia Erickson in front of her claim shack. (*Patricia Hillius, Stockton Family Collection*)

About Tex, He is a grass widow about 40 years old.[4] His wife left him seven years ago for another man. They had a boy 2 years old at that time. He is with his mother whom is married again now. Tex was broken hearted not for her so much but for his baby which he has never seen since. But is going to try and find some time. However, said he had never had much to do with any girls since but now [says] he loves me as much as he ever loved her. Everybody around Flatwillow that knows him is interested in the case and says he is all right. And guess would like to see us get married. I like him guess its because he is so good to me and he does act as if he thought I was all right. Of course I haven't known him long, as I only met him the day I came to Flatwillow and that is not quite 3 months yet. I know I don't love him and have made him no promise as yet and perhaps never will. How I wish you could see him. I would so love to have your opinions for he is pressuring me so. I feel as if I'm beyond the stage when I can love any more. Still I think it's wrong to marry unless you love some what. He has not much money for he said he never expected to marry again and consequently had only himself to look out for. He earns a good salary $200.00 per month. Besides he has been locating people and made some on that. Should he see any way to make good, he may start up in the land business at Flatwillow. You see so many people are proving up now and will want to sell out this coming summer. Mr. M. is after him strong to go in with him on this and of course he would like to too I guess. At the present time he is near Bozeman on a job and will not be through for six weeks or 2 months. He has black hair, brown or black eyes. 5 ft. 11 inches tall very quiet a southerner and therefore never sounds his R's. don't think he ever did drink much still of course I don't know. But anyway in one of his letters he told me he had quit entirely. For he knows I'm afraid of a man that drinks was surprised at this for I had never asked him to. Besides he is a very strong minded man and never allows anyone to dictate to him. It makes him so mad when I _____ or give in to Bessie on anything. He always says when he wants to do anything he does it. And that's about the case. I'm sending you a picture of him it's a very good likeness. He is the second man from the left.

I like Montana so well Perhaps its because I don't have any thing to do and have had such nice times and am feeling so much better. My neck is normal again too. And I must confess it did worry me some especially after the Doctor was so surprised. I didn't cough any. Everybody is saying I'm looking so much better guess I must be for I can't get my last summers dresses on. Weigh 118 strong after I had been here a few days only weighed 109. The gain of nine pounds is pretty good I think.

Monday morning

Didn't get your letter finished yesterday as the Beer girls came down and of course Dora had to take her sweet heart with her.

My I had an awful experience this morning behind my house we have a little box dug down in the ground where we keep our butter and milk. Well, the board we have over the box is about 8 inches longer than the box. Well after I had taken the board off and had put the milk in and was just trying to find a place for the butter, I saw one of the largest rattle snakes I have ever seen coiled up right by the box. It hid under that piece of board for shelter so you can understand [how] near the box it was when it was under that end that stuck out over the box. It seems the funniest thing that I did not touch it with my hand. Had 8 rattlers and the end was broken off so hard telling how many more it had had. I'm always the one that sees them. Last week I killed three but four is all we have seen since we came out and we or I have killed every one. Bess has never seen any and so she is scared to death of every thing so I'm glad she never does see any. But the scare I had this AM really made me sick. We never hear of any one get bitten, still such a close call makes any one hair stand on end.

Yes and down at the Hotel there was one in the front room one day. I was the one he was after then too. I never saw till it was right by my foot. Mr. Davis and Mr. Millsap never gets thru talking about how fast I got out of the house and of all the screaming I did. Whenever I get my eyes on one I'll always scream. Bess asks what the matter. I'll say snake. Then she scream is it coming my way? I almost have to put my finger on them they look so much like the grass. I'm going to send you the rattlers of the one I killed this AM.

We are getting our houses fixed up real cute. I think and we really are quite happy. Whenever we are gone for a day we are so glad to get back home.

Mr. Firey promised he would have a rug made for me out of old car carpets. I wish he would remember but of course poor fellow he has so much on [his] mind.

How sorry I am that he is not in a position to help you if you only could come out here we would have such a nice time. Just think Anna my land is only 1 miles from Winnett. Oh if the railroad would only come thru. The post office is not there now. It was but the post master had some troubles with Mr. Winnett and they had it moved about 2 miles farther out. But of course the town site is all staked out at Winnett and there is a little store there a hotel and saloon so we feel as if its town anyway.

Tell Mr. F. that land has been sold around here for $20.00 per acre all ready. Crops are looking grand. Have had more rain this season than they have ever had. No need of irrigation whatever. Millsap gardens are grand. Mr. F. ought to see it every thing is looking fine around the country.

Here is my house.[5]

Guess this will be all for now please write me soon wish you could advise me
Lovingly Julia

⚹ ⚹ ⚹ ⚹ ⚹ ⚹

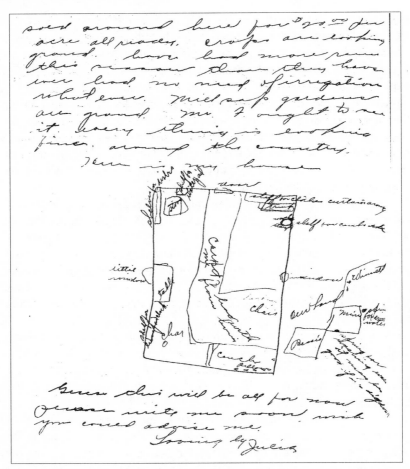

"Here is my house," Julia Erickson Stockton wrote above the drawing of her house that she included in a letter to her friend Anna Kittleson, dated August 27, 1911. (*Rene Graff Collection*)

January 30, 1912
Minneapolis

My dear Anna:–

Just a line before I go to bed. Have a _____ again—do believe I've lost about 10 pounds since I came home. Telephone work is to hard for me. I know now I cant stand it any more last week I had to stay home a couple of days. Sunday was in bed till 3:30. My how glad I'll be when the time comes to go back again if I only had a nice pal then how grand it would be.

Had a letter from Tex yesterday. The letter was mailed at Bahia—15 days from N.Y. and 4 days from Rio. Just imagine the distance nothing like that for mine he says Bahia was simply beautiful but _____ it be beautiful—not for me not for a man that I don't even love—but maybe Anna that is my last chance.

Was down to see Finsands Saturday. Joe is the same old girl . . . thin as ever.

Can't you come down before I leave. Wish you would Anna just for over Sunday if you can't spare any more time.

Its real late and I must go to bed or I won't be able to work tomorrow. Will write you again soon.

Love Julia

Have a phone in Tri State Calhoun 361 tell Hannah to call me up

Give me your box number again.

*   *   *   *   *   *

2-23-1912
Erickson, Minneapolis, Minn.

Dear Anna,

Can't you come down a week from tomorrow. That is the day I'll quit working. Had expected to work a few days longer but am afraid would be too rushed the last minutes if I did. Had intended to leave here on Saturday so as to spend Sunday with you.

So sorry you went to all that trouble about the rug. Said that more to have something to say than anything else. You remember Mr. Firey said he was going to send it to the cleaners etc. was thinking he worked that expense on the Milwaukee, my its too bad you should go to all that trouble.

Can you imagine Terry called me up a few minutes ago and wants to see me some time next week. Seems strange how these old flames of mine pop up every now and then—and how it never makes my heart jump any more. Guess it must have turned to stone.

Father is very poorly. Guess I told you before that it was his heart. Am so glad I came home for, oh _____ matters need attention—indeed—bills every where—Elmer is falling off the water wagon again still Anna—don't mind it like I use to. For I feel its near the end. Besides mother has decided its best that he hustles for himself after this.

Now Anna let me know if you can be here next Saturday or Sunday or any time after I quit—let me know won't you. Bessie leaves the last of this week so we won't be bothered with her.

Will tell you all the news when you come.

Lovingly, Julia

PS My telephone is Calhoun 361 in case you don't hear from me again before you come.

J.E.

After spending the winter with her family and working at the telephone company in Minneapolis, Julia returned to her homestead.

✶ ✶ ✶ ✶ ✶ ✶

March 15, 1912
Flatwillow

My dear Anna:–

Back at Breezy and honestly it seems awfully nice to get back again.

"Honey Boy" of course was at Musselshell to meet us and do you know he come in a single rig—You should have seen us—boxes—suitcases, chairs—carpet—3 of us in the seat and "Honey Boy" sitting on the carpet in front with his legs hanging over the dash board such a sight. I shall never forget it—it was a cold wind that day besides. It snowed so we were all pretty well in by the time we reached Flatwillow. It seemed so strange at the hotel since the Millsaps have moved out on their claim but the new land lady seems very nice.

Have my carpet down you should see what a dear little home I have. But Anna coming up from Musselshell and also from Flatwillow I was so lonesome for Tex. Really it seemed as if I could not stand it—and I would have given $5.00 to have seen Harry Shepard—would have anything to have Tex see my shack now.

The "Boys" had a nice big pile of wood chopped for us but do you know Alvin let our chickens starve to death only one hen and the turkey left—have not seen him yet but he has to make that all right [you] bet.

We are going to Winnett's to a dance tomorrow night. Honey Boy is going down after the girls. (Halversens)

The weather is simply grand today—a shinook again—something you Dakota people don't know anything about.

Mrs. Nelson (a neighbor) gave us about 40 pounds of fresh pork and said we could get all the milk there we needed aren't people just grand to us.

Tell Mr. F hello and wish he could see how nice my shack looks now. Hiram (Mrs. Nelsons brother) helped me clean the house this morning.

With love to all the folks and oceans to yourself. I am as ever.

Lovingly, Julia

Hellow from Bessie. Write quick

✶ ✶ ✶ ✶ ✶ ✶

April 9, 1912
Flatwillow Montana

Dear Anna:–

Will you please do me a great favor? My hair is turning awfully gray. Mrs. Nelson tells me that Ayers Hair Vigor darkens the hair. Wonder if you could please mail me a bottle if that does not do the work I heard Henna tea does then you let me know how much it is so I can send you the amount. Have not that much on hand till I've been down to Winnetts and cashed a check.

Had a letter Easter Sunday that father was much worse again. Oh dear, it makes me feel most awfully blue. Carrie and Christine has to change off sitting up all night with him. They telephoned for Ed to come and also Martin was coming up. My how I [wish I] could go home but that is out of the question.

Elmer and Belle are engaged and she is wearing a diamond.

Rec'd your card Sunday morning. Please write me soon. Love Julia

PS. Regular summer nearly dying with heat. J.E.

✶   ✶   ✶   ✶   ✶   ✶

April 26, 1912
Flatwillow, Montana

My dear Anna:–

As I have a chance to get a ride back from Winnett this afternoon thot I would write you a few lines before hiking in.

There has all kinds of new things happened but won't stop to tell you now only have been having a man here plowing the AM. — have a new lady neighbor with an auto. Some live wire "believe me Morris" she is married so of course she can't bake all our beans.

Planted potatoes this AM must not forget to tell you that—and next Monday expect to finish planting everything. You asked if you could send me some seeds. That would be fine and dandy. We got most of our seeds in Mpls and also got some seeds for vines we must have misplaced them some place—it was a package with 5 different kinds of vines in [it] so if you would not mind would just love to have some they have some seeds at Winnett but no flowers to speak of and no vines at all. Have planted sweet peas expect them up almost any day. Oh! This Montana soil just shoot things up anyway.

Well so you've had a card from Will. Now do answer just as sweetly as you can don't forget.

Have not heard from Tex yet. No one else has either so guess perhaps its not his fault. Anyway don't lose any sleep over it. But should think I ought to hear soon. Have not heard from home for nearly a week and then father was just the same. Doctor still says he can't get well.

Am counting the weeks till you come. Yes of course you can take a stage clear up to our door. Look who we are and what country we live in so why wouldn't the stage run by our door. How is every body out at Ida's now and how are you feeling, dear? Glad I'm in a country where there is no sickness, people out here don't even have colds. When ever I feel a little cold coming on I go out doors and practice deep breathing and its gone in a day.

When does Cora intend coming out here. Tell her the invitation is to stay as long as she thinks she can stand the simple life.

Every thing out here is beginning to look so nice. Having lots of rain and sunshine. Both indoors and out.

Bessie is much better now we had a talk one day.

Don't know if I've answered all your questions or not couldn't find your letter. When is Mr. Firey coming out?

Am sending you a couple of kodaks. Mrs. Nelson is our best neighbor and Ray Badger or the Badger Boys are the fellows that have the store at Winnett swellest dancers ever. They call on us girls _____ the other is the Winnett hotel. There is to be several new buildings there this summer.

The hair tonic seems to be doing wonders.

Cora and D_____ haven't been up as yet but expect to see them tomorrow if nothing happens.

Awfully glad Mabel and Cora are making ammends. It will be so much nicer for everybody—oh not to have that ice.

When you see Pete going by in his auto tell him. Oh you kid from me.

Well Anna as I must write home also must ring off hoping to hear from you very soon.

Lovingly, Julia

* * * * * *

June 1, 1912
Flatwillow, Montana

My Dear Anna:—
Seems an awful long time since I've written you but simply could not get my self to write to anyone. Of course when I don't write I don't get any letters and I've surely missed yours.

Want to thank you so much for the flower seeds.

They seem to be coming up fine and dandy. My garden too is doing fine and I'm real proud so far we have had a great deal of rain. Seems these dry landers _____ draw rain.[6] Guess that is what the ranchers think any way. People are just streaming in now. Last summer I knew everyone in the country and now every body seems strange to me.

We have 4 fellow right near us and they surely are fine and dandy to us girls.

Glad you want to call on Mother poor old soul. Guess she must feel most awfully blue. Wish I could get her out here if it only didn't cost so much. Father went at last. My but he did suffer poor father. I know it is better so but it was awfully hard to part with him. Father is father and we have only one.

It seems a shame that I was out here and could not have helped at home it was a long and hard watch.

Well this is June and isn't this the month you planned on coming out. and when is Cora coming? There is to be a celebration in Flatwillow the 4th. Wish both you girls could be here for that then right after the 4th guess the crowd will be going up to the mountains. They have planned on going July 2. But since they are going to have doings in Flatwillow guess they will wait till afterwards. We had a dandy time last year. So I'm quite sure you girls would enjoy it.

Guess maybe Bess and I will sell ice cream and lemonade again.

Bessie just called me over to kill a bull snake when she saw it she grabbed the broom. But she said it turned around and looked at her then she dropped the broom and run. He was a big fellow 4 or 5 ft. long.

Have heard from Tex now. He had been sick was just able to be up when he wrote. He says Reo is just beautiful and the climate down there is grand. He likes it down there except every thing is about 50 per cent higher there than in the States. So he is not contented and was going to come right back. But now had made up his mind to stick it out till the job is finished which I guess will be a year from this coming fall. He wants me to go down there in the meantime but I don't see it that way.

Is Mr. F. coming out when you do and has he mentioned taking us over into the Bitter Root Valley since? My that would be grand. But of course it's too good to be true.

Have you heard from Will lately. And did you answer him when he did write?

Have not seen anything of Bill and I do hope he will pass it up

Well now be sure and write when you find time and tell me when you intend to come out. Bessie too was saying she wished you girls would come out when there was excitement in the country We have had some dandy dances this spring and there are lots of good dancers around.

With oceans of love to you all I am.

As ever Lovingly, Julia

After the death of Julia's father, her mother came to live with Julia in Montana.

✶ ✶ ✶ ✶ ✶ ✶

May 9, 1913
Winnett, Mont.

My dear Anna:–

Received your 2 letters a couple of days ago and as you know glad to hear from you.

You must not think mother got that sore throat from you people. And if she hadn't been taken sick before she left for the claim I would never have called the doctor. And I think it's a good thing I did for his medicine is doing her a world of good I think. It's a tonic and also something for her heart. She is looking so much better than when she came and is getting quite a bay window on her again. Her neck is going down so what more can she want am going to take a snap picture of her with a low necked dress on so the people in Mpls can see for them selves. They had all kinds of excuses why she should not come out here saying there would be no doctor or anything out here. But we are going to have a very good doctor at Winnett and also a drug store so I can't see there is much cause for alarm. Besides mother feels contented now with me. . . a thing she could not do in Mpls even if they all were good to her. She could not feel at home so that too may have something to do with her feeling better

Yes she filed on a claim a little ways from Winnett. There is also another claim next to hers that is held as a dessert that has to be relinquished back to the gov. which is better than the one Mother has.[7] Mother wants to get a shack put on her claim so she can prove up on it but can't see how I can help her unless I could make something on my wheat. (which is looking very good at present) But then she may be able to make a nice little stake selling her relinquishment.

One can borrow 1/3 value on this land when one [commutes][8] and one of my neighbors said he could get $1400.00 on his and this claim joins mothers. He was the one that held _____ mothers claim as a dessert so you see land is worth something out here and will be going up now when these roads are coming thru. . . .

My wouldn't [it] be grand if your mother and John could come out in this country and take land around us some where . . . of course there is nothing left now unless its some thing that has been held as desserts. And contests of course so they might be able to get something. Why don't you come and file on the one next to mothers. Then I surely would do my durndest to have Mother prove up on hers. And we all could live together, wouldn't that be great. You see we could all go and live with each other. I don't know much about the Big Dry. Isn't that in Dawson Co.? There is lots of people going to Dawson as of course land is scarce around here.

I expect Tex to come down either tomorrow or next Sat. I feel almost like getting married for I need some one to help me. But of course one never knows what you're going get till after you got it. My hair is gray Anna and may not have many more chances. Things are getting real interesting with Luke and Daisy. They are real crazy about each other it really is funny. You better come out Anna maybe I can knock _____ you down to some one. The man that bought the store at Winnett is a batch and a rich one and also a Norwegian. About 40 years old real nice fellow. Now is there any thing better you are looking for. Oh, there is a lots to choose from here. So you want to come early. Easy go [to] get here. Stage drives right up to the door comes up 3 times a week. No excuses now Anna. Nothing stands between you and a man only a couple of weeks vacation of course you really should take a month anyway to get firmly established with some man.

Today I'm going to walk down to Winnett to mail these letters. Mother says she is glad she will have another chance to go to S_____. Gee that certainly was a rich one about her and Gust Anderson. You must be sure and tell the folks in Mpls about it. Mother says "you should see him now how nice he looks. Why didn't you get her to go so we could have had some fun["] Daisy and I are having lots of fun with her, time simpley flies.

Bessie is working for Mrs. Millsap now in the hotel and comes out occasionally to stay over night.

Well as we are getting hungry will wring ____off Hoping to hear from your soon.

Lots of love from us to you all

Lovingly

Julia

✶   ✶   ✶   ✶   ✶   ✶

[No date: Probably late June, early July 1913]
Wednesday

My dear Anna:–

I know you have been having all kinds of thots but can't explain by letter and this won't even be a letter. Have been sick, away on a trip, married and goodness knows what else. Please don't blame me for anything. I really am not at all to blame. Am now camping with Tex and will be here for 4 or 5 weeks perhaps one thing you simpley must come and see us here it's a dandy place. And I never would get over it if you didn't.

You go to Lewistown and take the stage out to Forest grove. Stage leaves on Tuesdays, Thursdays and Saturdays and it might be such a thing that we could come in and get you if Tex didn't happen to be busy. Anna oh please come.

Am writing this the stage is coming and I want to get it off this morning sure. My headaches something awful and have been for several days simpley can't think.

What kind of time did you have in Rio? Didn't get your letters till a few days ago.

In haste Julia

Julia Erickson Stockton

In the last letter from Julia to Anna, written March 11, 1917, she and Tex (now called Bill) were preparing to sell the homestead near Winnett, Montana, for an anticipated $4000 and planning to start over about 50 miles away where Julia could "homestead another 160 and Bill 640 acres." They had two children: Patience, nearly two, and the new baby, Mary Carolyn. Julia's living children, Bill Stockton and Patience Hillus, provide the rest of the story. Tex (Bill senior) died three years after Julia's last letter to Anna was written, leaving Julia a widow with four children to support as well as a homestead to manage. For three years, Julia and her children tried to make a go of the homestead, but when a fire destroyed their house, the family moved to the nearby town of Winnett, and the homestead became government property once more. The Great Depression made life even more difficult for the little family, but Julia managed to support herself and her children by doing laundry and working odd jobs in Winnett (French 2000, 1A, 9A).

How can Julia's high hopes for homesteading be reconciled with the unfortunate circumstances of her later life? Some might suggest that Julia's experience is representative of many failed homesteaders for whom homesteading meant a hard life and broken dreams. On the other hand, had she remained in Minneapolis would her prospects there have been any more promising? Perhaps she would have avoided the disappointments and the hard physical labor, but she would have forfeited the great adventure of her life.

Ida Gwynn Garvin, Montana — *1916–1920*

Homesteading for a forty-eight year old widow[9] with seven children would make for a more difficult situation than most, but if that woman also had tuberculosis, homesteading would seem to be an impossibility. Yet Ida Gwynn Garvin filed on a claim in Choteau County, Montana, in November 1916.

Ida chronicled her homesteading experiences in the letters she wrote to her mother, Adaline Gwynn, who lived in Zanesfield, Ohio. Homestead records and family lore help piece together her story.[10] Unlike most homesteading women, Ida was not seeking adventure by moving west to stake a claim on Montana land, but she shared their desire that a homestead would provide economic security. Even with the backing of her family, Ida's decision to homestead was a bold move for a woman in her circumstance, requiring self-confidence and bravery. Although her mother continued to send her money and her brother's family provided additional help, Ida and her oldest children, Gwynn and Nita, contributed to their own support.

In 1916 Ida had spent time in the Nobb Hill Lodge Sanatorium in Colorado Springs, leaving all seven children (Irma, Dan, Gage, Edwin, Amer, Nita, Gwynn) in the care of her mother. Letters Ida wrote almost weekly to her mother from 1916 until 1920 reveal her poignant story. The sanatorium proved too expensive for a lengthy stay, and Ida was eager to escape the confinement and the complaints of fellow patients. Ida had a brother, John, who had homesteaded in Choteau County, Montana, in 1914. In May of 1916 she left the sanatorium and traveled by train to Loma, Montana, to stay with him and her sister-in-law, Ethel. Ida's early letters from Montana suggest she did not mean to stay there permanently, but by September two of her sons, Gwynn, a teenager, and a younger son, Amer, left their grandmother's home in Ohio and joined their mother in Montana. The plan was for Gwynn to help John with work on John's homestead and for Amer to be cared for by Ida and Ethel.

During the summer and fall of 1916, the idea of Ida filing on land was conceived. Perhaps John had suggested homesteading near him as a solution to Ida's dilemma: she needed to be where the air was dry, and eastern Montana certainly met that requirement. With the help of John and his wife, she could acquire a piece of property and provide a means of support as well as future inheritance for her children. One can imagine that Ida welcomed both the opportunity to provide for her little family and the change from the antiseptic life of the sanatorium. In November she wrote of having found her land. By December when she left for another winter in Colorado Springs, Ida had signed the papers to take over a relinquishment on property near Loma.[11] This time Amer went with her to Colorado Springs, while Gwynn stayed in Montana to help his Uncle John and to prepare the new homestead for Ida's return the following spring.

Her letters reveal that Ida was a semi-invalid when she first moved to her claim, able to take occasional walks, but as the years passed her condition apparently worsened, so in the final years she speaks proudly of being able to sit up in bed part of the morning. Thus her view of homesteading is that of a keen observer rather than a participant in the work going on around her. Consistent themes in her letters are the weather, her physical condition, and the activities of her family. Unlike most women homesteaders, the delight of living close to nature was inhibited by Ida's limited ability to experience it firsthand. In spite of the fact that she was indoors most of the time, her letters contain vivid landscape descriptions and detailed weather observations. In spite of the sad circumstances of her life, Ida did not complain in her letters. The letters show that she had a sense of humor and kept up with local and national politics, reading as widely as was possible on the frontier by using local libraries and subscribing to newspapers and magazines.

It is beyond the scope of this book to print all of Ida's weekly letters to her mother; therefore, I have selected the letters that provide the greatest insight into Ida's homesteading experiences, her character, and the circumstances of the family. The letters appear chronologically as best as I can determine. I have excerpted parts of some letters relevant to her homesteading to omit repetitious and less relevant information and have omitted sections of letters unrelated to homesteading. In the case of letters dated only by month and day, not year, and unclear postmarks on envelopes, I determined the order from their content in relation to other events. Ida's Montana letters are always dated from Loma, the town nearest her claim and the town in which she stayed during the winter with her brother, John, and his wife and son. Presumably to save space, Ida rarely used paragraph breaks and started writing on the same line as the salutation, separating the salutation from the letter with a :–. These features have been retained in the following reprinting of her letters.

Ida's correspondence with her mother began January 3, 1916. Apparently they had lived close enough to each other previously that they did not need to write to keep in touch until Ida's tuberculosis required her to enter Nobb Hill Sanatorium in Colorado Springs. The content of most of the early 1916 letters has to do with details of her life at Nobb Hill Lodge. The first mention of going to Montana occurs in a March 5 letter, when she writes:

> I don't know when I will go to Montana. The doctor advises extreme caution about making the change but I shall pack up and go as soon as I feel at all satisfied about the weather conditions. John said he thought it would be safe to come any time after the 10th but I'm afraid of running into a big snow storm if I start that early.

By late April, Ida eagerly anticipated her release from the sanatorium and her new life in Montana. It is at this time that we meet her in this first reprinted letter.

✶   ✶   ✶   ✶   ✶   ✶

319 Logan, C. Springs, Col. April 25" 1916

Dear Mamma:– Your letter arrived this A. M. and will try to answer. I suppose you received my card containing the joyful news that I was about to leave this place. Just think no more sick people, kicking about the meals, no more pillows smelling of formaldehyde, no more board bills, no more cranky nurses. I am surely delighted at the prospect, tho I have some very good friends here that I hate to leave, feeling as I do of course that I will never see them again. I have the pictures all ready to send and when I strike some one who is going to the office, I will have them mailed. City postmen are not so accommodating as rural ones and do not take packages and stamp them for you at the office. Some of the people say the picture is very good, but Mrs. Pound says to tell you it does not do me justice, at least as far as health and complexion are concerned. So you may imagine I look healthy. I am sending a picture for each household. I am feeling quite healthy at present. My cough is better than it has been since February and I am much stronger than I was at that time. I feel much more equal to the trip to Montana than I have felt at any time since I have been here. I walked two and one half blocks yesterday, played cards till nine o'clock, slept all night without waking, and feel fine today. I am going down town in the auto this after. And get my tickets and make all arrangements for my trip. Then tomorrow evening at seven I start. I thought I had explained that "T.B." or "the bugs" was the pet name for the tubercular bacilli, and chasing the cure, chasing the bugs, or killing bugs, means that you are absorbing the fresh air and sunshine which are supposed to be fatal to the aforementioned T.B. I really feel at present that I have my bugs on the run and that when I get where I won't hear so much about it I will improve even faster. I am awfully glad tho, that I came here in the first place and that I stayed as long as I have. I have acquired lots of information that will be useful to me, and tho it comes high I do not think I should have got it any other way. We are having a little rain and thunder shower but it will soon be over, and fifteen minutes after it stops you would never suspicion it had rained. I must close. Direct my next letter to Loma.

Your loving daughter, Ida

* * * * * *

Loma, Montana. May 8" 1916

Dear Momma:– I received your letter Saturday and was very glad to hear from you. Sorry you had to have colds again, but hope you are over them by this time. We are all feeling quite foxy. My cough is improving some every day. If I only keep on mending I can come home this fall. This is a quiet and pleasant, tho cool, morning. Saturday was hot and in the evening there was a terrific wind storm. I momentarily expected for a short while, that my house would start rolling merrily across the bench and presently land in the coulee. But nothing happened and the wind finally blew itself out, for a season, sometime last night. John's[12] had company yesterday. Their nearest neighbor, Mr. Mackey, went a fishing and left Mrs. M. alone so she came over here to spend the day. Then some friends, whose house you can see cross country nine miles away, came over in their auto. They have a real house and barn, about the only ones anywhere about. At least every other family in the country has an automobile and John's are beginning to want one pretty bad. Elmer is the best baby I ever saw. He sleeps alone in his little bed in the front room and never wakes all night. Last night he slept eleven hours. He doesn't sleep so much in the daytime but amuses himself with considerable assistance from Ethel, and hardly ever cries. Did you ever see grasshoppers at this time of year? There are oodles of them here, and I tell John he will have to hurry and raise something for them to eat, for they are beginning to starve to death. Buffalo grass is said to be fine pasture, but the trouble is that there ain't none. I like the looks of Montana much better than other places I came through on my way here, especially western Nebraska. . . . What do the children think of my picture? As to not looking happy, you must remember that having a picture taken is a serious matter.

Ever, Ida

* * * * * *

Loma Montana May 17" 1916

Dear Mamma:–

I received your letter yesterday, and will mail my answer tomorrow. It seems a little primitive to get the mail three times a week but that is better than to have to drive five miles to Loma for it. This is the first place out from Loma. We come over a large hill into the coulee, and the road runs along that for quite a distance between two groups of little round hills, shaped something like apple dumplings; then up onto the "bench" and here we are. The bench is a high, wide and level prairie dotted with shacks, and straw stacks that look to have been threshed last week instead of last summer. When I see them I can readily believe this is a dry country. It will be a "dry" state soon as they vote for state wide prohibition this fall and there is no doubt that it will carry as the women vote and the rural vote is solidly dry.[13] The weather is pretty good this week so far. Last week was fierce—rain, snow, hail and high wind every day. I am getting along fine—as well as I can possibly expect. I have had two or three cards from C.S. *[Colorado Springs]* They seem to be getting along about as usual. I am monarch of all I survey at present. John's have gone automobiling. . . . I had an invite to go along but letter writing is about all the dissipation I indulge in at present. I have been reading a good bit as there are bushels of magazines here and some books. Ethel has Palgrave's "Golden Treasury" and I have been committing some of the selections, especially Shakespeare and Wordsworth. . . .

Hoping to hear from you soon–

Your Loving Daughter

✻ ✻ ✻ ✻ ✻ ✻

Loma Montana May 29"

Dear Mamma:– I received your letter Saturday and was glad to hear that every one was well and getting along so good. . . . The weather here is more summer like than it has been. Last week we had a forty hour rain which included about two inches of snow, and since then it has been warmer and the wind doesn't blow all the time. We have just had a little thunder shower and the air seems fresh and cool. The farmers are feeling happy over the rain and are counting on enough extra bushels of wheat to buy an automobile with. I counted twenty shacks this morning from a slight elevation in the field back of here. Some of them were a long way off of course. . . . I am feeling quite foxy at present. I take a walk every day and think I shall take an auto ride the next chance I have. John and Ethel went for a joy ride last evening with Mr. Dodge a bachelor neighbor who has a new Ford, but the baby was asleep so I stayed with him. . . . I have heard the coyotes several times in the early morning, but they were some distance off. I hope to see one ere long. I saw a jack rabbit loping across the prairie this evening. Hoping this finds you all well — Ida.

✼ ✼ ✼ ✼ ✼ ✼

Loma Mont. June 9"

Dear Mamma:– Your letter arrived yesterday and was very glad to hear from you. This is a very pleasant day and I am feeling real well. The morning was clear and bright but not at 11 a.m. The clouds are beginning to gather. It has just got dry enough to plow again and we hope it won't rain today. . . . This is p.m. and we have had a hard shower with some thunder and lightning but not alarming. The grass on the prairie looks somewhat green but not green like real grass. The wheat is a beautiful color. About the only birds we have are the prairie sparrows who have a mild subdued twitter and trill, and the meadow lark, which looks like the eastern meadow lark, but has a more elaborate song. There were some fine northern lights the other night, some what to my surprise, for I did not expect them at this time of year; but they say they are often visible in the summer. There are big doings at Havre the 4th and John and Ethel want to go but as they don't have an auto I don't know whether they will go or not. Another bird I forgot to mention is the curlew which makes an awful lot of noise. There are some frogs in the reservoirs but they do not rival the eastern form in the volume of music that they put up. I hope this will find you all well.

Love to all Ida

✼ ✼ ✼ ✼ ✼ ✼

Loma Montana July 1" 1916

Dear Mamma:– I will try to write a few lines this morning before mail time in answer to yours received a day or two ago. It is not raining this morning but is beginning to cloud up already. Yesterday was clear all day—the first one of the sort for nearly two weeks. John has not worked except to pull weeds since Tuesday week. It has not been very warm, but the garden stuff grows very fast. Every thing is such a good color—I don't think I ever saw such beautiful dark green wheat. High water in the three rivers has done some damage in the surrounding country, not on the "benches" as they average one hundred feet above the rivers, but especially to the railroads which are mostly contained in the narrow river valleys. The wagon road is washed out at one place between Loma and Ft. Benton and that highway is no thoroughfare at present. John hitched up the team and took me across the fields to the river bank a few days ago. It was a scene quite different from what I had been gazing upon for the past two months. The narrow green valley, at that time partially submerged, enclosed by the two lines of high, almost perpendicular hills, with the turbulent Marias, bank high, roaring through it, presented a picture sharply contrasting with the grayish, daisy sprinkled prairie behind us. Then there were trees, real trees! I also went over to Mackey's on that trip and got weighed, and figure that allowing for the difference in clothes, etc. I have gained 2 lbs. since coming here. My weight was 123 lbs., and I feel that I have gained much more strength in two months here than I did in five at C.S. I must close and get this out to the box. Hoping this finds all well — Yours Ever, Ida

As Ida's appreciation for the landscape increased and her health seemed to improve, she began to revise her plans for returning "home" to Ohio the following year. When an uncle came out to Montana and filed on a claim, the idea of Ida filing her own claim took form. In July she wrote the following to her mother.

If I could find a claim that was not too far back I should take it as I expect I ought to stay here awhile longer. If I could get located somewhere and have Gwynn, Gage and Amer, I *think* I would be satisfied for awhile. One trouble is that schools are few and far between, so I think the girls at least are better off where they are for the present. Anyway I will keep a "lookin round" and see what I can do.

In early September two of Ida's sons, Gwynn and Amer, took the train to Montana. Ida's letter telling of their arrival states that Amer "seems to like it here all right" and Gwynn "thinks this is a fine place." Of herself Ida reports, "I work a little now, wash dishes, look after the baby some, and wait on myself and Amer, but most of the time I "kill bugs" (the slang term for recovering from T.B.). Later in the month, it is clear that she is actively pursuing her plans to homestead.

≠ ≠ ≠ ≠ ≠ ≠

Loma Montana September 24" 1916

Dear Mamma:– I received your welcome letter last evening. I began to think you had forgotten me but it seems evident that you did not get my letter before-the-last so had nothing to answer for a space. This is rather a gloomy day, rained some this morning and the clouds refuse to roll by. John finished hauling the wheat that he had in "Norwegian grain bins." So is ready for rain. NGB's consist of a circle of wire fencing lined with straw holding 400

This family portrait was made before Ida Garvin became a Montana home-steader. Her mother and brother John would later support her homesteading venture. As teenagers, Gwynn and Juanita (Nita) helped their mother homestead. Standing, left to right: John, Harry, Quincy, and Thurman Gwynn (Ida's brothers). Seated, left to right: Norman Garvin (Ida's husband), Ida Gwynn Garvin, Ira Gywnn (Ida's father), Adeline Root Gwynn (Ida's mother), and Amy Eleanor Gwynn (Ida's sister). Children left to right: Irma, Gwynn, and Nita. (*Faith Mullen Family Photo*)

to 700 bushels of wheat and can be seen in every stubble field at present. The rest of his wheat is under roof and he will leave it until he gets his seed-ing done. The long expected Ford is at Ft. Benton and he will bring it home when he comes back from the State Fair. He is going to Helena Tuesday morning. Ethel wanted badly to go but is afraid to take Elmer on account of Infantile Paralysis. In the letter you did not get I told you about a "relin-quishment" some distance from Ft. Benton that John heard about when he was at Great Falls for sale for $800. And I may buy it if we find it as repre-sented when we go to look at it—that is if we find nothing better in the mean time. It doesn't seem like there is any satisfactory land left for filing. I wrote to the commercial clubs in several towns in north east Montana in regard to homesteads and they all replied that they did not know of any land that had not been filed on except in the mountains, thirty or forty miles from market. The Ft. Assiniboine military reservation up by Havre is to be opened up some time, but no one knows when; and there will probably be a hundred or more entries for each claim. Some relinquishments on this side of the river have sold this summer for twenty dollars per acre and they were at least ten miles from Loma. The claim we were going to look at is across the Marias from here and is supposed to be fifteen or twenty miles from the railroad, but if I find nothing better soon, I shall probably take it. I can get the money at the bank for six months and by that time we should be able to sell the Chardon property. It seems to me this ought to be a good time to dispose of it as times are good, and it will not get any more valuable as time passes. Gwynn is getting brown as a young Montana Indian—is much more tanned than he ever was in Ohio and there hasn't been a real windy day—a real Montana windy day—since he came. We had our first frost on the 14" and like yours it was a sure enough freeze, the thermometer registering 26 degrees. This is Monday morning and it is the warmest morning for sometime. It is still pretty cloudy tho the sun shines out occasionally. John and Ethel are washing; Gwynn is pulling Russian thistles. I wish you could get some one to do the washing this winter; it must keep you tired out to do so much. Of course it is a bother to take it away but most anything is better than to do it yourself. I suppose the ache in my shoulder is caused by my bad lung. The doctor said once to put a mustard plaster on it and I have several times and it seems to relieve it for a while; but the last time I did so my temperature came up so I stopped. I think it will be well when I stop coughing. I must close for this time and go out with Amer to see the automobile he is making. Hope this letter will get through all right but will write every week after this whether I hear from you or not. Love to all

Ida

✸　✸　✸　✸　✸　✸

Ida's October letters express some frustration with the continuing search for her land. On October 9th she wrote the following.

I haven't made any land deal yet. There is one piece not far from here that we like pretty well but the man asks more than I want to pay. I may take it yet but won't until after the state land sale at least. Not that I really expect to get any of the state land as all the farmers are so prosperous this fall that they are on the alert to gather in any Montana land that is lying around loose.

In her next letter, October 16th, Ida gives the following report.

We all went in to the land sale Friday but did not make any purchases as land has riz. Some outsiders came in and run up the more desirable quarters to considerably more than their appraised value. . . . Some of the farmers are "sore" over the situation but others who wanted more land just as bad are quite contented as they count this makes their present holdings decidedly more valuable than they had considered them. I think every week that I will do something definite but so far have been disappointed. I think I will either make some kind of a deal in a few days or postpone it for awhile.

Finally, in her November 20 letter Ida had positive news.

Well we went up to Havre on a land hunt but did not find any thing that looked good, so are going to Benton this after. and buy that relinquishment over east here. John says he don't think I can do any better in northern Montana at present. It's the only thing close to the railroad at any price. We went out from Havre about thirty miles to look at a place for $750 but it was not as good land as this down here and was very stony besides being far from town. The real estate man would not even take us out to the reservation to look at the land that had not been filed on, so it must have been pretty bad . . . we are borrowing the money for the claim for six months which will give us till the last of May to sell the Chardon property.

✶   ✶   ✶   ✶   ✶   ✶

Loma Montana December 4"

Dear Mamma:– Your letter came Saturday and as ever I was very glad to get it. This has been a lovely bright day, with a high and rather cold wind. The weather has been fine for the past week—even Sunday was pretty fair. Thanksgiving was a very nice day here and the festivities went off as per schedule. I had been somewhat "dancey" [14] for a few days so was in bed most of the day, but was able to eat a pretty good dinner, the main part of which consisted of a turkey and two ducks. My indisposition was I think, the after effect of the Havre trip, and consisted of a high pulse and general trifflingness. My temperature was not much above normal at any time. I have entirely recovered now—feel unusually well today—but am still keeping pretty quiet. I got my "papers" today and am now a full fledged Montana homesteader. By a lucky turn John got $150 taken off the price so it is costing us $1350.

There isn't much doing here in the work line at present. The ground is frozen too much to plow and they can't haul wheat as the elevators are full and are unable to get cars. Somebody gets in a car of coal once in a while but it is hardly ever possible for a person to get over a 1000 lbs at a time so nobody has much ahead. I suppose I will start for Colorado about the middle of the month but haven't set any date yet. I have not heard from Miss Standish and am feeling considerably put out over the fact, as I wrote her almost two weeks ago. Mrs. Pound who is at a boarding house in the Springs sent me her landladies' address and I am going to write to her this evening. I would rather go to Miss S.'s than to a boarding house as I think it would be much better for Amer there, as it is clear out of town and he would have almost as much freedom as he has here. . . . I must close as it is getting late.

Love to all— Ida

By December 23 Ida was in Colorado Springs and Amer was with her.

✳ ✳ ✳ ✳ ✳ ✳

By the end of April 1917, Ida, feeling some improved but "quite disgusted with her experience," left the sanatorium with Amer. Back in Montana, she stayed with John and Ethel until she felt strong enough to move out to the claim. Once her older children, Gwynn and Nita, came from Ohio to join her, the family settled into a routine. Gwynn was kept busy working with the land and animals; Nita was doing much of the inside work: cooking, sewing, and looking after Amer, with help from Ida when she felt well enough. Limited because of her illness, Ida must have felt hopeful that homesteading was a way the family could, by working together, support themselves and achieve a small measure of independence.

During the summer months, Ida felt well enough to walk out on the prairie and to help with cooking and dishwashing. As the year progressed, Gwynn and Nita made friends with young people in the area, attending dances and taking occasional trips to the nearby town of Loma. Ida declined her mother's offer of financial assistance, sure that sale of the hay they had grown would bring in enough money for them to pay their bills, but when her mother sent the money anyway, she was grateful. In October Ida wrote the following: "There is a hint of autumn in the haze and in the yellowing leaves on the cottonwoods by the river, but there isn't any 'feel' to the seasons here. There is just two kinds of weather, good and bad; and each is the superlative of its kind." By the end of 1917, the little family was surviving on the claim, pleased that a chinook had melted the first snow of the season and filled the cisterns built that summer. In spite of thirty-below-zero temperatures, Ida wrote to her mother that "we came thru in fine shape."

✳ ✳ ✳ ✳ ✳ ✳

In Colorado Springs, Ida's thoughts often turned to plans for her homestead. She wrote the following on February 5, 1917:

John and Ethel both think I ought to have Nita come out to Montana next summer, and I really don't see what else I can do. Of course there won't be much to do, but I will need someone to do all there is to do. There is no possibility of hiring anything done, not even the washing, and we will have a few hands off and on, and they will expect some eats. John thinks we can easily make arrangements for her schooling next year, and I will certainly leave no stone unturned in that direction. Of course there is plenty of time to discuss the subject, between now and spring and I am anxious to hear what you all think about it.

* * * * * *

319 Logan Colo. Springs February 12" 1917

Dear Mamma:– I will begin to answer your letter before I get it this time. I think by the stir outside that the mailman, otherwise "Ben Hur," has arrived but the mail hasn't been distributed yet. We are having fine weather here now. It isn't just a succession of lovely days like last February here, but one can stand one or two bad days in the week when the rest of the time is so nice. If I were called on for my ideal weather I should say at once "February in Colorado." I am still resting. The doctor came out Friday, professed himself well-satisfied with my improvement and said for me not to "weary in well doing," but to stay right on in bed. He is coming out this week to go over my chest and I am in hopes he will let me get up then. I am getting tired of wearing a kimona and having my hair braided down my back. I had a very interesting letter from Ethel, Saturday, and feel as if I were as well posted on Montana matters as tho I were on the spot. She wrote Monday and said that was a fine day, temperature 44 most of the day, and she had hung her washing outdoors and had given the house a good airing. They were all quite well tho Gwynn had frozen his face. The mail has been brought in consisting of your most welcome letter and a long epistle from Nita. Sorry to hear of so much sickness but hope you will all escape this time. My tray is coming so will stop writing and eat my dinner. I guess my homestead is getting on all right but don't think anyone has been near it this winter. It is somewhat inaccessible—I have never been there myself. There has been between forty and fifty acres broken and we are going to put it in spring wheat. There is a "shack" on it built new last year, but it is not finished inside. It is 14x18 and has a shingle roof. I hope to get it plastered but may have to do with "ceiling," and will have a sleeping porch built on one end. I suppose you noticed the article in the Exam. about Miss Lottie Grubs and her Montana homestead. Her town, "Big Sandy," is about twenty miles north of Loma and the interview gives a pretty good description of homesteading in Chouteau Co. Was very glad to hear that Quincy's had a Victrola. I think they are a very fine affair. I don't hear as much Victrola music as I did last year when I was in the house. There they don't play it as much as they did then. Hoping this will find you all well, I must close.

Love to all Ida

✶ ✶ ✶ ✶ ✶ ✶

Loma Montana April 30" 1917

Dear Mamma:– Here we are back to Loma. We got here Saturday morning and found John, Gwynn and the Ford waiting for us, came out to John's and have been resting since. I don't think I was as tired as last year but I cough a good deal and have got my throat irritated so am a little uncomfortable. We struck winter as soon as we left Colorado and came the rest of the way through a snow storm which continued with a few intermissions, till some time yesterday. Today has been cool and cloudy but is clearing off this evening. The season is not so far advanced as this time last year and the farmers are somewhat discouraged. Still John has got a lot of plowing done. Well there is some exciting news. John's sold their farm today. A man came along and made them a pretty good offer and they have gone to Loma to make the contract. They both feel a little dizzy I think, now they have make the plunge and hardly know whether to be glad or sorry. I myself, feel like the Babes in the Wood, but really think they are making a good deal so could not ask them to hesitate on my account. They are to give possession in thirty days and of course their plans are very vague at present. I suppose Nita will be starting west tomorrow, and if she makes as good time as the boys did, will get here Friday morning. It is much easier to travel east and west in this country than north and south, as the roads go straighter and make better connections. I had to stay all night in Billings and also in Great Falls when I came up which made the trip long and also more expensive. We struck a hard snow storm in Wyoming, five or six inches deep, which delayed us more than two hours so if the connections had been closer we should have missed them; but as it was it only made us a little late getting to bed. Gwynn went over to our place to work this morning, and will be able to keep right on as his occupation here [working for John] is gone. We will take the horses and farm implements and go to farming in earnest. It seems we are bound to have some trouble to get a road out from our place and I hope we can get that settled before John goes away. Everything looks natural here, Elmer is as fine and good natured as ever. It seems to me everybody is a lot older this year than last, both here and in Colorado, but perhaps it is I who have aged. I must close as it is supper time. John's are back from Loma but I have not seen them yet. I hope this finds all well.

With best love Ida

* * * * * *

Loma, May 28, 1917

Dear Mamma:

This is a rainy morning. We have had considerable rain lately which is nice for the wheat, but not so good for moving. We have got moved however and like our new place very much. We have a nice little shack 14x16, built like a regular little house, with a shingle roof, not like some of them, on the lines of a boxcar. Then we have built a shed sleeping porch 12 x 14, so we have lots of room, or would have if it were not for our numerous grips and suitcases.

We are not far from the Missouri and can see miles and miles on the other side but can not see the river as it is much lower than this. On the other sides we are pretty well encircled by a low range of hills which limits our view. At present we have no near neighbors, and are two miles from the road way back from everybody, as it were. John's don't seem to get started east very fast. It is awfully hard for John to get away. He thought he would be comparatively free when he sold the ranch, but his responsibilities are about as great as ever.

Every body but one has been having a sick spell. Gwynn almost escaped but had a slight touch. They decided it must have been the water in John's cistern that caused it but of course we can't be positive. No one was very sick—plenty sick enough, they all thought—but kept having one attack after another. I haven't heard from John's since Friday. But every one here has apparently recovered. Gwynn was going over to John's after a load of oats this morning, but it is so rainy I'm afraid he won't get started. There is a steep hill to go up before we get to the road, not very high but straight up, and it is the same as impassible when it is wet. If it were on our land we would cut it down but the owner so far refuses to have any thing done to it. Gwynn is getting along nicely with the work, but of course there's lots to do. John was over several days last week, and just now Ted Eastlund is here. They have been building fence and cementing the cisterns. We have got our crop fenced now, and the other fencing is not so imperative. Nita has made a little garden but its been too windy to sow seeds most of the time. So glad to hear you were better. Don't work too hard.

Love to all, Ida

*   *   *   *   *   *

Loma Montana June 18, 1917

Dear Mamma:–

As Monday is the day I write to you will get busy, tho I have no letter to answer. The reason of that is that we haven't got the mail. Gwynn intended to go to Loma this afternoon but he has so many other things to do that I am afraid he won't get off. We have had a hired man for the last few days and I am in hopes he will stay a week or two longer. The children call him the Scandihoovian but he is an Austrian. He knows nothing about farm work but can dig post holes and we are going to set him to digging a big cistern when they get the fence done. I am feeling pretty well this week, better than I have lately. I take a short walk on the prairie every morning and hope to be able to increase the distance gradually till "someday I can walk home to Kansas City" as "Sam" said. The wheat looks beautiful and green and is growing nicely at present. We haven't had any rain since I wrote last but it begins to look hazy and we can hardly see the mountains and that is a pretty good sign of rain. It has been nice and warm all week, quite like summer. There was a high wind yesterday which blew down a big feed barn that was being built at Loma. Gwynn walked over to town in the afternoon and got there just after it fell. The man whose farm we have to go through to get to the road had nailed up the gate, so he went down to see John about it. They have got things fixed up temporarily now, and the gate is open again. The old Dutchman won't sell a road to us so I reckon we will have to have one condemned. We are to have the hill cut down now in a short time and then I guess we can stand it for awhile tho its provoking to have to open two gates. John was out one day last week. He said he had concluded it was impossible to get away at present and had written to tell you so. I'm sorry to have him give it up even for a time, but I guess it can't be helped. He certainly is a busy man. He has opened war on the saloon at Loma and expects to put it out of business shortly. Ethel came back Saturday. They have built a garage on their lot and will live in it this summer. Gwynn was there yesterday and says they look real nice. It keeps Nita busy to cook for the hired man, whose name is Mike. He has a gorgeous appetite and glares at us if we take off the last piece of meat. One nice thing about living in the west is that the hired man doesn't expect to sleep in the house. Most folks have a bunk house but we had to put Mike in the barn. Amer is getting along fine except that he has to wear his shoes on account of the cactus and that doesn't suit him at all.

With love to all

Your affectionate daughter, Ida

＊　＊　＊　＊　＊　＊

Loma Montana July 17" 1917

Dear Mamma:– This is still a dry country, and hot—my, my! There is a breeze most of the time except in the early morning and it always cools off a lot as soon as the sun goes down but it's hot and that's all there is to say. Gwynn is getting thin but doesn't complain, and Nita seems to get along fine, tho she growls some. She is doing a two weeks washing this morning and has the clothes ready to hang out at half past nine. Gwynn and Amer are hauling water. There is a "chataqua" at Loma this week and they are going in this after. And Nita is going to stay at John's a day or two. It will be her first outing since she came out, except a trip to Benton. The wheat is still looking a lot better than one could expect, but it certainly can't amount to much. John was out Sunday and thot it might make ten or twelve bushels to the acre, but I don't see how it can fill at all. If we cut it for hay will probably begin the first of next week. Oh well we may have better luck next year and Montana is just the place for me that's certain. Of course I feel a little wilted by night, these hot days, but I sleep fine, eat anything I can get hold of, and walk a half mile at a stretch without getting out of breath. I didn't go out this morning as it is so very hot and so I did the dishes for exercise, and expect to help some about the dinner as Nita is pretty busy with her washing and getting ready to go to Loma. It looks awfully hazy and misty today, we can't see the mountains in either direction, but the sun boils down on us hot as ever. Mont. is noted for thunder storms and last year at this time we were having two a week reg'lar, but there has been no heavy thunder at all this year. Havn't heard of any hail either and that is another thing Montana is celebrated for. It is really too hot to write so will close for this time. Love to all. Ida

＊　＊　＊　＊　＊　＊

Loma Montana August 10, 1917

Dear Mamma:– I suppose you received the card that was my sole contribution to the cause last week. I think Gwynn carried it around awhile before he mailed it,—he seems to be getting forgetful. The weather is about the same, hot in the middle of the day and cold at night. Still no rain, but the wind has been blowing from the east for two or three days and the prophets say that means rain. We are hoping to get the cistern cemented and some more work done on the road this week but Gwynn had to go threshing today so is getting a bad start at his own work. Nita went too and I guess they must be getting supper as she has not come home. We haven't sold the hay yet but will probably sell part of it at least for twenty dollars in the field. There is about twenty five tons of it. The cow did not do us much good. She gave so little milk and drank so much water that we turned her out with the range cattle. I guess John will take her to Loma when she is fresh. We talk of buying a cow but they cost expensive. We get some milk at the neighbors when we go after it. Uncle Charles is at John's now and came out here yesterday. He is looking fine and is entertaining as ever. I tried to talk him in to coming east with John's but he thinks he has to go to California. He offered to send us some potatoes from his ranch, and I told him we would be very glad to get them, but they are so far from the station that I think it is doubtful if he can get them started. We would be very glad to see the Ohio beans, etc., but expect it would be pretty expensive to send them so far. We can't get them now at the store even at the fabulous price we paid this summer—25 cents per lb., but reckon they will have some later. . . . We are all in our usual health. I am feeling real well but am not walking so far as I did as I am short of breath, climbed too many coulee banks I guess. Ida

✶   ✶   ✶   ✶   ✶   ✶

Loma Montana Sep 17″

Dear Mamma:– At last we have had a rain. It came just when you had the frost and rained steady for twelve hours, and as it did not get cold afterward I suppose it will rain again ere long. We have had no frost yet tho we heard of frost not far away, more than two weeks ago. I am feeling rather bum this morning as the old cow kept me awake last night. She is fresh now so Gwynn brought her in and shut the calf in the barn, and she took it pretty hard. I don't know whether John is going to take her or not, guess he hasn't decided yet whether he wants her. She seems like she is going to do a lot better than she did last year, if she doesn't bawl her head off after the calf. It is very nice to have milk again I can tell you. Was glad, as ever, to have cheering news about the children. Nita did not get started to school. She may go later but it is rather doubtful. Board and lodging is so very high in these parts, and tho she could probably find a place to work for her board the plan does not seem practicable under the circumstances. We are very anxious to get the plowing started and John had engaged a man who owes him to start work with his tractor, but he went off to Canada on a land hunt just before the rain and hasn't got back tho I guess they are looking for him. It don't look like there ought to be so much work on a wheat farm but it doesn't seem possible for Gwynn to get caught up. We hope next year that all these extra jobs will be done so he can put in his time at the straight farm work. He will have to build some fence next spring but not so much as this, and he won't have the never ending job of hauling water. I hope your frost was not so bad as it seemed at first. It is surely unusual to [have] such early frost two falls in succession tho I suppose that of last year was some later than this one. It would seem to make little difference whether it frosts here or not except that it would make winter seem nearer. There will have to be some more work done at the house before winter to adapt it to the chilling blasts, and Gwynn is going to take up part of the floor and dig a small cellar. I rather dread it and think I shall go to Loma to escape the tumult. Hope this finds you all flourishing. With best love. Ida

✳ ✳ ✳ ✳ ✳ ✳

On November 19th, Ida wrote the following.

. . . I feel much more encouraged about our prospects than I did three weeks ago. We have put the forty that was broke last year in winter wheat, and will put that much more of this falls breaking in spring grain, probably spring wheat and oats, which will give us eighty acres of crop next year. Then we expect to get all the rest of our plow land broken next spring and put the whole place in winter wheat next fall, and if the next two seasons are anything like fair we should get some of our debts paid and have a pretty good start. . . .

Loma Mont. December 27"

Dear Mamma:— I hear somebody saying mailbox so I will hustle up and write a few lines on the chance of getting them mailed. We are having winter again, not quite as fierce as before I guess but pretty frosty. I was in hopes that the nice weather would last till after Christmas as I had an invitation out but it got cold Saturday night quite suddenly and has stayed so ever since. I was invited with John's to Mark Waters' but it was too cold for me to venture out. I haven't heard whether John went or not. The children, that is Gwynn and Nita, went to the community dinner at the schoolhouse and had a fine time. They are all the real "young folks" in the bunch, nearly all the rest are married people but they seem to have a good time. Amer and I stayed home as usual and had a nice quiet time. Amer got a nice lot of Christmas presents, more than he needed I guess. Ethel sent out some things and he got the top from Alta so he has a variety. He still had his old teddy bear and a most disreputable looking specimen it was. So it disappeared Christmas eve and the theory is that Santa took it with him. Amer says he wishes he had teddy but he can stand it not to. . . . I must close as I think the procession is about to start. Ever Ida

✗ ✗ ✗ ✗ ✗ ✗

The little family stayed on the homestead, or ranch as they sometimes called it, through Christmas and New Years, 1917, and the month of January 1918, but by February Ida had moved in to Loma to live with John and Ethel. She wrote of seeing a particularly colorful "aurora" and of the children who were still at the homestead. About the third week of March she was reunited with the children on the claim. Her letters in March encourage her mother to visit Montana in the summer and list some things they would see and do when she came. A gap in the letters during late April, May, and early June suggest the duration of Adaline's visit to her family in Montana.

The summer passed with the usual homestead activity. Ida's July 1 letter reports that Gwynn and John were shingling the roof, while Nita canned "sarvice berries" and did the wash. Amer was busy playing with a new wagon. The crops were doing well, although the weather was hot and dry. The harvest began in late July after an addition was built onto the barn and a new fence was built to prevent a neighbor's cows from invading their wheat. In late August, Ida's brother John "thinks he will start out with his family to find some place where there is something doing." Nita, who is to be left in charge of John's Loma place, was "pleased with the idea of getting out of the brakes[15] for the winter." Ida and Amer were to join her in Loma so Amer could start school. Gwynn was to stay at the homestead to plant the winter wheat and rye. October and November letters discuss the influenza epidemic.[16] Talk of the war and the prospects of local boys, including Gwynn, being drafted were concerns in the latter part of 1918.[17]

✗ ✗ ✗ ✗ ✗ ✗

Loma Montana February 13, 1918

Dear Mamma:– Your letter received and was glad to be assured that you were not frozen up or buried in the snow in that frigid land where you dwell. It has been real warm here since I wrote last, the snow is gone except in patches, and it has been very muddy. This morning it is froze up but isn't very cold at that, the wind isn't blowing at all. John is expecting to make the trip to Benton today in the Ford and I imagine he will find it rough going. The Benton road is never very good and I suspect it is not very bad. I am feeling pretty well now but don't try to stay up much. Have got to the point where I can be pretty comfortable lying in bed. John thinks I had better stay here till after the next storm, and I certainly won't try to go while the roads are so bad. The children are getting on nicely I guess. They were in and stayed all night the night of the play. They all look fine and Nita is in danger of being a fat lady one of these days. I think she is heavier than her aunts were at her age. Have you got to see Mary yet? Ethel was to call yesterday on a woman who had broken her ankle. Her husband drinks and she makes the living but now he has to work and do the housework too. His wife said it was wonderful what a man could do if he had to. One usually looks with suspicion on a man's cooking but if they have the brains that they are popularly supposed to have, it should be an easy matter for them to learn. Anyway I shall always maintain that anyone can cook if. . . . I hope the storms have subsided and enough of the snow gone off by this time so the schools can start again, and the mail get along regularly. They don't try to have school here in the country in Jan. and Feb. tho they might easily have had this year. Ever— Ida

＊　＊　＊　＊　＊　＊

Loma Montana March 22" 1918

Dear Mamma:– I was somewhat surprised to receive your letter last evening as that is two or four days better time than letters have been making. I received the last one last Monday and was too trifling to answer till yesterday and, I fear, did not do a very satisfactory job then. I came home a week ago today and this is the first afternoon I have not had limp. I think I was not quite so well for a day or two before I came home as I was coughing a little more and got tired more easily than usual. I am feeling pretty good today and hope to be out a little before long. Don't think I shall tho while the wind keeps up its present rate of speed. The weather is mild with scarcely any precipitation but the wind blows hard nearly all the time. If it keeps on it will dry up the mud after while and the ground will be ready for the spring seeding. Am so glad to think you are coming out this summer but think Papa was right in advising you not to come till later; for tho I hardly think the spring is disagreeable here as with you, still the wind and the mud make it bad to get around. I only hope Papa will decide to come too. I think he will find Montana not half bad and will really enjoy the change from the effete

Ida's children. In back row, from left to right: Irma, Gwynn, and Juanita (Nita). In front row: Dan, Gage, Edwin, and Amer. (*Faith Mullen Family Photo*)

east. I know he will like Ethel, and John will be delighted to show you both the sights of Loma and surrounding country. John helped Gwynn bring out some lumber yesterday and think he will get out here to make garden and help Gwynn build some fence this spring. He's an awful busy man tho, and I shall look for him when I see him. Ethel wanted to make garden in Loma, but nothing grows well in the river valleys without irrigation, while up here on the "bench" things do splendidly if there is anything near the normal rainfall. Was so sorry the pictures were failures. Maybe someone else will happen along with a kodak some time soon and have better success. . . . Our old cow has made a dash for liberty just at milking time after hanging around all day, and can now be seen on the edge of a coulee bank about a mile away with some range cattle, and Gwynn is dashing off in that direction on "Billy." So I muchly fear supper will be delayed and I am hungry. Hope this finds you still all enjoying your excellent health. Love to all Ida

* * * * * *

Loma, Mont. April 2, 1918

Dear Mamma:– This is a most beautiful April morning. The meadow larks and crows got here Monday and all signs point to the fact that spring is here. This seems exactly like an April morning in Colorado but there is some difference in the scenery—the Maria's bluffs are not a very good substitute for the rampart range of the Rockies. Gwynn rode in a few minutes last evening. He says the wheat is beginning to show up nice and he can probably begin work on his oats ground this week. We haven't heard from John since he went back nearly two weeks ago. He thought then the roads would not be fit for the long trip in the Ford before the 10th, but we are rather looking for him most any time now as the roads around here are drying up fast. . . .

Mr. Merrick sent me a big bunch of papers—Outlooks and Christian Science Monitors. The Monitor is an all around newspaper with editorials on every possible subject, with of course a bit of C.S. leaven in the lump. It is quite "Boston" and much more literary than the average daily. I like it very well tho the suppression of the partisan spirit makes it somewhat colorless.

I have been pretty well this week, not much temp or cough. I think I'll get my bed moved out on the porch in a day or two. Hoping this finds all well and enjoying the spring time.

Your loving Ida

* * * * * *

The following letter refers to her mother's visit and mentions that she brought another of Ida's children, Edwin, with her.

Loma Montana June 24"

Dear Mamma:– I received yours of the 17" and was glad to hear that you had such a pleasant journey. John seemed kind of worked up because he didn't hear sooner but I felt sure you were getting along all right. Glad to hear that every one was in fairly good health. . . . I am just about like I have been lately, no temp and not very much cough. I sit out doors awhile in the morning and find it very pleasant. Last week was another hot one tho not quite so bad as the week before. There was no more rain till last evening when we had a shower lasting about two hours but it did not rain very hard at any time. Guess we will have to resign ourselves to the fact that this is a dry year in Montana. You ought to see our new barn. It is really a dinger. They started building Wednesday and got it enclosed, doors and all, except the roof by Saturday night. Gwynn is laying shingles all by himself today as Charles is working out at Thomases and John had to go and see a feller. I think they can get it done this week if John gets out to help. I guess Charles is going back to Kansas in the near future. This morning is a little cooler than last Monday and I hope it won't get quite so hot this week. I have got my north window made and it is quite an improvement. From my experience the first summer I thot the south and east openings were all I needed but see my mistake now. . . . Ethel was out a little while the other evening. She says the Red Cross work is going rather slow tho they have a nice cool place to meet in the bank basement. I haven't had any callers since you went away. Tanners sent word that they were coming down yesterday afternoon after Sunday school but I suppose the clouds scared them out, tho there would have been plenty of time as it didn't start raining till about ten. Suppose Edwin is glad to be home and having a good time. Amer misses him a lot and talks about him as much as he used to about Bob.[18]

Love to all Ida

* * * * * *

Loma Montana August 21" 1918

Dear Mamma:– I received your letter and as ever was very glad to hear from you. Also received the papers last evening. I get them quite regularly but nearly always forget to acknowledge them. We had a little shower in the night and it has been quite cool all morning, but the sun is shining now and the clouds are breaking up and it seems much warmer. It still gets pretty hot here sometimes but not hot as it did in June and July. Well, we have threshed and our wheat crop amounted to 136 bushels, near four bushels per acre counting that we had in 35 acres. Gwynn took a load to town yesterday and it tested 60 lbs. to the bushel. Wright's had 50 bushels of winter wheat and are threshing their spring wheat today. John has several plans for getting us all thru the winter but nothing definite as yet. I think he and Ethel are liable to start out in the Ford one of these fine days to seek their fortunes. Everybody wants to go to the coast this winter and I expect every body who can leave at all will go away somewhere. Gwynn thinks he may be able to get work from one of the cattlemen. . . . I am just about the same, cough quite a bit especially at night, and my throat is not entirely well. I think I am "fatter" than when you were here. Tell Edwin that the kitty came back all right and seems to be pretty well satisfied with his new home. Amer came in a while ago with one hand all scratched up and a piece bit out of his little finger so I guess the kitty is able to take his own part. We are having lots of excitement about snakes lately. Nita and Mrs. W. started to kill a small bull snake in front of the door one day and it came thru a knot hole into the house and they had to finish him up in the kitchen. Then yesterday while Gwynn was away, Amer was digging in a hole that Gwynn started for a cellar, when he heard a rattle snake under the house. It was quite near him and it seems a wonder he was not bitten. Nita then rushed for the front armed with the 30-30 and when the snake started to come out she shot it. It was not very long but quite thick and had six rattles and a button. It was pretty creepy of course, but we did not get the thrills out of yesterday's adventure that the former one, with Mrs. W's able assistance, afforded. Mrs. George Wright was over one day last week. She is lovely as ever and her baby is awfully cute and dear. Hope this finds you all well and having pleasant weather. Love to all Ida

⚡ ⚡ ⚡ ⚡ ⚡ ⚡

Loma Mont. September 4"

Dear Mamma:– Your letter and card received yesterday. Was glad to hear that you had got home safely, or comparatively so, and had so pleasant a visit. We are getting along about as common. Gwynn is trying to get started plowing stubble this morning, but had to chase his broncs all over, and seems to find it hard to get organized. Nita has ironing on hands and pears to can, but her "canning sugar" has been delayed and unless it gets in so John can bring it out this morning she will have [to] put them up without it. Amer is getting along pretty fair, is some fatter than he was last spring. He is a little put out because the "Wright kids" got started to school and he did not. We are still expecting to go to Loma but don't know just when. John's may start off the 12th after he registers, but I doubt if he is ready by that time. We had an all day rain Sunday, preceded by a dreadful all night blow. It didn't rain nearly so hard as it blew but dampened us up quite a bit. I am feeling pretty well, the best I have for some time, tho I am rather stiff and aching since the rain. It is rather cool here now especially at night. Mrs. Wright takes the children to school and goes after them which will keep her pretty busy I reckon. Nita saw her last evening and she says the teacher is quite disgusted because nobody will board her. Mrs. Atwood is "keeping" her for the present but thinks that is all she can do. It seems that every body round who has a house has poor health, and the ones who live in shacks have large, or at least some family. It seems to me Mrs. Neighbor might take her, but Nita says she hates to cook so bad that she don't think there's any chance. Mrs. N and Mrs. Hinegar were down here, on an errand, not long since, so I can't say that I don't know any of my neighbors by sight. Suppose the children are starting to school this week. I must close for this time. Love to all Ida

    ✳ ✳ ✳ ✳ ✳ ✳

Loma Mont October 16"

 Dear Mamma:— Your letter received and was glad to hear you were having nice weather and good health, was especially glad to hear of Papa's improvements. I am not so very well have some cough and some afternoon temperature. We have been having some lovely days but just now it [is] quite gloomy, has been raining a little but not much. Are you having much excitement over influenza? All the schools in the county are shut down, also the schools in the Falls[19] and several other cities in the state. All gathering places were closed in the Falls except saloons, and there is quite a sentiment in favor of shutting them up. I do not think it reached the proportions of an epidemic anywhere in this part of the state and only hope that the quarantines may keep it from becoming epidemic. There are perhaps a half dozen cases in Loma but in ordinary times they would just be "common colds" and not very bad ones at that. It was reported yesterday that the barber, who had been ailing, had developed pneumonia. The saddest thing in connection with the disease so far as it has affected these parts has been the deaths in the various soldier camps and especially the death of Dr. Parrish of Benton who went to Camp Ogelthorpe Ga. about two weeks ago. The Havre bunch *[John, Ethel and Elmer had moved to Havre]* are getting on fine, all busy as bees, especially Elmer. I had a rather disconcerting caller a few days ago, in the person of Mrs. Hansard, where Nita visited last spring when you were here. She is a very strenuous lady and has no patience with the "rest cure." She also recommended two sure cures—besides exercise—which she kindly offered to procure for me but which I felt obliged to regretfully decline. Is there much excitement over the peace talk? I would surely be glad to think that the fighting would be over before winter but suppose it is necessary to show the Kaiser that it is easier to start a war than to stop it. Some of the younger boys around here expect to be sent to the State University for a course in mechanics but don't think any of them have gone yet. Gwynn hasn't got his classification yet so far as I have heard. I forgot to tell you that Mrs. Hansard evidently has matrimonial designs on Nita in favor of her oldest son, Frank H., but the propaganda so far has failed to make any impression on either of the principals so far as I can observe. I must close for this time hoping this finds you all well. Love to all Ida

✼ ✼ ✼ ✼ ✼ ✼

Loma Mont. Nov. 10"

Dear Mamma:– Your letter arrived yesterday and I was glad to hear that the epidemic had so far passed you by. Our folks are getting along pretty good I guess so far as I can hear. Gwynn has been at the hotel in Benton since Wednesday evening. Ted went down with him and stayed till yesterday when we hear that he came back, but he never showed up here, and Nita does not see him when she goes down street, so we don't know what has become of him. Thursday afternoon Ethel took Elmer to the hospital and yesterday Mrs. Mackey took John down to Benton so that they are all now under the doctor's care. I am awfully glad that John finally went for he would get up and chase around whenever he thot he was better. Mrs. M. reports Gwynn and Elmer both improving and thinks they will probably all be home tomorrow. Mackeys have surely been friends in need. Amer is sick this morning but I guess it is just a case of indigestion. He was quite sick at his stomach last night and hasn't got up yet this morning tho he ate some breakfast. Nita has just come in with the morning paper which announces the abdication of the Kaiser and the virtual closing of the war. Of course it isn't unexpected news but none the less welcome for that. The idea of another winter of war was more than I could bear to think of. This is a lovely morning and seems almost summerlike after the cold snap, tho we still have a considerable quantity of the beautiful with us. The snowfall over the state varied from two to seven inches, we probably got about three inches. Some of it may be with us the first of March, or it may all vanish in a couple of hours if the west wind starts blowing. The sun however will never make way with all of it unassisted. The chief excitement in Loma is not the ending of the war, but the arrival at Baldwin's of twin girls. They were doing fine the last I heard. I will write again in a couple of days to let you know how we are getting along. I am just about the same.

Ever Ida

✼ ✼ ✼ ✼ ✼ ✼

Loma Mont December 10, 1918

Dear Mamma:– I received your letter containing the Christmas money, for which many thanks. The pictures also arrived in good order and I need not say I was delighted to get mine. It is real good I think and I was especially pleased to see the wide and winning smile. *[The photograph may have been of one or more of Ida's children who were with their grandmother in Ohio.]* The weather is still fine here tho it has been rather cold for the last day or two. We are all in hopes now that it won't snow till after Christmas. I am feeling real well don't cough much except "spells" which seem to come from my stomach. I was up awhile yesterday morning and also today. Yesterday I felt so well that I had a notion to stay up, but feared I was not really as well as I felt, so went back to bed. Suppose Edwin and the other kiddies are excited over Christmas. Amer and Elmer are both expecting Santa to bring them guns but I have no advices at present as to what his intentions are in the matter. I can hear the geese squawking all over town this after. Alphonse Martin, the Canadian Frenchman who lives on the river bend above Loma, raised a lot of geese and has some kind of scheme to have them put up as prizes in the local solo games, and as a result they are getting distributed around all over town. John has got one but it doesn't seem to be as vocal as some of the rest. Ethel and Elmer are out at Walter's this week and John is keeping back [on the claim]. Lena W. is quite poorly since she has got home and Don came in and got Ethel to go out there and do for them. Gwynn was home Sunday. He likes it real well out there but is afraid his job won't last long as there seems to be very little to do. Amer says they are going to have a little Christmas tree at school, and they each drew a name to get a present for, just as they used to do in Granga [Granger?], Co. He got the name of one of the banker's little boys. He has a great curiosity about who got his name but hasn't found out yet. Ethel expected to have a tree for Elmer, and also intended to help on the tree at the church, but I don't know whether she will be able to carry out her plans or not. A dry country certainly has its charms, especially in the fall and early winter. It is amazing to an easterner to see one perfect day succeed another for weeks at a time. Even when it gets pretty cold—it must have been near zero this morning—it doesn't seem in the least like winter. It seems much warmer this afternoon. I am writing this in bed with the windows up and haven't stopped once to warm my hands. Hoping this finds all well. Your loving Ida

*   *   *   *   *   *

The year 1919 began with Ida writing letters to her mother from Loma where she was still at John and Ethel's home. On January 8 she reports that the weather was "almost summerlike," and "John was as proud of the winter as if he had ordered it." Worries about nearby cases of influenza and family finances were added to Ida's usual reports on the weather, the family, and her health. She hopes they can "get along without calling on [her mother] for anything more" and thinks they could "borrow another hundred at the bank—at 12%." February was still mild and Gwynn, who was working on a neighbor's ranch, came in every Sunday to visit the family. Sometimes he borrowed his Uncle John's Ford to "take a girl to the dances." Ida thought he was getting to be "quite the society man, that is for him." March brought a belated winter with considerable snow, but Gwynn planned to move back to the claim by mid month and the others planned to follow "as soon school is out and the roads are good." Ida proudly reports that Amer, a first-grader, was reading "very well for a beginner," but he was eager to "get out to the ranch."

By the end of May all were back on the claim; however, there was bad news about Nita who had been hospitalized after a "strenuous week" followed by "dancing most of the night Saturday," then taking a "long car ride in the broiling sun Sunday afternoon." The doctor diagnosed the problem as "nerves" and sent her home in a few days. Other letters mention a drought and each shower that brought relief from it. News of the wheat crop, the horses Gwynn was training, and the heat characterize the summer letters of 1919. Ida writes that her friend Anna Howell had "cut loose from Montana" and of her regret at seeing her go because she "came the nearest [to] being a friend that I have had in Montana, outside the family." In a late August letter Ida admits that she had been ill but that she is now "feeling pretty well"; however, she relates that she did not "sit up at all, except to eat."

In September arrangements were being made for Amer to stay with a family in Loma so he could go to school while Ida remained on the claim with Gwynn and Nita. A rare reference to her children in Ohio with grandmother Adaline appeared in a September letter, promising to answer the "much prized" letters from Irma "all at one fell swoop." Ida writes in one letter that she "was very much obliged for the money as it will purchase what we will have to have for the winter." Apparently the homestead's income was not enough to cover the family's expenses and Adaline was once again helping out. A highlight for Ida occurred when some "aviators" who had put on a show in Fort Benton flew over the homestead. She wrote: "At last I have seen an airplane, and would not have had to stir from my sleeping porch to do so tho I did go to the door for a minute or two." By mid-December Ida was back in Loma as were John and Ethel. The letter mentions that Nita took the teacher's examination, but the results would not be known until after the holiday. On December 3, the land commissioner came out to the Garvin claim to determine whether requirements for "proving up" had been met. "If the proof goes through," said Ida, "I will be a full-fledged land owner." Another letter from that month describes Christmas preparations and a much colder winter than they had the previous year.

✶ ✶ ✶ ✶ ✶ ✶

By the end of April, Ida, and the three children had moved back to the claim.

Loma, Mont. April 30, 1919

Dear Mamma:–

"The wind she blow from the north, east, west

and the south wind she blow too."[20]

But still no rain. Last evening was the worst of all from four o'clock till about eleven. At one time the dust was so thick I could not see the bluffs. I moved in the house pretty early in the game and let her blow. The east wind last week blew steady for forty eight hours and I felt quite frazzled when it was over, but it didn't blow up the dust like the Chinook does. Today is calm and peaceful with thunderheads rolling up on the horizon accentuating the deep blue of the sky. I feel kind of lazy today but am not coughing any more than common. Had no fever yesterday. Gwynn got off to Havre all right and a letter from Ethel says they were very glad to see him. . . . The weather is quite warm for April and some of the bushes down by the river look quite green, which is unusual for this time of year.

Love to all, Ida

✶ ✶ ✶ ✶ ✶ ✶

Loma Montana June 24

Dear Mamma: I received your letter and was glad to hear you were all well and had good prospects for crops. Hope you have had plenty of rain by this time. Montana crop prospects are bad. John's came down Sunday, and they said they only saw one piece of winter grain besides ours that would be worth cutting. We may have to cut part of ours for hay but are still in hopes it will fill out. John's are looking quite well. Ethel's hard work hasn't cost her any pounds and John has put on a few since I saw him before. They went on to Loma to

Ida Gwynn Garvin. This photo was taken possibly in 1916 or 1917, when Ida was at Nobb Hill Lodge Sanatorium. (*Faith Mullen Family Photo*)

stay a day or two and Amer accompanied them for a visit with Elmer. It has been dreadfully hot here. I thot Saturday was the worst day I ever saw. There was a hot wind blowing from the southeast and the sun fairly sizzled. Ethel thot Sunday was hotter and it sure was hot enough—the thermometers in Loma were reported 116 in the shade. I have got used to the heat and feel pretty chipper most of the time. Have not had more than a half degree of fever the past week which is doing pretty well for such hot weather. Nita seems to feel the heat a good deal, and looks pale but has picked up in flesh.

We have four little colts this year. Gwynn is working two of the mares today and the colts are making a lot of noise in the barn. Yesterday was the first he had worked them since the colts came and they don't know what to make of it. Gwynn has been helping Wright dig a well down in the coulee. They got considerable water at 25 feet, rather strong, but no worse than the Loma water which people and stock seem to thrive on down there. Wright's folks seem pretty cheerful tho you can see they are homesick for Iowa. I think they will stay here till they prove up at least.

You were right about me being less lonely here than in town. Gwynn is lots of company and I much prefer the scenery out here to look at for a steady thing to that of Loma. John has just stopped on his way home. Ethel is going up on the train tomorrow and take Amer along for a two weeks visit. They are taking the oil stove this trip, and with Nero, he had a car full. Hope this will find you all well.

Love to all Ida

* * * * * *

Loma, Mont. September 5, 1919

Dear Momma:– Your letter received and was glad to hear you were well and having so many outings. I have been afraid you were staying home to cook while the rest did the going. Nita has lost the pen so I have to write with a pencil. The heat is not so bad at present, but no rain. Some days are quite cool but mostly it gets hot in the middle of the day but starts cooling off about four o-clock. I am about as I was when I wrote last; feel fairly comfortable but don't sit up. I am not awfully weak as I can walk across the room without much effort. My limp has been about normal except one day when I had a degree of fever. Johns got around to see us Friday when I had about given them up. They had been having trouble with the Ford and were afraid to come down for fear they couldn't get out again. As it was Gwynn had to pull them up the hill with a team. School began this week but Amer hasn't got started yet. Ecklunds are going to stay in Loma this winter and Gwynn thinks Mrs. E. will take Amer when she gets settled. There are several families moving to Loma to send their children to school. John's scheme at present is for Ethel and me to live in Loma this winter while he, Gwynn and Nita go out to work. Lots of people are leaving, some for good, and some expecting to come back in the spring. The Loma barber, Brillhart, and family have gone to Akron, O. for the winter, Thurman's [one of Ida's brothers in Ohio and his family] might chance to meet them. I enclose a "poem" that was in the Loma items last week. . . . I will have to close for this time so good bye, Ida

Text of the enclosed poem:

The Right Spirit
(By Geo. W. Devany)
My vision of wheat and homesteading are O're,
I'll live like a hermit on dry land no more.
Hauling water all summer, buying feed in the fall,
Will try the patience and purses of both short and tall,
We are frozen out, dried out, and beaten by hail,
Overcharged by the merchants—no wonder we fail.
We have snow in the winter, and rain in the fall,
And when moisture is needed we have none at all.
We have hauled off the rocks and broken the sod,
But through failure of crops we are broke, by God.
Now what will we do without credit or gold?
Bid farewell to the desert and go back to the fold?
We left the Willamette account of the rains,
And come to Montana—homesteaded the plains.
But alas, we regret having come to this state.
So, I guess we'll go back before it's too late.
Lyman Palmer is going with his family of four
Carl Huston goes and will return never more.
Clarence Cox goes with his wife and two boys,
And Geo Cummings will be there, though not making much noise.
H.G. Howard had gone to the Valley for hay;
But when he gets there I think he will stay.
Why should he return to the scene of defeat?
For on the Willamette there is plenty to eat.
Now last but not least there is Horace Armstrong,
Who will join friends in the Valley 'fore long.
Good luck to you, Horace—. May you see many Junes,
And grow bounteous crops of Italian prunes.
Winter is coming, and with it the snow.
I would not stay here, but I've no place to go.
So Heavenly father, please send down your manna.
For I'm going to stick, be heck, to Montana.

Loma Mont, Oct 2

Dear Mamma:– I will try to write a few lines this morning in answer to yours received a day or so ago, tho I don't know when I will get my letter mailed. At last we are having some precipitation, showers, all night drizzles and also two or three inches of snow. It has wet the ground down several inches and also revived the spirit of the citizenry to some degree, tho the numerous individuals who did not have their seeding done are beginning to squirm around. Gwynn is just about half done and thinks he can start in again this afternoon. It is cloudy today and has been sprinkling a little but I don't think it will rain before evening anyway. The snow fell the 26th and 27th and it was quite wintrish but did not get so cold as we expected it would.

We have not heard whether John's came down or not. Gwynn got the yard cleaned up—some, at least,—and some water in the cistern. The children had used the place for headquarters this summer and it was in bad shape. They had thrown all sorts of trash in the cistern and Gwynn had a time getting it out. Amer did not get home Friday as it was raining and blowing when Gwynn came home, and I don't know whether he will get out this week or not. Maybe if John is there he will bring him out.

I am just about as usual these days, have some temp at least one day in the week. I feel about as well as I did before I was so sick in August, but have to be more careful about what I eat than I did before. The clouds keep gathering up and the sprinkles are coming faster, perhaps we will have another long drizzle. The old timers are predicting a long hard winter but they always do that. I seem to have lost my dread of winter, have not thot of it at all this year. . . .

With love to all, Ida

*   *   *   *   *

Loma, Mont. Oct. 30

Dear Mamma:– I am back in Loma once more, came in day before yesterday. Yesterday was the day set but it had begun to Chinook so we hitched the old mares to the bob sled and came along. It was good sledding, not jolty at all and I did not mind it a bit. Yesterday the snow was nearly all gone, but today it is snowing again and looks like winter might be here to stay. Of course nearly every one thinks we will have more nice weather tho everyone is glad to see some precipitation. Up to the 28th there had been 1.8 inches at Great Falls in this month, and in the 12 months ending September 30 there was only 6.75 inches. There is said to be more snow in the mountains now than at anytime last winter.

I have taken a little cold since the storms began, have a little sore throat and a sore place in my side but the moving did not make me any worse. I am not coughing as much as last week. There is quite a difference in comfort between living in a house and in my old sleeping porch in the winter time. John took Nita into Benton yesterday but the superintendent decided not to give her a school til after the examination which comes the first week in December. Then if her work is not too bad Miss M. will give her a permit. The question lists are gotten out by the state board who also do the grading, and it is usually some months after the examination before the certificates are issued. . . .

The state land sales are about over in the state for this year. There have been over 15,000 acres, mostly grazing land, sold at an average of $15.71 per acre. An 80 between our place and the river, entirely unimproved sold for $20. So that does not look like Montanans were entirely discouraged. My date for proving up has been set for December 2nd. The commissioner from Benton will come down here.

Amer seems to be well and happy but I don't think he is getting along with his lessons as well as last year. I think there are few primary teachers better than Miss Kelly.

Love to all, Ida

*   *   *   *   *   *

Loma, Montana, November 19

Dear Mamma:– Summer again in northern Montana. At least it seems so by contrast tho there was a heavy frost this morning. Friday the Chinook began to blow, continuing till sometime Sunday night. It took off all the snow, filled reservoirs and cisterns and dried off the ground to some extent. Since then it has been mild, clear and calm, and everybody feels pretty good. We are hoping, tho hardly expecting, that it will be good weather till Christmas. Another 10 days or so of severe weather and I fear the situation would have been acute, what with scarcity of fuel, feed and money. As it is one reads sad stories of suffering children and starving cattle and horses. I had a spell of stomach ache yesterday not awful bad but quite persistent. I feel as well as usual this morning but not as hungry. Had a little fever one day since I wrote last but my cough is better than it has been. Elmer is having a fine time playing since it turned warm. He and that little Gifford boy are great chums, and today Bobbie Gray, the Farmer's store manager's little boy has come up to play with him. Ecklunds have a boy about the same age but so far he has not got into the game. Amer isn't such a regular visitor as he was awhile, guess he likes to play with the bigger boys. He generally gets around to the window to say a few words to me but that's all I've seen of him so far this week. Gwynn is in town today, quite happy over his cistern full of water. Now that he don't have to haul water he don't have much to do and comes in quite often. . . .

Ethel is canning meat these days. She has three dozen quarts and has another quarter to can. Lots of people are canning meat as most everybody has killed a beef or two, being in a hurry to get rid of surplus cattle owning to the scarcity of feed. Cattle will surely be scarce next year as they are being killed and shipped out in such great numbers. . . .

John went up to Havre yesterday on the train and came back this morning. He says conditions there are the same as here, the snow gone and the ground wet down from a foot to 18 inches. Will have to close for this time and rest up before dinner. Hoping this finds you all well.

Your loving daughter Ida

＊　＊　＊　＊　＊　＊

Loma, Montana, December 3rd

Dear Mamma:– I will try to write a few lines this morning. We have been having very cold weather but it is warming up some this morning. Yesterday was the coldest we have had so far, various thermometers being reported from 34 to 20 below, according, I suppose to the time when their owners got up. There is several inches of snow on but the past few days have been clear and very still. Thanksgiving morning was 20 below, our first experience with such low temperature on that date. . . .

Well, I got "proved up" all on scheduled time, and will be a full fledged land owner one of these days if the proof goes thru. Thanks to John and the land commissioner Mr. Hans Rudolph of Fort Benton, my part was very easy and consisted of saying "yes" or "no" as occasion demanded. And signing my name.

December does not mean to be as good to me as the preceding month I guess. The afternoon of the first I was taken with a bad spell of pleurisy and have been hobnobing with mustard plasters and hot water bags since. I feel greatly improved this morning after a good nights sleep. Had some fever yesterday and my face is beginning to feel hot now.

Nita is going this evening to take the examination. It will last two or three days, I don't know which. She was in a few minutes ago but I forgot to give her Thurman's letter. . . .

The coal miners in Montana were supposed to go to work yesterday but they didn't go. We still have a ton or more and most everybody has a little but it is getting scarce. There is a car of Pennsylvania coal in today at $22 per. I guess I will have to stop writing for this time, will do better next week.

Your loving daughter, Ida

* * * * * *

Loma, Montana. December 31st 1919

Dear Mamma:– Your letter received and was glad to get so favorable an account of your condition. I hope at least that you are fairly comfortable by this time. You were lucky to get the Dutch lady and I hope she will continue to help you out as long as she is needed. My side is much better but I have a good deal of fever and don't sleep very well. All the rest seem to be getting along fine. Amer stayed here till after Christmas and then went out to the ranch. That is the only place that really seems home to him I guess. Like Edwin, he and Elmer were very happy over Christmas. They each got a sled and not very much else, and were perfectly happy and contented, as I think most children are at Christmas if they get anything at all. Santa Claus is a great institution and I appreciate him more and more as the years go on. . . .

Winter, in the form of a light snow, descended on us yesterday and this morning was considerably below zero. I rather look for Gwynn to bring Amer in today as it is bright and calm, and if it snows again soon it will no doubt get very cold indeed. The kids with new sleds welcomed the snow but the rest of us were not enthusiastic. These two weeks of warm weather made a nice breathing spell but we should have liked a January like last. The ice is just gone out of the rivers, now I suppose they will freeze up again. There is said to be lots of snow in the mountains, enough to keep the water in the rivers up to normal next year. . . .

I guess I will have to stop for this time as I am getting rather warm. Hoping to hear of your continued improvement.

With much love, Ida

* * * * * *

The winter of 1920 passed much as those of previous winters spent in the town of Loma, with Gwynn and Nita moving between the homestead and John's place in town while Ida stayed in town with Amer. John had gone to visit his and Ida's mother, Adaline, in Ohio, but Ethel and their son, Elmer, stayed in Montana with Ida. Ida's health seemed about the same. She could only sit up in bed in the afternoons, ran the usual temperature, and had the usual cough. In February Nita heard the results of the teacher's examination. She had passed, received a "temporary certificate" and had "the promise of a school," but when the family moved back to the claim in early March, Nita went with them. Ida says vaguely that "there were too many personal obstacles in the way" for Nita to take a school at that time. Ida's health rallied some after the move back to the claim, but a cold wet spring caused her to worry that she doesn't "seem to improve much." She reports coughing and shortness of breath. John, Ethel, and Elmer moved to Havre in late March and all settled in for the summer's work.

No letters from May or June of 1920 exist in the family's collection. Whether they were simply lost or the gap indicates that Ida's mother visited her again is unclear. The letters before and after the gap do not mention a visit, however. Ida received her homestead patent in June of 1920. It seems unusual that she would not have written home to her mother about what must have been a momentous event. However, further evidence that her mother did not visit is found in a July letter in which Ida mentions that she wishes her mother could come for a visit after the threshing was done. Although July was hot, it was not dry and the wheat prospects looked so good that Ida thought perhaps they could "pay out on our current expenses."

In September Ida reports that she is "coughing her head off" and not sleeping well but that she is "not getting any worse which made [her] hope that [she will] feel better some of these days." Gwynn was working away from the claim, first for John in Havre, then for a smelter in Great Falls.

✳ ✳ ✳ ✳ ✳ ✳

Loma Mont, March 11, 1920

Dear Mamma:– Well, the semiannual flitting has again transpired and here we are again, back in the breaks. It did snow for about four days most of the time and when it warmed up Sunday it was decided that we would make the trip the following day on a bob sled. The Chinook got the start of us however and the sledding was far from good, taking about three hours to make the trip. I got rather tired of course, but feel no special bad effects from the trip. The after effects of my cold still trouble me a little but in general I am just about as I have been since I got over the pleurisy. It was too bad Edna had to get sick on your hands. I hope she is quite well by this time and that the strain has had no bad consequences for you.

We are getting along quite nicely since the move, tho Nita seems far from husky. There isn't much that she has to do just at present, and I trust she will soon get stronger now she has got away from Loma. I imagine she doesn't feel exactly that way about it, but feel sure from past experience, that is how it will turn out.

It got very cold when it stopped snowing the mercury getting down to 36 below Saturday morning. It was rather cold Saturday night—zero perhaps, but by afternoon Sunday it was 40 above—some change in so short a time. It has been real pleasant all week but today is cloudy and rather "drizzly," making it a little cold on the hands to write without fire. It has been so long since I had a lead pencil in my hand that I hardly know how to manage but as we have so far neglected to provide ourselves with ink there is no alternative. The stock is looking better than I really expected to see. I think everything will get thru all right now. There has been no more flu in Loma, but two families in the country have been down with it. They were all thot to be improving when we heard last, tho the Baldwin twins—one year old—were still quite sick. I hope this will find you all well and getting along fine. Love to all, Ida

✯ ✯ ✯ ✯ ✯

Loma Mont. March 17th 1920

Dear Mamma:

. . . I am feeling rather stronger than for some time past and am not running quite so much limp on the average. I always feel better after I make a change, guess I will get a tent and move around over the prairie. I think I should enjoy camping down by the river awhile, for a change, tho I felt when I left Loma that I did not want to see any bluffs or sagebrush for quite a while.

The sun is shining brilliantly today but it is pretty cold with a cold east wind. The snow is all gone except patches in the north side of the coulee banks. The little prairie sparrows are beginning to twitter but none of the migratory birds have returned. The magpies of course we have always with us. . . .

We are getting along pretty smoothly tho some clouds have arisen already so soon, but they have drifted by, temporarily at least. Nita's health is improving and she seems more like herself, and if her friends would let us all alone I think we should get along nicely. Amer is staying at Ethel's now and will probably come home when she goes to Havre. If I keep on feeling chipper I shall try to have him go on with his lessons out here.

We brought the Bohemian's little Jersey cow out here with us when we came, but have got word that her owners are coming back this week so she may be snatched away from us any moment. It would be quite a blow, as she is a dandy and gives almost pure cream, and there is no sign that we will have a fresh cow, tho we have been expecting one for sometime. The B's have three babies however, and doubtless need a cow as bad as anybody. I surely hope that this will find you all getting along fine.

With love to all, Your loving daughter Ida

❊ ❊ ❊ ❊ ❊ ❊

No letters are available from May–June of 1920.

Although Ida did not include the year when dating the following letter and the postmark on the envelope is obscured by the stamp, it appears from its context that this letter was written in the fall of 1920, which makes it the last known letter Ida wrote to her mother. The letter contains no hint of worsening health, but three months later Ida died in the hospital at Fort Benton.

Loma Mont. October 28

Dear Mamma:–

This is another beautiful autumn day, in fact that is about all the kind we have at present. It rains once or twice a week and once we had a little snow but are still to have our first storm. Last year it was real winter at this time. It freezes a little most every night and the leaves have almost all fallen. A year ago today I came to Loma in a sled. It doesn't seem possible at all today, when I look out on the "happy autumn fields."[21] But of course I don't know what it will look like tomorrow.

We haven't heard from John since he came down after his car tho he said he would be down before the first of November. I hardly think now that he or Ethel either one will be down till after election.

I had one letter from Gwynn since he went away. He had got work at the smelter and said they would stay there "for awhile." I hope it will not be long as I do not think that kind of work will agree with him, and then there are a good many accidents. Yes, I have been getting the Examiner right along but always forgot to mention it. You need not bother to send the Enterprise as it is so very seldom I see a name in it that I recognized. I guess the people that I know down there don't get into the papers. Where does Joe stay now? Does Maggie live alone in Huntsville? I suppose Walker Cline is still the village barber. The Loma barber closed his shop and pool hall and hied him to Great Falls for the winter. I guess there weren't enough men left in the vicinity to make a living off. He was also the fisherman of Loma and had twice brought me a fine fish for my dinner, so I rather regretted to see him go.

I have been overworking my digestion lately, guess I had got to thinking subconsciously at least, that I could eat anything, and yesterday I was pretty sick. It was not an "acute" attack but I felt pretty miserable and had a high fever in the after. I slept pretty well however and feel "almost" well as usual today.

I just got the mail and there was a letter from Ethel wanting Gwynn to come up election day and stay while they came down here, but as he is at the Falls I guess he can't go. There was also a note from Gwynn saying he would come up Saturday and kill the pig. Must close

With much love Ida

✶   ✶   ✶   ✶   ✶   ✶

Ida died three months later, at the age of 53, on January 29, 1921. Unfortunately, no letters remain that tell of those final weeks. Among the undated and incomplete correspondence of Ida is the following sentence written in shaky handwriting on a single sheet of paper: "The supplications of Christians ascend to the throne of Grace in behalf of suffering humanity the world over and insofar as it is God's will, they will be answered." One wonders whether this might not have been something Ida wrote as her illness worsened and she began to face the possibility that this time she would not get well.

The Montana air had not cured Ida's tuberculosis, but with the cooperation of her family, she had achieved her goal of providing property to leave her children, and she had led a life more vibrant than she would have if she had stayed within the confines of the sanatorium. Her children, Gwynn, Nita, and Amer, inherited not only the land but also the experience of helping to earn it. Whether her other children, left behind in Ohio, admired their mother's courage or felt abandoned by her absence is not known. In any case, although Ida's independence was limited, all of her children experienced independence at an early age.

5 · Looking Back: Single Women Homesteaders' Memoirs

....

After time had passed, a few women looking back at their home-steading wrote about their experiences and created a record for posterity. For readers, memoirs provide an opportunity to understand the home-steaders' experiences in greater depth and from a more distant point in time than do the articles and letters they wrote while homesteading. This distance from the events described is a crucial factor in interpreting a memoir, a genre in which the distinction between history and fiction may become blurred. People may misread memoirs if they assume their writers are "obligated to fact" (Mansell 1981, 64). Actually, memoir writers, like writers of fiction, must select and may even alter their experiences as they create a story that fits their memory of what happened. Memory can be tricky, as anyone who has compared a childhood experience with a sibling who shared it has probably discovered: at the very least, each of you recol-lects different details, and you may even disagree on the basics of what was said and done or on the significance of the experience.

Women writing memoirs had the advantage of seeing the long-term consequences of their homesteading experiences. The fact that they attempted to recreate that part of their lives suggests the writers were aware of its historical significance. In spite of, or perhaps because of, that aware-ness, a few removed the rose-colored glasses that tinted the earlier accounts in promotional literature. But more often they romanticized their home-steading days, and their accounts deemphasized the negative, unpleasant, or ugly aspects of homesteading, although common sense suggests home-steading had plenty of each. As one scholar notes, writers of memoir often resurrect experiences to create a "personal myth" in honor of their lives (Kazin 1981, 43).

Scholar Thomas P. Doherty offers another explanation for the opti-mistic nature of memoirs: "American autobiographies tend to be warmly reassuring: the very fact of an autobiography testifies both to the value of the individual and to possibilities for success in the culture (failures do not get published)" (Doherty 1981, 95). In addition, the intended audience for most women homesteader memoirs was family and community members, people whose opinions mattered to the writer. For all these reasons, it is understandable that women writing memoirs of their homesteading lives wanted readers to hear the culturally approved message that homesteading was a vehicle for personal achievement and happiness.

The stories in this section are set in varied landscapes from sagebrush country to the high mountains of Wyoming, Montana, and Colorado. Some of the authors traveled long distances from homes in the Midwest to homestead in the West, others traveled short distances across state lines. All were educated, creative women who combined their careers with home-steading to succeed. Their stories hold our attention with their exciting narratives, their detailed descriptions, and their vivid character develop-ment. In the memoirs, more than in any other genre, single women home-steaders' writing can be appreciated as literature as well as history. Here women become protagonists in initiation stories that encompass standard features of American literature generally reserved for masculine protago-nists: journeying, adventuring, establishing new homes in the wilderness, improving their economic and social status.

Recalling their experiences from the distance created by time and know-ing how their homesteading experiences shaped the rest of their lives, these women wrote not only about what happened to them in these brief life-changing years but also about the life-lessons they learned from home-steading. The wisdom of following your heart is one theme that resonates throughout these memoirs. Dr. Bessie learns to trust her intuition in the face of family disapproval. Katherine Garetson takes "the leap [into home-steading] as one who shuts his eyes and jumps" (1989, 2). Madge McHugh Funk admits that her decision to go west was primarily influenced by the romantic promise of the Zane Grey novels she read. Others stress a more calculated form of risk-taking. Alice Hildreth Zehm says she and her sister "thought of [filing on a homestead] for some years" before doing so and credits her grandparents with imparting the pioneering spirit to her and her sister (Prairie County Historical Society, 602). Florence Blake Smith recalls the elation of learning that she could homestead but also empha-sizes how carefully she weighed the pros and cons as she made her deci-sion. By embracing life's risks as well as its opportunities and tempering their enthusiasm with common sense, Bessie, Katherine, Alice, Florence, and Madge discovered a strategy for living life fully.

Dr. Bessie Efner Rehwinkle, Wyoming — 1907

When Bessie Rehwinkle started writing accounts of her pioneering adventures as a lady doctor, she intended them as a family record for her children. Fortunately, she and her husband recognized the historical value of the memoirs and published them in 1963. Several chapters in the memoir, *Dr. Bessie*, tell of her homesteading experience. Before she homesteaded, Bessie revealed her pioneering spirit by following in her physician father's footsteps, attending medical school and establishing two successful medical practices in her native state of Iowa at a time when women doctors were rare. Although Bessie was unmarried, she had adopted her three orphaned nieces and was their sole support.

A nationwide financial crisis in 1907 caused Bessie to lose the second Iowa practice she had worked so hard to establish, but it proved to be the catalyst she needed to fulfill her lifelong dream of going west. Remarkably, Bessie, a single parent, successfully combined homesteading and a medical practice in the frontier town of Carpenter, Wyoming. Bessie's professional status was an important factor in her ability to prove up on her land and achieve her goal of economic security as well as fulfill her desire for adventure. Her medical training allowed her to be self-supporting and independent, qualities that characterized an increasing number of women of the time. From 1907 through 1909 Bessie was content with her busy life as adoptive mother, physician, and homesteader, thinking she might never marry. However, a young minister visiting the area was brought to her for medical attention after he was thrown from a horse. That was the beginning of a three-year courtship, which culminated in their marriage in 1912 and in Bessie's leaving her beloved homestead to join her husband's ministry in Canada. Their Canadian adventures compose the remainder of her memoir (Rehwinkle 1963).

Dr. Bessie, Chapter VII
I Follow the Advice of Horace Greeley and Go West

The panic of 1907 had ruined me financially. I had lost all my savings, my home, my office, and everything else except my clothing and office equipment. But life had to go on, and "hope springs eternal in the human breast." To have hesitated or given way to self-pity would have solved nothing, but only added confusion to my disaster. My girls required food, clothing, shoes, and shelter, and I had assumed this responsibility for them, and so there was but one thing to do, and that was to gird myself with new determination and start all over again, just as other men and women had done in similar circumstances. I still had my practice, and by now was well established and had reasons to feel fairly secure, though I knew that competition would become more intensified with the addition of the fifth doctor in the field, who had the backing of a wealthy family and influential friends in the community. Taking everything into consideration, therefore, it would seem that the normal thing to have done was to remain where I was and try to regain what I had lost.

But I decided to do otherwise. I decided to make a radical move, leave Moville and go west.

On the surface my decision seemed most unwise and foolhardy. My good father was very unhappy about my plans and tried his utmost to persuade me to change my mind. He had been on the frontier in a new country, and he knew what I was facing. He felt that I was throwing common sense and experience to the wind and plunging headlong into another disaster. But a woman is not always guided by experience and common sense but by intuition, and usually she comes out all right in the end.

So it was in this case. In the end my "foolhardy" decision and "poor judgment" proved to be the wisest thing I ever did, because as a result of this decision I was eventually led to my greatest happiness, which could never have come to me had I remained in Moville.

My decision was not made on a sudden impulse, nor was it a mere whimsical feminine notion, but there were a number of appealing reasons which prompted me to act as I did.

The first and most immediate, of course, was the financial losses which I had suffered in the current panic.

The second was a personal one. I had always had a desire to go out "where the West begins." The adventurous lure of the West had intrigued me since my childhood days. My father had been a pioneer in the early days in western Iowa and later in South Dakota. In fact, my grandfather and great-grandfather had been pioneers, beginning in the State of New York and finally landing in Iowa, when the territory was opened for settlement. My brother, also a doctor, had gone west to a new community in the state of Washington, and this same restless pioneer blood was also coursing in my veins.

In the third place, it just so happened that a special opportunity was beckoning me to go west at this very time. The Federal Government had opened large areas of Government grazing lands in the Western states for homesteading, and this included land in Laramie County, of southeastern Wyoming. When it became known that the Government was making free land available for anyone willing to settle on it, great excitement spread throughout the farming communities of Iowa, Nebraska, Wisconsin, and neighboring states, and the reaction was somewhat similar to a mild gold rush. Thousands of young farmers or prospective farmers rushed out to file on some of this free land, hoping that in that way they might secure a farm for themselves and their growing sons, which would have been impossible in the older communities of the East. As a result the prairie was soon dotted with homesteader shacks. New towns sprang up where a short time before large herds of Hereford cattle, and before them the buffalo, had roamed.

Among the new communities established at this time were such places in Wyoming as Carpenter, Burns, Egbert, Campstool, Hillsdale, Hereford, Grover, and other places in the adjoining areas in northern Colorado.

But besides the free homestead land offered, there was also made available additional cheap land from land grants that had been made to the railroad companies and from the so-called school sections.

The Union Pacific Railroad Company alone had received a subsidy from the Government in land grants to the extent of 20 sections of land for every mile of railroad built. This amounted to 5,000,000 acres in Wyoming alone; in addition to this, two sections of land in every township had been reserved for the support of public education in the state.

This land was now placed on the market. The sale of these lands was handled by land companies. It was in their interest to attract as many prospective buyers as possible.

To make the country more attractive, these companies were anxious to provide or cause others to provide the essential social services, such as schools, churches, medical care, and the like. And so it happened that I was approached and urged to go out west and locate in one of these new communities. The community that had been selected for that purpose was a place called Carpenter, so named after the chief promoter of this project. Carpenter is located on a branch line of the Burlington Railroad, about 30 miles southeast of Cheyenne and about six or seven miles from the Colorado boundary. As a special inducement I was promised that a homestead adjoining the town site of Carpenter would be reserved for me. All this seemed very promising.

This together with the other reasons mentioned prompted me to make the momentous decision. And once I had made up my mind, I lost no time to act upon it, and promptly went out to Cheyenne and to Carpenter to file on the homestead that had been promised me.

This was on July 6, 1907.

Next I made arrangements to have a house built on this land, which could serve as my home and office at the same time, and had a well drilled and such other essential improvements made, necessary for the establishment of a home. Then I returned to Moville and carried on as best I could while waiting to be notified when my new residence would be ready for occupancy.

When I received notice to that effect, I took immediate steps to move there. I had my office equipment and other belongings packed and shipped ahead of me, spent a few days with my father in Pierson, and after that returned to Moville to say good-bye to my friends, including especially old, faithful Uncle Ira, and then took the local train with my three little red-headed nieces to Omaha, where I changed onto the main line of the Union Pacific, which would take me directly to Cheyenne.

I had to buy one full-fare ticket for myself and two half-fare tickets for Elsie and Ina, hoping that Reta would still be free. This almost exhausted my resources. I could not afford to take a sleeper or to eat in the diner, and so we had packed our lunch and ate in the coach as most people did in those days.

Trying to sleep in a day coach was never very pleasant even under the most favorable conditions. But it was not because of the uncomfortable seats or the stifling atmosphere in that overcrowded coach that kept me awake. During the night that followed, a tempest was raging within my soul which drove sleep from my weary eyes. While the Union Pacific train was roaring westward, my thoughts were also racing to and fro, now forward, ahead of the train to the unknown country and the uncertain future to which I was going, and then back again to what I had left behind, to my father, my friends, and to everything of my past. And the warning words of my father, "You are headed for disaster, and you will come to want in that God-forsaken wilderness," never seemed so frightening before.

And then when I looked upon the peaceful faces of my sleeping little girls, wholly unperturbed about what was happening and unconcerned about the future that was disturbing my soul, apparently feeling absolutely secure as long as they were with their Aunt Bessie, my responsibility frightened me even more.

What if all my plans would collapse? What will become of them? What will become of me, so far away from everybody?

But merciful nature finally insisted on her rights, and despite the storm that was raging within my weary head I fell asleep, and never was I more grateful for the wonderful gift of sleep. I did not awake until the sun was coming up over the eastern horizon from which I was racing away. As I looked out of the car window, I got my first glimpse of that endless, treeless prairie which was to become my new home.

We arrived at our destination late in the afternoon. When the conductor called out, "The next stop is for passengers for Carpenter," and the train came to a halt, I stepped out of the coach and looked for the town, but there was none. In fact, the train had not stopped at what was to become the town of Carpenter, but about two miles west, at the Baxter Ranch, because there was no depot or train stop at Carpenter as yet.

As we stepped off the train and looked around, the only human habitation to be seen was this ranch house with a cattle corral and some barns. All the rest was prairie, nothing but the endless prairie. And I said to myself: "And so this is Wyoming, my new home, the glamorous West of cowboys and cattle about which I have heard and dreamed so much."

There was no reception committee at the depot to greet us. Curiosity had caused a few people at the ranch to watch the incoming train to see whether new settlers had arrived. That was the only change in the monotony of their daily life. They stood and gazed at us but said nothing.

It was too late to drive out to my homestead, and so we spent that night at the ranch. The next morning I engaged a man to take us to our new home. As I approached the house standing there, isolated and with no other human habitation in sight, a feeling came over me similar to what I imagine Napoleon must have felt when he landed on barren St. Helena and saw the ship that had brought him there disappear on the distant horizon.

Then, as I stepped over the threshold of my new home, I felt that this should be a moment for prayer. But my mind was crowded with a thousand thoughts concerning the problems confronting me, so that I could not find proper words for such a prayer. But I know that God knew what I would like to have said. He answered this unspoken prayer again and again in the years that followed.

This was on the 18th day of December, one week before Christmas.

A new chapter in my life was about to begin.

Dr. Bessie, Chapter VIII
I Establish a New Home on the Wide-Open Prairie
of the Real and Legendary Wyoming

The new chapter of my life which began with our arrival at Carpenter was to be an interesting one, though raw and rugged at times. It is fortunate for us that we do not know what each chapter contains before we have lived it. How grateful we ought to be that our knowledge is limited to the here and now and the past, and that the road over which we must travel opens its vistas only in small segments at a time! If all the mountains and valleys of obstacles, hardships, sorrows, and failures were known to us at the beginning, we would never have the courage to start, but be frightened into inactivity, frustration, and despair. But living day by day with the difficulties of each day, we are able to go on and in the end accomplish what in its totality would have seemed utterly impossible. The achievements of each day give us strength and courage to go on to the next.

My new home was a very plain and modest one-and-a-half-story dwelling, consisting of three rooms downstairs and one large, unfinished room upstairs. The kitchen was large enough to serve as a kitchen, dining room, and general living room. The room which might be called the front room served as my office and as a general sitting room, when I had no patients or was other wise not professionally occupied in it. The third room was a general-utility room. It was my examination and treatment room. It was also my dispensary, where I kept my supply of drugs and where I filled my own prescriptions. The room also served as a very necessary emergency two-patient hospital for patients who had come a long distance and who had to remain for a longer period of time, either for observation or for treatments. The upstairs was one large unfinished room under the rafters of the roof, which was the common bedroom for me and for my nieces and also provided enough space to store our clothes and other personal belongings.

Of course, there was no plumbing in the house, no hot or cold water, and no bathroom. What is ordinarily called a cellar was a large hole in the ground under part of the house, but it had no retaining walls and no cement floors. However, it was cool and dry in summer and warm enough in the winter to keep potatoes and vegetables and other food supplies from deteriorating. Refrigerators and iceboxes were not known on the prairie in those days.

All water for use in the house for washing and cooking and for my professional use had to be carried in from a well in the backyard and had to be heated on a small kitchen stove. A small heater and the kitchen stove kept us warm in winter. Later I added a barn large enough to provide shelter for two horses and a cow, and a small chicken house, and a coal shed.

This little complex of buildings was my new home, plain and modest in the extreme, and primitive in the conveniences it offered, unprotected by shrub or tree on the windswept prairie, and isolated like a little atoll on the endless expanse of the wilderness.

And yet this was my home, my very own. I had built it, part of the inside finishing I had actually done with my own hands, and here I intended to stay. And more than that, with it I had also become the proud possessor of a homestead of 160 acres of land. At least, that is what the Government had promised me. But unfortunately it was later discovered that the surveyors had made a mistake, and a resurvey had to be made. As a result of this mistake I lost part of my land, and my homestead was reduced to 93 acres. But I still had the advantage that it joined the townsite; and there was every possibility that the town would expand in my direction and that eventually my land would be included in the town.

The feeling of being a landowner was a new and an exhilarating experience to me. To be able to say that this fine stretch of land is my own, my very own, does something to one's ego. It gives one a sense of security, of stability, of belonging, and of being a part of the land itself. One no longer lives in a community, but has become an integral part of it. Its weal and its woe suddenly become identical with one's own. I am sure that so long as America retains a healthy core of land-owning farmers and home-owning citizens, so long communism will not become a threat to our country. Many times I would go out in the evening of the day and with a feeling of inward satisfaction and pride survey with my eyes my new estate, happy in the thought that all this was my own, that I was a part of this new community and was contributing my share in converting a wilderness into a civilized habitation for men, women, and children, just as our pioneer forefathers had done when they took possession of other parts of our great country.

But as I look back now, I realize that those were the dreams of a youthful idealist. All pioneers are idealists and enthusiasts. If they were not, they would never have the urge or the courage to leave the old, established homeland and risk their fortune in a new, uncharted world. Eventually, of course, all such idealistic dreams are realized, as the history of our country sufficiently shows. But it is not as easy or as glamorous as the storybooks about the westward trek of the covered wagon often picture it. It is a slow process and a hard day-by-day struggle, and only the strongest are able to survive.

Wyoming, as is well known, is one of the great prairie states of our country, and Laramie County in the southeastern corner of the state, where Carpenter is located, is no exception.

It was in December when I arrived here: the prairie grass had turned to a drab, monotonous brown. As far as the eye could see, there was not a tree, a shrub, or a hillock, or any other obstacle in sight to break the monotony. Far in the distant horizon to the east, however, one could discern a long high ridge, or mesa, resembling a range of low mountains of a very peculiar geological formation, composed of a whitish-gray friable rock and at places carved by nature into freakish formations, sometimes resembling a church spire and at other places looking like the battlements of an ancient castle, or taking on the form of a gigantic prehistoric animal. In many respects these were like similar formations found in the Badlands of South Dakota. They seemed to be the remnants of ancient islands in a prehistoric island sea.

In the far west the dark outlines of the Rockies with their snow-covered peaks were visible. And in between these two barriers lay the monotonous solitude of the grayish-brown wilderness resembling in its undulating surface the calm of the great sea. . . .

This was the Wyoming of which I had read and heard so much and which it had always been my youthful ambition to visit someday. Now I was here, not as a tourist for sight-seeing, but as a homemaker and as a young lady doctor to practice my profession. And here an interesting new world was opening to me in the years that were lying ahead. Here I was to learn much about the stark realities of life and about human behavior in adversities, about what it takes to build a new country and what it had cost in sweat and tears and suffering to make America what it is. What I was witnessing here had been the experience over and over again of previous generations of pioneers in other parts of this continent. And what I learned here, I learned not as a spectator or a journalist representing some wealthy New York paper or magazine, but I was one of the actors on the stage of the great drama, and one who shared in every detail the hardships of primitive frontier life with the other homesteaders that had come here to build for themselves a new home. Here I learned that pioneering in a new country is not a glamorous experience, as so often depicted in movie and novel, but a hard day-by-day struggle and a most unglamorous struggle for one's very existence. And it is not a struggle with gun and rifle and beautiful horses and cowgirls against Indians and wicked gangsters, but a life-and-death struggle with the most primitive enemies of man, namely, against hunger and drought and dust storms and grasshoppers and hail and blizzards and cold, and against failure and frustration, loneliness and despondency. The people that survived in this struggle were not the 40-hours-a-week type, nor had they heard of the slogan that the world owed them a living. If this philosophy had prevailed in those days, America would still be a savage wilderness. If we are to erect national monuments to honor our nation's heroes and heroines, who made America, we ought to erect such monuments to the heroic men and women who with their sweat and brawn and indomitable determination laid the foundation of the rich and wonderful heritage we now enjoy so bountifully in this our beautiful America.

Dr. Bessie, Chapter IX
Sharing the Hardships of the Homesteader on the Western Prairie

The cost of moving my little family and household goods from Moville to Carpenter had completely exhausted my financial resources. I had only enough money left to buy the most essential supplies necessary to start housekeeping in my new home. When I had paid for them, I had exactly 75 cents left. That was my total cash possession to begin life with in this new country. There was no chance to borrow from the bank if the need should arise, because there was no bank. Nor was there any possibility to buy groceries on credit, because the operator of the little store was just beginning himself and could not afford to sell on time to others. And here I was a stranger in a strange land without a friend or acquaintance who might assist me in a dire emergency. And besides that, winter was upon us. It was only one week before Christmas. And so it was not a very pleasant thought to contemplate as to what might happen to us if there would not be an early demand for my professional services. And the prospects for that didn't seem too promising at this time, partly because of the sparseness of the population. Newcomers were steadily arriving, but the number of those who were already established was still comparatively small, and they were scattered over a very large area. There were still miles and miles of open grazing land in all directions without a single occupant in sight.

To this must be added the fact that the people who were there did not know that a doctor had located in their community. I had no way to make my presence known. There was no telephone, no newspaper, no school or church, and not even a post office. But sometimes strange things happen which help to solve our problems in the most unexpected manner.

Early in the morning of the very next day after my arrival, even before I had hung out my shingle to advertise my presence, there was an urgent knock at my door. When I opened it, I was confronted by a man with an anguished look on his face, and he said: "Are you the new doctor? I was told by some workman at the tent that one had located here, and I was directed to this house. I have a very urgent case. One of my horses is very sick, and I might lose him if I am not able to get immediate help. I have only one team, and if I lose this horse I am ruined."

When he stopped for a moment, presumably to await my response, I explained to him that I was a doctor indeed, but not a horse doctor. "I am a doctor for people," I said, "and not for animals. And I know nothing about horses."

"But," he interrupted impatiently, "if you can cure people, you can also cure horses, because horses are very much like people. I will tell you how my horse has been acting, and you tell me what you would do for a man under similar circumstances. I am sure you can help my horse."

Before I could say any more, he began to describe the symptoms of his sick horse. As I listened to the vivid account he gave, it occurred to me that it might possibly be suffering from an acute case of colic, and I told him what might have caused it.

And he continued, "What would you do for a man under such circumstances?" I told him. Then he urged that I give him the same, but to make the medicine dose four times as strong as I would prescribe for a man. "Well," I said, "I will do as you wish, but only with the understanding that you are administering this medicine at your own risk. I have not seen your horse, and what is more, I know nothing about sick horses. And I don't pretend to be a horse doctor. If you are agreed to that, I will give you the medicine."

He was more than ready to assume full responsibility. I filled out the prescription for him and gave him directions how to use it. With that he hurried back to his sick horse.

My charge for the consultation and the medicine was 75 cents, and I felt uneasy to take even that.

That horse was my first patient in Wyoming, and the 75 cents the first professional fee I earned on the Western frontier.

But that was not the end of the story.

The next day the man returned to tell me that my medicine had been effective and that his horse was saved. This man was my friend ever after and my best publicity agent when I needed one most. He told everybody how this new lady doctor had cured his horse even without seeing it, and he was sure that if she could cure sick horses, she would also be able to do something for sick people.

The 75 cents I received for my services doubled my financial holding, and I now had a total of $1.50 in my treasury.

The first winter on the prairie was a hard winter, and it is not so pleasant to recall the memories of it.

In the first place, it was a very cold winter. The winter of 1907 is remembered for that. At one time the thermometer registered a low of 38 below zero in our parts and even went down to 54 below in other areas of the state, and thousands of sheep and cattle perished. We were not prepared for that kind of winter.

My house was a typical homesteaders construction, built without my personal supervision and not adequate for a severe prairie winter. Our bedroom upstairs was unfinished and neither the rafters nor the inside walls were covered with plaster or boards. Even the downstairs was not completely finished. There were no storm doors or storm windows or a windbreak of trees and shrubs outside to help protect us against the icy blasts from the northwest.

But that was not my only problem. Even more serious was the question of making a living. My resources were exhausted upon my arrival, as already stated. My practice was slow, in fact, very slow in getting started. Either people were not getting sick in this healthful climate, or they lacked confidence in me as a doctor because I was a woman. And I had already learned before that it required time and patience to overcome old and deep-seated prejudice against women doctors.

But even babies seemed to have postponed their arrival, which was more serious for me, because for baby cases women generally preferred a lady doctor to a man, and these cases gave me an opportunity to gain the confidence of the people for other cases. As a result of this situation our daily fare for a considerable time was rather Spartan in character, with very little variation. One day it was potatoes, pork and beans, and prunes, and the next day it was prunes, turnips, and pork and beans. Salt pork provided seasoning and necessary fats, and the homemade bread spread with molasses was our dessert. We didn't count calories, nor were we much concerned about vitamins and about a balanced diet. It was a matter of satisfying elementary hunger, the most urgent drive in human life. But I was surprised how quickly we learned to adjust to this rather rugged Indian mode of living. Nor did we suffer any adverse consequence as a result.

But necessity not only enables one to adjust to the most difficult situation, it is also the mother of invention. It forces one like Robinson Crusoe to make the most of all available resources. In the course of time I discovered, or better, invented many variations of preparing the same simple foods to make them more palatable.

Gradually as the dreary winter months wore on, my practice began to improve, and with it our standard of living. However, it required about two years before we were back at the level we had left behind in Moville.

The wide expanse of the level prairies had its own peculiar fascination and even grandeur for one who has learned to recognize that beauty. But to most newcomers it had the opposite effect and appeared to them as a most dismal and God-forsaken wilderness altogether unfit for human habitation.

The immensity of the area one can survey with unaided eye, the enormous distance from horizon to horizon without any evidence of other living things besides oneself, the oppressive silence broken only by the occasional melancholy hoot of the night owl or the weird howling of a pack of coyotes in the distance or by the roaring blizzards—all this in itself is enough to cause even the most stouthearted to become depressed and discouraged.

But necessity taught me to solve even this most difficult problem. At such times I would gather my little nieces around me in front of the kitchen stove and read stories to them. In the course of these weary wintry evenings I read a variety of stories, among them such as *Uncle Tom's Cabin, The Young Carthaginian, David Copperfield, Robinson Crusoe, Swiss Family Robinson, The Crisis* by Churchill, and others like them. As a result these evenings became the most precious hours I spent with my little girls. As we read these stories and we became absorbed in the struggle, defeats, and victories of our heroes, we forgot all about our own troubles and were thankful for the relative warmth and the comfort of our humble cozy home.

As a whole, my experience on the frontier was about the same as that of every other homesteader, with the only exception that I had my profession, and therefore a potential cash income, which gave me a certain advantage. . . .

I was once caught in such a fearful prairie blizzard, and I shall never be able to erase that horrible experience from my memory.

I had been called to a farmhouse some distance from home to the bedside of the wife of a young homesteader. After I had done for her what was possible, I left medicine with instructions how to care for the patient until I would return in a day or so, and made ready to return home.

I was already late, but the sky was clear, the weather was calm and mild, and a beautiful starry heaven above gave the prairie a most peaceful appearance. All the nature lay, as it seemed, in a restful slumber. I was well acquainted with the road from Carpenter to the place where I was at this time, and so I had no misgivings about the drive home, even though it was dark and the hour was late. But before getting into my buggy I looked up once more to scan the sky and make sure about any possible change in the weather. This was standard procedure in the winter months before any one would start on a long drive over the prairie.

And as I looked around, I noticed a large, dark bank of clouds hovering over the distant northwestern horizon, but it seemed very far away, and even if it were a storm cloud, it would require hours before it could possible arrive here. That would give me ample time to reach home. And so I started on my homeward drive.

All was going well. My horses were trotting along at their usual pace while my thoughts were still with the patient I had just left. But presently I noticed a change in the atmosphere. The serene calm was abruptly broken by a sudden gust of wind, followed again by a calm and then another gust which was increased in velocity. This was followed by some sporadic snow flurries, not serious yet, but an indication that a storm was on its way. Realizing that these changes were the forebodings of something worse to follow, I urged my horses on to a faster pace, because I was still a considerable distance from home.

But then suddenly the storm broke, and broke with all its fury, as though 10,000 demons had been unleashed from their chains in the lower regions. Snow began to fall in shovelfuls, driven over the prairie by a 70-mile gale and roaring past and around me with the thunderous notice of a fast-traveling freight train. It was a cloudburst of snow combined with the elemental forces of an icy tornado, one of the most deadly weapons nature has in her destructive arsenal. It seemed as though the forces of the universe had conspired together to destroy every living thing that happened to be in their path. Neither man nor beast could long endure this frightful icy bombardment. The swirling snow blotted out everything around me. The road was vanished. I could no longer see the horses before me. I lost all my sense of direction. My eyes became blurred, my hands numb, and my face burned from the frozen pellets to which it was exposed. There was no escape either from this unmerciful blast of snow or the piercing pain of cold. The pace of my horses had become a creeping walk. I was completely bewildered and no longer able to guide them, and so I relaxed the reins and let them choose their own course, hoping that their native instinct might lead them back to their own stall. Time seemed to have come to a standstill. This was the longest night in all my life that I can remember. As the moments passed, the storm grew in ferocity and the cold increased in intensity. My whole body was becoming numb, and I began to feel an almost irresistible drowsiness creeping upon me, which I recognized as the first stage in the process of freezing to death. My horses were beginning to show signs of fatigue, moving at a very slow walk or even coming to a stop. I urged them on with all the energy I could muster, knowing only too well that if I would be left stranded here, I could not possible survive until morning.

How long my horses and I had been battered and buffeted by cold and storm I knew not, but hope was beginning to fade. Both my team and I were growing weaker, and I was becoming aware that we were fighting a losing battle. And then I thought of my little orphan nieces at home all alone, and what would become of them if I would perish here in this blizzard.

Then suddenly something happened that gave me a new gleam of hope. I thought I had seen a very faint glimmer of light ahead of me. My horses were heading directly for it, and presently they came to a stop. Yes, it really was a light and not a phantom like a desert mirage created by a crazed imagination. But though safety and rescue were now within reach, I could hardly move. My body was rigid from the cold that had penetrated to the very marrow of my bones. My hands and joints were so stiff that only with the greatest difficulties could I climb out of the buggy. I was covered from head to foot with an icy sheet of snow, which had frozen into a crust so that I had become a human icicle.

I managed to get out of the buggy and reach the house before me. I knocked on the window from which the light came, and called for help. A man opened the door and assisted me into the house. But as I staggered to safety through that open door, I suddenly discovered to my great astonishment that this was the very place I had left sometime before. For more than two and three hours we had wandered over the prairie, but in some miraculous way the remarkable instinct of my faithful prairie broncos had led them back to the place from which we had started and thus had saved my life and also their own.

My team and I found a safe shelter in this homesteader's shack for the rest of the night, but it required hours before I was completely thawed out and warm again in all my body.

I was able to return home and to my frightened little girls the next day. The storm had subsided, and the Wyoming sun shone brighter than ever before. The snow that had been so frightful and deadly only a few hours before now lay like a downy blanket over the prairie, glittering in the brightness of the sun like myriads of brilliant diamond crystals scattered over the landscape like manna that had fallen from heaven. My soul was filled with a song of thanksgiving for this wonderful deliverance. Daniel's escape from the lions' mouths was not more miraculous than my escape from the roaring lion of the prairie blizzard.

I had many other unpleasant, long, and hazardous drives in wind and rain, hail and snowstorm, but none was comparable in frightfulness to the experience I had in that blizzard. But after that I always felt a degree of uneasiness about night driving. There was always the possibility of getting lost on the prairie, running into some stormy weather, or meeting with some other unforeseen mishaps which in either event might mean spending the night on the open prairie, a thought not too pleasant to contemplate after what I had experienced.

After describing her own struggles to establish her home and medical practice in Carpenter, Bessie devotes several chapters to describing life in the growing settlement. These next excerpts summarize the community's progress.

Dr. Bessie, Chapter XII
Social Life in a New Community

All these developments of which I have been speaking in the preceding chapter had taken place in the comparatively short period of the first few years of our history. Carpenter, a mere name for an unrecognizable spot on the wide-open prairie, had overnight become a buzzing little town and a self-sufficient community. The prairie round about had blossomed forth in new farms and new homes, and young enterprising farmers were busy breaking up the thousand-year-old sod, planting and reaping new crops that had never been grown here before. And where for millennia the earth had been covered with the humble buffalo grass and the uninviting cactus plant, golden fields of wheat were now waving in the breeze, and corn, alfalfa, Mexican beans, and a variety of vegetables had taken their places.

We had developed more rapidly than even the most optimistic promoter had anticipated. And more than that, the progress we had made was not limited to the material and the tangible side of the community life, but we had also made most gratifying progress in welding the scattered settlers and the townfolk together into a self-conscious community. Carpenter was becoming not only the business but also the social center for the many scattered homesteaders for miles around. We were conscious that together we were building a new place on the map of the state of Wyoming, and we were beginning to feel that we belonged together and that we were a community of people with common interests. Carpenter was becoming for us a real home. . . .

It is true that the life in the early days was bleak and prosaic, as I have pointed out before. But it would be a mistake to assume that this was the whole story and that we were a miserable, pessimistic community with life nothing but a dreary succession of cheerless drudgeries and failures, without ever a ray of cheer penetrating the clouds of gloom. Nothing is farther from the truth than that. On the contrary, we were a happy and forward-looking people, despite hardships and reverses.

Katherine Garetson, Colorado — 1914

Katherine Garetson defied common sense and conventionality, even among single women homesteaders. Instead of choosing to homestead land in an agriculturally promising area of Colorado, Katherine, then in her late thirties, filed on 160 acres high in the Rocky Mountains, near Estes Park. Only two and a half acres of her land were deemed suitable for cultivation, a fact that caused her difficulties in proving up on the homestead.

But prove up she did, after five years…two years longer than required thanks to the Forest Service contesting her claim. The following excerpts from Katherine's memoir tell of her first optimistic year (1914) when she had two lively companions—her friend A.A. (Annie Adele Shreve) and a Great Dane named Gypsy—as well as the trials of the subsequent years alone on the claim. During the second year, A.A. went back to teaching, and Katherine proved brave, inventive, and tenacious in enduring financial difficulties, loneliness, and severe winters alone on her claim. In 1915, her cabin became the Big Owl Tea House. Such notables as Edna Ferber, Cornelia Otis Skinner, and Enos Mills signed her guest register (Dings 1989, iii).[1]

Katherine's memoir of her homesteading days shows her evolution from a dreamy and naive woman to a realistic and seasoned homesteader. The theme throughout her narrative is her love of the natural world, as the following description of a day when the "weather gods" were with her shows:

> From sun-up to sun-set I lived on my hill and learned it from the brooks at its base to its crest. There were different nooks where I had built up cooking places of flat rocks. I chose my nook with reference to wind and sun. There I sewed or read or wrote or dreamed all day long; I would sit so still that wild things would play very close to me. And then I was half in love (Garetson 1989, 43).

As the third year of her homesteading drew to a close Katherine decided that she "was in no hurry to go someplace else to live after final proof. I loved my home, my land, the whole mountain world (1989, 65)."

Katherine lived on her homestead from 1914 to 1917. Elizabeth Dings, wife of one of Katherine's nephews, wrote a brief biography explaining what happened after Katherine received her patent. Financial problems brought on by World War I forced her to move to Denver to work. Using the stenography and typewriting skills she had learned in her St. Louis jobs, she worked first for a state senator, then for the Secretary of State in the liquor license department. She spent vacation time on her Big Owl homestead but never returned to live there permanently again. After Katherine died in 1963, her sister's family preserved her typed story and photographs, but it wasn't until 1981 that Katherine's nephew, McClelland Dings, brought these documents to the Estes Park Historical Museum where they were copied and preserved (1989).

Homesteading the Big Owl
Chapter I: 1914

One midsummer afternoon I stood on the porch of a mountain cabin and felt myself whipped and tossed and spattered by a violent storm of wind, rain, thunder, and lightning. I wish that everyone could put into his life one storm of the high mountains. My sublime mood was interrupted by the onrush of two drenched human beings who, bent double, came running through wind and rain to the shelter of my porch. One of them was an old man who was terrified by the storm and cheerfully admitted, when I had taken him indoors, that thunder and lightning were horrible to him. As he dried out by the fire, he told me he was a road mender. Road mending seemed to be the only way my old man could earn a living while holding down his "claim." As he steamed in front of the red fire, I listened to his husky voice as to one who brought an answer to prayer. He told me how he had chosen his homestead, what he hoped to do with his land, what he considered a Rocky Mountain quarter section to be worth, and many other matters that interested me intensely. I know now that every American with a spark of romance in his make-up has at some time of his life cherished this idea of taking up a claim. What the old man said would have caught the attention of anybody, I believe. The words fell on peculiarly fertile ground because I was seeking escape from the return to St. Louis. Before he went away, he tugged at some old papers in his pocket and finally produced two pamphlets for me. They had been published at Washington; issued by the General Land Office of the Department of Interior. One was "Vacant Public Lands of the United States," but the other pleased me most; it was entitled, "Suggestions to Homesteaders and Persons Desiring to Make Homestead Entries."

Was it not incredible that a whole estate could be had at no cost, save living in the land where you loved to be! More than once I had discovered a deserted, one-room log hut that had been the claim cabin of some settler. These hovels, set in wild flower gardens alongside mountain brooks, had impressed me with the romance of the simple life as pioneers know it. Later, my road mender and I had several arguments while he filled in ruts and I sat on the embankment and prodded him. At his suggestion I sent a dollar to the nearest land office (it was in Denver) and received a plat of the township in which I was visiting. This showed which quarter sections had been home-steaded. There were plenty of little squares still not crossed out. By hunting up Government section corners (grass-covered heaps of stones built up like monuments), and learning to tell approximately how certain lines would be run by a surveyor, I soon located the one hundred and sixty acres that became my heart's desire. It was over two miles south of Long's Peak Inn and the summer cottage where I was staying.

Filing a three-year residence claim is the most serious thing you can do, aside from marrying, I think. The more I thought, the more I feared. At last I deliberately took the leap as one who shuts his eyes and jumps. It took less than twenty minutes after I reached the land office in Denver to make out papers, swear an oath, pay sixteen dollars in fees and hear the register say, "The land is yours. All you have to do is live up to the requirements of the law."

The trouble that lay heavy on my heart the day the road mender gave me the tip about claim staking was nothing more nor less than how to earn a living. A financial upheaval had interrupted my life, made safe by a prosperous father. Like all good American girls, I could sew and cook and read and write and think. I was average. My home was in St. Louis and I had observed other lives carefully enough to be overwhelmed with the knowledge: "The city is so hard a place for people who are poor and sensitive that many choose to die by their own hands."

I went back to St. Louis for the month of September and acquired a girl companion and a dog. The girl I chose. I chose her because she was steadfast, and keen for adventure; she was gentle, not talkative, earnest and good-looking. We called her A.A. [from Annie Adele Shreve]. The dog somebody else chose. It happened to be a Great Dane, named Gypsy.

And so I took up the homestead in the Rocky Mountains, hoping the land would become valuable as summer cottage sites. The quarter section lies in northern Colorado eighty miles from Denver. Less than a year after I began living on the homestead, the Rocky Mountain National Park was created by an act of Congress (1915). My north line was the south boundary of the National Park. An increasing number of tourists came to our region in summer so that the cabin was converted into a tea room. This served the same purpose as road mending did the old man who gave me my first lessons in homesteading. The nine months when the tourists were not with us were to be spent fighting the wildness of winter in the wilderness, together with the more profitable occupation of making salable articles for the gift shop connected with the tea room.

For about seven weeks, including October and November, up to Thanksgiving, while the claim cabin was in process of building, we lived in the cottage where I had spent the summer. That was over two miles north of the claim and close to Long's Peak Inn. This summer house was heated by fireplace only. During those cold October nights, we suffered more than we ever

Katherine Garetson (left) with A.A. in front of Katherine's homestead, which they christened the Big Owl. (*Estes Park Museum*)

told. When the log would burn low, about two in the morning, my poor short-haired Dane would come to my bed, shove her head under the covers; then shiver and shudder till my bed rocked. I was apt to be awake and very miserable myself, so I'd build a cracking, blazing fire and the two of us would crouch in between the andirons with a steamer rug wrapped around us and our bodies close together. When we had a snow it was dreary. We had to lug the absolutely necessary implements and utensils close to the blaze. Indeed, we made a moveable wall of household plunder around the hearth. We had an oil heating stove which guarded the outskirts of this domestic circle. Cooking went on at the fireplace as well as on the heater. With this introduction to mountain snow storms, no wonder we dreaded the winter.

The fact that I was planning to spend the winter in as high a valley of the Rockies as can be inhabited the year round, although my house wasn't built, and roads sometimes became impassable overnight, worried me less than it did the permanent residents of the region. Now and then I nearly lost my nerve. For the most part, I drifted along, blown by the kindness and enthusiasm of friends.

The region was sparsely settled. Long's Peak Inn was the most distinguished habitation in our high mountain valley. At that time, the Inn could accommodate about fifty guests, but only in July and August were so many people there. During the rest of the year, Enos Mills, guide, lecturer and naturalist, lived there completely alone, absorbed in his arduous task of becoming a writer. He had a devoted servant in Alfred (Oberg), a Swede.

Alfred's cabin was devoted to domestic arts. To cooking, serving meals, washing and mending. Alfred had a shining face. It was amazingly clean, always, and bright and sweet. As Mr. Mills's own cabin was lined with books, the food for his alert mind, so Alfred's was packed with food for the body: the winter's supply of potatoes in sacks, and tubs of eggs, (Alfred always coaxed a flock of hens through the winter), bushel baskets of carrots, parsnips, turnips; shelves of dry old onions with shining skins of sunset shades and many cans of vegetables, brightly labeled. And there were Hubbard squashes piled in a corner with cabbages. As I remember that cabin of Alfred's, it often had a line stretched across the corner behind the stove, where woolen underwear and socks slowly dried. Every wet cloth would freeze solid if taken a distance from the stove. The mop itself had to be dried before it could be put away. The only luxury in Old Original was Alfred's phonograph, a mighty good one and well cared for. After the evening meal had been cleared away, the phonograph did duty for awhile, usually winding up with "My Little Gray Home in the West."[2] Then Alfred would bring out a sewing box and mend until he fell asleep. He had the most amazing assortment of buttons and needles in that funny old box. I used to suspect that he had been collecting the contents for forty years.

While we camped in my sister's summer cottage, we were neighborly with the Inn family. Alfred had much concern over my preparations for the winter, and Mr. Mills, while pretending that it was a matter-of-fact thing for a woman to brave a Rocky Mountain winter, must have been aghast at times over the foolhardiness of my exploit. Nothing would have induced me to go into that undertaking had I known what things could happen; what the life was like.

Alfred told me that I would freeze to death on a single bed. He wagged his head with a "No, no, that won't do!" when I said I had bought cots for A.A. and me. I must have a double bed and tons of comforts below and above my body, and furthermore, learn the trick of rolling up tight in the covers so that no speck of my bodily warmth could escape. He told me I must secure a tank that would hold at least fifty gallons of coal oil. Wood—stacks and stacks of poles for stove wood, must be placed around the house like a barricade, and a lot of it sawed up before the first deep snow came. He showed me how to swing an axe; how to lift and wriggle a pole on to a sawbuck; and how to saw with the big coarse-toothed saw.

Two men were living at Long's Peak Inn the early part of my first winter in that mountain home; two men besides Mr. Mills and Alfred. One was the manager of the Inn, and the other was a newspaper man from Chicago. Charlie, the manager, was a long, thin, likeable man in his twenties. He had been frightened by an illness, so had come out from Ohio to get strong. Mr. Sherman was an editor of a Chicago paper, on leave of absence.

Charlie and Mr. Sherman were our companions, and our only companions, until the first of January. And then, they both went away! In November Mr. Mills had left for a four month lecture tour, and Alfred was absorbed in the care of his "shickens," his eternal soup making and muffin baking. The men from the inn were good comrades and we saw them almost every day. They must have found my naivete appealing. My ignorance was colossal.

That first winter was unusually pleasant as to weather—what the hill folk call an "open winter." Indian summer lasted with but few light snow storms to break the glory till December. In that I was lucky but knew no better than to take it as a matter of course, knowing nothing of the hardships of a cold and snow-bound autumn.

Frank and Otto, who were building my cabin, dallied with the work, relishing the opportunity of building something more like a bungalow than a homesteader's shack. I did not want a bungalow. They merely took it upon themselves to elaborate my plans, thinking there was a lot of money back of me. We thought my plan could be carried out in two weeks. It took eight, and at that, the boys went away disgruntled, calling the work unfinished. But they had taken all my money.

The original claim cabin consisted of one large front room with many windows on three sides. The back of the room had no windows. The wall space was taken up by two chimneys and a door. The door led into a lean-to which was ten feet wide and stretched the length of the main room. This lean-to was divided into three rooms: the middle one, lined on two sides with shelves, was the store room. On either side of the store room was a tiny bed room. One of these was A.A.'s and the other, mine. They were very, very small.

By the last of October our friends made it emphatically understood that there was to be no more foolin' about bringing in winter supplies. The road might be blocked with snow any day. A.A. and I had been glad to offer as [an] excuse for not getting the supplies, the unfinished house. Now the roof was on, the windows in, the crates of stoves and trunks of bedding had been brought up from the freight depot forty miles away. There was no longer any excuse. Truth is, we were staggered at the idea of getting together all the food we would need during six months. How to begin!

The tearoom at Katherine Garetson's homestead, the Big Owl, was a convenient stopping place for tourists on their way to Long's Peak. (*Estes Park Museum*)

One morning as we breakfasted on the east porch of that summer cottage, warm enough that November morning in the level rays of the rising sun, we naturally fell to making the list, everything to be brought from the general store in Estes Park, ten miles down the mountain. One of us had an inspiration: "let's count the number of weeks on the calendar till June first.

Then, let's make out seven different breakfast menus; ditto, luncheons; ditto, suppers. We can figure amounts of food needed by the two of us for each meal and multiply that by the number of weeks." As we are both of us generous by nature, the portions were liberal. The list went to the store. In addition to canned goods, we bought a whole big cheese, realizing that it would be perfect food in case we ran out of everything else nourishing. Because breakfast food is a part of the breakfast menu, we ordered quantities of seven varieties, I never eat it; A.A. can, but not with condensed milk for cream! There were many mistakes similar to the breakfast food one. Afterwards, we learned that the town bench warmers made merry over the list. We bought enough food for a family of eight, when all we needed was a six month's grub stake for two girls and a dog.

On the thirteenth of November a wagon drawn by four horses pulled up the mountain, bringing a tremendous load of provisions. I had never seen so many tin cans, sacks and boxes of food outside a grocery store. I felt as if I had invested in a department store. This stuff was piled in one corner of the main room of the cabin amidst shavings and boards, crated beds, stacks of water pails and coal scuttles, tubs, dishpans, and brooms.

Our first night was the most tragic of my life. Coyotes, wild with excitement over the light in the wilderness, howled and shrieked to blood-curdling tunes. We bravely went to work to have supper. Although the cook stove had been set up, no table was built so we laid boards over carpenter's horses and found some boxes to sit on. We decided to cook just one thing for the evening meal and that happened to be spaghetti stewed in diced bacon and tomatoes. We unpacked the new skillet and after washing it carefully, turned into it a can of tomatoes, the bacon and then the boiled spaghetti. The skillet wasn't iron—or at least the inside of it was enameled with some strange preparation.

When we sat down to our first meal, we tried to be jolly; probably we were silly; we were both afraid of the night and the long winter ahead of us; and we were desolately lonely and homesick. We each took a mouthful of the spaghetti and stopped. It was vile. The strange enamel had soaked off—perhaps the acid of the tomatoes had helped it—and the flavor of our one and only dish was nauseating. It didn't really matter because neither of us could have eaten that night. We couldn't even swallow water. The new coal oil lamps burned queerly. Without ceremony we unpacked the bedding and crawled in— to cry, to turn, to toss about, and to wonder why we ever did it. . . .

Our wee bunkrooms were furnished with an iron army cot, the tiniest drum heating stove made, and a wash bench with a mirror over it. At one end of the large living room we had a big Wilson heater (air-tight drum) and at the other end a cook stove two feet square. After we had settled ourselves for the winter, you could see at a glance when you entered the front door that the stoves gathered about themselves respectively, the kitchen para-phernalia and parlor furnishings. A six-foot table of pine boards had one end near the heating stove so that it served as library table, while the other reached almost to the cook stove and was dined upon. A kitchen table near the cook stove had shelves about it and above it so that the corner became a kitchen cabinet, complete. I never minded the shining dishpans hung on the wall, but before that long winter was over, I came to hate the coal scuttles and the slop pails

We had rough benches for window seats and two big willow arm chairs were in constant use. If we had one guest for a meal, somebody sat on a box; if there were a lot, we pulled the window benches up to the table. The yellow pine boards of the walls were left unstained so that we had a bright, golden interior. The many six-paned windows had dark blue draperies of denim which served as shades at night.

After the utensils had found their own pegs on the walls, and all the canned goods were lined up on the store room shelves, we were as tidy as a ship and realized that we had set sail on a voyage that might prove full of hardships—an arctic expedition, it would seem, from the serious manner in which I set my face towards it. And by the time we were settled, the all-winter snows began.

Homesteading the Big Owl, from Chapter II

My own acquaintance with this land of sky dwellers began as a tourist. As a guest at Long's Peak Inn, I had visited the beaver colonies and studied their works. These particular colonies and lakes were on the moraine west of my homestead. The most dismal attempts at nature study were the evenings when we seriously endeavored to see the wiley beaver at work on the moraine lakes, gathering winter food, building dams and repairing their houses. We would forego the evening dinner at the Inn, carry a paper bag of unpalatable sandwiches, raisins, chocolate and oranges, trudge down to the moraine and long before the set of sun, station ourselves on boulders project-ing into a lake. No whispering allowed. The children were repressed until they were sulky. And so we would shiver away the sunset, anticipating the moment when the beaver would emerge from their hiding places and per-form upon the water. Very seldom did we see anything but the jump of a frog. A long time after the dinner hour at the Inn, we would gather our picnic group. It wasn't pleasant to gulp down the cold lunch. Then we would run home in the dark—chilled and drained of enthusiasm for nature study.

When I took up the claim, I had an inspiration! I would make a tea room for my place with the special purpose of serving hot suppers to these beaver students. The colonies were not a ten minute walk from my place.

Therefore, when it came time to name the place, we all felt bound to emphasize the beaver suppers in some way. We had to decide on a name before the stationery was printed. And we wanted to order signs painted. We had bought a turkey and had a Thanksgiving celebration less than a week after we moved in. Mr. Sherman, Charles, Alfred, A.A. and I made up the dinner party and before anyone departed, the name was to be decided on.

We started out with the beaver idea and wore it threadbare. "Beaver Colony Tea House," "Beaver Hut," "Beaver Lake Lunch room," were quickly discarded and so was the extreme of these, "Beaver, Bacon and Buns." Mr. Sherman preferred to make something out of the combination of our names, Katherine and Annie Adele, so his best suggestion was Katakinn—which, of course, meant nothing. I know better than anyone what it was all about and suggested "Last Chance," "Little Money," "Rough and Ready." Charles facetiously contributed "Raisin Reserve" because we had been so sure of having enough raisins that we had them sent from every direction—particularly a ten-pound box of fancy ones from California.

"What's the name of the hill?" some one asked.

"Big Owl for the great horned owl nesting there."

"Then why not Big Owl Lodge?"

Every resort in those days that was not an inn was a lodge. We were worn out with considering fifty names, so "Big Owl Lodge" won the vote. Thereupon Mr. Sherman clinched the decision with:

> The Big Owl Lodge,
>
> You cannot dodge,
>
> You should not if you could,
>
> So near the road,
>
> So a la mode,
>
> Its eats so very good.

They tell me that the trappers used to speak of my hill as, "The green hill where the big owls nest." It was named "Big Owl Hill" in a poem by our valley poet, Charles Edwin Hewes. The first time I met Mr. Hewes, he told me of his experience on my hill one afternoon when a great horned owl rose up from slumber very close to him and hovered over him like the Roc in an Arabian Nights story. His wings, he said, spread for one yard. I know how thrilling the incident was and how he came to talk often of that Big Owl Hill.

DUTCH LUNCHES

TEA PARTIES

THE BIG OWL

TO END THE RIDE

Two Short Miles South

of

Longs Peak Inn

ARTS   NEEDLEWORK   CRAFTS

The menu cover for Katherine Garetson's tearoom at the Big Owl also featured arts and needlework. (*Estes Park Museum*)

Of the great horned owls I, myself, have intimate knowledge. One summer day, years ago, when I was at Long's Peak Inn, I rambled off towards the south after breakfast. Following no road nor trail, I was soon lost in rough country east of Cow Creek. At noon I began to work my way back, crossing the creek on two fallen trees and stumbling into a tangle of old and young spruces, growing thickly among fallen timber and willows in a swamp. Now, I know that I was then on the spot afterwards designated as my northeast corner. I scrambled up some crags and looked into a pleasant cove by the stream. Here was a miniature Greek outdoor theatre, with the semi-circle of crags arranged like tiers of seats, and a lovely flowered open space for a stage. As I slid down into this charming place, there was a muffled noise of shirring wings that frightened me. I saw before me several great humps of white and tan feathers on that stage, and I slowly realized that I was intruding upon the noon day quiet of four huge, bewildered owls. One by one they lifted their large, puff-ball bodies, spread out their wide wings and escaped over the rim of my amphitheatre, leaving me shuddering from the startling stunt. It was unexpected and uncanny. They looked so powerful and mysterious. That was my introduction to the north end of my land and to my own big owls. Little did I dream then that I would some day—years after—own that wild, rough bit of the hill. I was frightened and plunged straight westward, finally coming out on the main highway leading to the Inn.

And so, when Mr. Hewes called on us one day in February and after introducing himself and his companion to us, related his experience of the owl on the hill, I had my yarn to contribute, and we agreed that the great birds had first claim to the hill, and it was only fair that the hill be named after them. It was worth something to me at that time to be able to agree with a neighbor about anything under the sun, for I was growing like other people who dwell in a mountain fastness, critical and suspicious of everybody.

Properly speaking, the only neighbors we had were the folks at Long's Peak Inn. On beyond that group of log buildings, a mile north, was the Wind River Ranch. That first winter of my homesteading it was deserted and dilapidated. Camped in the one log house of the group that could be made habitable, was a family of four. Their cow made them noteworthy. We seldom saw a four-footed animal at that altitude in winter. Ted Harding, the father of the family, was employed to gather wood for the Inn—and this was a whole winter's occupation. He had a wife and two babies. A.A. made excursions once a week to that place for a gallon of milk as long as she could break trail through the snow. When the ground became rough from old snow melted and refrozen into ragged ice, and snow drifts alternated with long bare stretches of frozen trail, we found it took her all day long to make the round trip for the milk, and so at last we gave up trying to have fresh milk and took to "tin cow"—the custom of the country.

There was a gulch between the ranch and our place where surface water moved so slowly that a great sheet of ice was formed. Several times A.A. had slipped and fallen in trying to cross this slippery, uneven field and had spilled the milk. We were unable to find a way round it because of the thickness of the timber and the network of willows. Many a tumble we had there—our feet thrust out straight before us and we sitting down hard. One day Mr. Sherman came along just as we had fallen. He named the spot "Alabama Gully" because, he explained, "Alabama" meant "Here we rest." It sounds like the Bible. To this day it is known as Alabama Gully; it marks the half-way place between Big Owl and Long's Peak Inn.

On beyond that ranch where lived the cow, there dwelt a very pleasant young man, Julian Johnson. He, too, was a homesteader. Half of his claim was lovely Lily Lake. The north shore of this lake rises abruptly into a rugged little mountain whose crest resembles a cluster of Gothic church spires, while off toward the west towers the snow-capped range.

These two inhabited places, the Wind River Ranch and Lily Lake, were so far from us that we hardly counted them in our community. Far up the mountain above Long's Peak Inn was the Hewes-Kirkwood Ranch, home of the poet Charles Edwin Hewes. Due to his habits as a recluse, we failed to think of Mr. Hewes as a neighbor; in fact, we never thought of him at all. As an actual fact, I had three companions, A.A., Charlie and Mr. Sherman. No other human associates. The men went away the first of January: Charlie to the Pacific Coast; Mr. Sherman back to work in Chicago.

Thirty or forty miles away down the mountains lay the valley towns. I had no knowledge of any of these settlements, and knew no soul down there. Denver was eighty miles out on the plains, but I did not know anyone there. From my mountain eyrie stretched a thousand miles of unknown country; clear to St. Louis my thoughts of human relationship must fly!

The days when A.A. went to Wind River Ranch for milk were long for me, left at home alone. As the afternoons shortened, I grew restless before she came home. One evening, I lighted the lamps early and climbed the hill in hope of seeing her on the white road at dusk. When I looked back at my home, I cried out with delight at the picture it made; it might have been a wood-chopper's hut in a Black Forest fairy tale. And, again, it made me think of the picture of "Home" on a Christmas card—a frosted card, of course. Icicles hung from the eaves to the snowdrifts; the windows glowed with light red and warm; from the chimney shot up spark-besprinkled smoke; and the trees behind the clearing were wearing white hoods.

It began to snow. By the time I reached home the big flakes were coming thick and fast. It was after nightfall before A.A. came in looking like a cotton wadding Santa Claus. Her cheeks and eyes were brilliant. Elf locks that hung as far as her chin were white, like Rip's. She wore a tight fur cap, a sweater and bloomers. Altogether, she was such a loveable sight that I couldn't help wondering how I could endure life without her anywhere. Being without her for a few hours brought on such loneliness.

We had held a housewarming two days after we moved on to the claim. The guests were few in number; Alfred, Mr. Sherman, Charlie with two girls in a buggy from the Village. Preparing the feast was like getting up a circus in a barn. But everyone was in high good humor even if we did sit on boxes and eat from boards laid across carpenter's horses.

Alfred came down once after that event, when the first great snow set in. He rushed down in the morning after the big flakes began to come fast, fearing that we would not know how to prepare for the storm. He taught us to think fast about all the things outside that would be needed inside during a three day storm which might be immediately followed by another. We carried in loads of stove wood; filled every container with water; put saw, axe and shovel indoors. Alfred was violent in his denunciation of any mountaineer who left his axe out when it might be buried by snow and lost till spring. After that sweet helpfulness in time of storm, we saw nothing of Alfred except on mail day at the Inn.

The manner in which we worked steadily towards Saturday, and let our excitements increase till that night, reminded me of the way city working men and women look forward to "Saturday night." Saturday was our mail day: letters had to be ready to send by four o'clock and by six or seven the carrier was met with his incoming pouch. Nothing mattered on Saturday: life was a scramble. And on Sunday morning we were more apt to be cross than happy. We had to get ourselves in hand for another week of mountaineering, and learn to regard the back-home, city interests in their true light: of no consequence, so far as we were concerned.

I am sure the majority of brides act as I did about my new house. I tried to be a perfect housewife. I observed the old time weekly regulations: on Monday I washed; on Tuesday ironed; cleaned lamps and scrubbed on Wednesday; mended and fussed about on Thursday; Friday wrote letters; and Saturday cleaned house hard. This naturally made Saturday the worst day of the week, even had there been no matter of mail! I was always tired and out of breath when we went out at noon for the weekly journey. We had to go to Alfred's cabin, the Old Original at Long's Peak Inn, over two miles north. The Inn was the Long's Peak Post Office. Alfred would make a gala day of our coming and serve a meal (often a delicious dinner) at about three o'clock. Then we sewed. He played his phonograph. It seems to me that that went on for many a restless, fidgety hour, till one of us, during repeated trips to the point of vantage outside the cabin, sighted the two mountain ponies and the mail wagon. Up to that point, we were all friendly, talkative, affable. As soon as the pouch was brought in we were all silent. Sorting out the handful of letters was so solemn a matter, we did it with lumps in our throats! It seems to me somebody was invariably disappointed. Never did all the right, hoped-for letters come. We would load up our shoulder packs, light the lantern and start home, often in a high wind. As soon as we had lighted the lamp and built a fire in the heating stove, we'd sit down and try to digest the week's mail. The room always looked the same way on mail night; mittens, caps, overcoats, overshoes, haversacks, and wrappings from parcels and newspapers in confusion on table and benches. We often had a loaf of bread sent up on the mail wagon from the village store. About nine o'clock one or the other of us would build up a hot fire and broil bacon, making sandwiches with the fresh bread. How many a night I stood over the heater eating bacon sandwiches, while A.A. and I told each other how "mean" certain innocent individuals were for not having written. Perhaps the Saturday excitement of mail did us good; on the other hand, it may have interfered with a settled content which this life in the mountains could have brought us, had we been able to throw off all interest in the life from which we were hopelessly cut off.

When we first moved down to Big Owl, we found it pretty hard to break away from Alfred's cabin at dark on Saturday night. I remember one such night when we were trooping along silently, farther and farther from the friendly neighbor. We had got safely across Alabama Gully and on to the county line, half a mile from Big Owl. To our horror, coyotes, down in our woods ahead, started their wild barking. Gypsy answered with her deepest baying. Now, we were sure one lone coyote would not attack us, but there ahead of us, perhaps in the road, maybe surrounding our house, was a whole pack! It was a long way back to Alfred's cabin, and if we went back, where could we sleep? All the rest of the Inn was closed for the winter—and let me tell you here and now, that when a mountain cabin is properly closed for the winter, it is uninhabitable. It is barely possible that there was only one coyote. We heard that one coyote can so change his tune in barking and howling that he sounds like half a dozen. This certainly sounded like a craziest yelpings of a whole chorus.

"Don't be bluffed!" A.A. and I recited together, and away we walked straight down towards the enemy, Gypsy stepping high, ahead of us, every sense alert. Not a shadow of a beast did we discover. When we came to the house, we were so tired and frightened it would have been easy to drop down outdoors, rather than enter the dark interior. One never knows what is hiding in a dark building. Neither of us admitted to the other this fear, so once we had entered and built up the fire and lighted the lamp, we were glad we had had the trip to the post office and the thrill of an adventure at the end.

It seems to me that I had an unbearable amount of ignorance to fight against that first year. I had a great deal to learn about country conditions as well as those conditions peculiar to the mountain region in which I had settled. We discovered that our wood was spicy and burned furiously, giving forth a quick, intense heat. But in a few weeks the stove gave forth more smoke than heat. It became almost impossible to start either fire. For a

ICED DRINKS		SANDWICHES	
Lemonade	25	Ham	15
Grape Juice	25	Lettuce	15
Iced Tea	25	Peanut Butter	15
Budweiser	25	American Cheese	15
Orangeade	30	Swiss Cheese	20
Orange Juice	30	Tuna Fish	25
Gingerale	35-25	Sandwich Relish	25
Pop---Root Beer	10	Chicken	30
Gingerale		Ham & Cheese	30
Coca Cola			

SALADS		HOT SANDWICHES	
Head Lettuce	30	Broiled Ham	25
Lettuce & Tomato	40	Bacon	25
Asparagus Tips	40	Hot ham or bacon on Toast	35
Pineapple & Cheese	40	Toasted Cheese	30
Tuna Fish	45	Cinnamon Toast	25
Fruit	45	Buttered Toast	25
Chicken	50	Club Sandwich	75
Shrimp	50		

The Big Owl menu had amazing variety. (*Estes Park Museum*)

whole week we shivered, coughed, denied ourselves warm water for any purpose whatsoever and subsisted on cold, ready-to-serve food. With difficulty we could create sickly fires; and then, we kept the lamps burning most of the day, hovering near them like moths.

But the torture of those mornings! I'd turn out of bed into a zero room and let in the great dog to stop her scratching on the door. While I tried to create a blaze by stuffing many newspapers and fat pine chips and matches and kerosene and kindling into the two stoves, Gypsy expressed her mad glee over getting inside. She would lope around the room for all the world like a bare-backed horse in the circus, while I, a sleepy equestrienne in a sooty bathrobe, would stand gasping, as if ready to leap on her back—and often did it when she dug her claws into my bare heels! And I would sit disconsolate and shuddering on the icy front porch, strangling, while great clouds of green and yellow smoke belched forth from perfectly cold stoves. A man from over the Range stopped in one day (he was taking pictures of big game) and listened to my woe. He calmly said: "All you need to do is clean out the stoves and take down the pipes and blow out the chimneys. It's customary to clean out the pitch once a month."

Yes, it's customary, I know that well, now. But that is the job I am reserving for my worst enemy when I have enticed him into my employ. It is rather fun to turn a stove inside out and scrape the lids and pipes until the long, sticky black streamers are blown away down the hill. Making mud pies is fun, too. But at neither pastime do I really care about being caught.

Among the red letter days of that first winter, the day we learned to clean out the pitch from the stoves is by no means the least important. After the soot was scrubbed out of the room and all three of us had washed a number of times, we had a warm room for the first time in weeks; a meal of better than half-cooked food; biscuits that were not veiled with a blue unholy cast of countenance in place of natural brown. And our kind guest smoked good tobacco all afternoon while we sewed and listened to stories of the habits of bobcats and mountain lions.

Homesteading the Big Owl, from Chapter V

. . . It was apparent that everyone who heard about us wanted to see the Women Homesteaders, but the encouragement they had to offer was: "A homesteader can't stick it out." This tea-rooming was my first experience in coming forward to meet the public. Our adventure created more interest [than] I was prepared for and my equilibrium was upset. Our secluded winter had made us more timid than we naturally were, so we were at the mercy of the first arrivals who were seeking "personalities." It was astonishing how many wanted to tell us about some other homesteader they had known who had had to abandon the claim before final proof. The usual story was: the homesteader ran out of money and there was no way to earn it in the claim; he lost his health; he could not endure the hardships and the loneliness, or else he lost faith in the undertaking.

As their first exhilarating summer on the claim came to an end, Katherine and A.A. came to a turning point.

Apparently the summer season was on the wane. A.A. went for the mail, bringing back an overwhelming sack of bills, duns, threats and such-like. It seemed I owed everybody who had ever supplied us with merchandise relative to homebuilding or tea-rooming. The bubble of our California dreams burst. Nor did we see how we were going to stay on the claim another winter and keep from starving.

A.A. had teacher's training. She set about securing a position in Wyoming while I put my wits to work to dispose of the dog. We argued that I had to stay at Big Owl to hold down the claim; but she and Gypsy were supernumerary.

Our parting was not only heartbreaking but prolonged. A.A. missed the one stage out of Estes Park by a few minutes; having twenty-four hours to wait, she walked back to Big Owl, weeping and footsore, her silk stockings worn and torn. Her skirts muddy. Early the next morning—indeed, before daybreak—we started out together with Gypsy, ignoring the tea room entirely. I walked half-way to the village with her, until she was picked up. . . .

The ensuing days and nights were distressing. In my loneliness I clung to Gypsy. There were almost no visitors. Tourists had turned their faces city-ward. . . . I was terrified at the approach of winter. My credit was gone. I had no money. Debts, debts, debts. I could see no way of feeding myself to say nothing of the poor dog.

After finding a good home and reluctantly giving away Gypsy, Katherine is left alone.

The experiences that follow are all part of a nightmare. I discovered within myself a great capacity for suffering. . . . Cooking and the consequent dishwashing I gradually reduced to nil. Of course I degenerated and lived like a stray dog. The nights must all have been stormy and black. I was really afraid to stay so many miles from human beings; so I would light my lantern and trudge up to my sister's house near the hotel to sleep there on one of the stripped beds. I would try to eat food from a knapsack packed at home. This supper I would spread out on the stone hearth after dragging in a log and building a fire. . . . There was rain and wind on those nights. After choking down supper I'd sit like a Buddha on the hearth and gaze into the embers. . . . I remember few details of that fall, must have spent whole days in a stupor, or grieving. Tired out. Beaten. Certainly I neglected to provide wood, food, snug quarters for the winter.

One day my new friend Bill explained to me that I'd better go back to my folks for a few months. I was docile by that time. After the traveling money came from home in response to his telegram, he sent the Allens Park mail carrier for me one glorious day. We went down the south Fork of the St. Vrain Canyon to Lyons where I boarded a train without knowing enough to buy a ticket. . . . I spent a few hours in Denver and had time to buy a book to absorb myself in during the long ride to St. Louis. I picked up *Two Years Before the Mast*. Perhaps *Les Miserables* would have afforded more gloom. Dana's must have been the right book for me at the critical time, for I read it in determined fashion, refusing to think of my own plight. After I had been with my relatives a little while, they looked at each other in grief and amazement. The first year of homesteading had told on me.

After recuperating with her family in St Louis for a few weeks, Katherine regained her enthusiasm for her homestead and realistically determined that what she needed was a benefactor. She made a list of "very rich men who might take a long chance on a good land proposition, Out West." The

very first man she told about her project gave her a check for the thousand
dollars she needed to pay her debts and get started again. Bolstered by
this experience Katherine was back on her claim by February to begin her
second year of homesteading, but this time on her own.

Homesteading the Big Owl, Chapter VI

. . . From sun-up to sun-set I lived on my Hill and learned it from the brooks
at its base to its crest. . . . Although I was a wild thing out of doors, I
became a lady when it was a matter of presiding at home. I cooked carefully; I made out menus for each day—did it thoughtfully and wisely when I
had pushed back the morning coffee tray. I ate regularly, daintily, and with a
book from which I read aloud in lieu of conversation. . . .

This solitude threw me on my own resources. I didn't care. It gave my
imagination full swing so that I dwelt in a bright world created to my own
taste. I accomplished a lot in the way of making articles for the summer gift
shop trade. I intended to go right on with the original project even though
A.A. had arranged to go home to St. Louis and would not be with me all that
coming summer. . . .

The great undertaking of that second spring was clearing the land and
fencing and putting in the crop. Even more serious for homesteaders than
getting money for improvements is the difficulty of finding men and teams
and implements. . . .

The last of May, my residence became a ranch house. This man [that she
hired] came every day with two and three teams and with five or six men to
help. I fed them at noon. It meant baking bread every other day; peeling
whole dishpans of potatoes; and making pies and coffee enough for a small
army. . . . The eight days of the land cultivation were brimful of joy and
excitement for me! How I lived! We put in three acres of oats and one of
potatoes. . . . Then came the inspector from the Land Office who measured
the fenced fields and assured me that I had four acres under fence. He was
very much impressed with my buildings, expressing the wish that more
homesteaders would take the residence on a claim as seriously as I did. . . .

It was June before my ranch hands departed. And with June came
tourists. My rich friend now received a report from me on my financial condition. Immediately came a check from him to pay the whole cultivation
expense. He believed in me. He was kind. I think, too, he had caught the
spirit of my adventure.

The tearoom took in little money that summer, and that winter, 1916-
1917, "went from one storm to another," creating severe hardships for
Katherine. She describes it as "the dreariest winter ever known in the

mountains." During that time she began the practice that she claims she adhered to "religiously when living alone"—the practice of reading aloud and talking to herself. To avoid "discontent" she divided her day as if in school with specific times for each of the tasks needing to be done, but she was frustrated when her clock "froze solid" and she could only estimate the time. She was dangerously short of food and wood for the fire. In April she sent a message to the general store in Estes Park requesting that supplies be sent as soon as possible. They were delivered on June 12.

Homesteading the Big Owl, from Chapter IX

It looked as if the three year homesteading period would end in a blaze of sunlight—striking contrast to the bleak third winter. . . . I was in no hurry to go someplace else to live after final proof. I loved my home, my land, the whole mountain world.

One night I went outdoors as soon as supper dishes were washed. I had not thrown off the consciousness of the long September day with its warm sunlight on clumps of yellow aspens. I was wondering how I had managed to live alone in the High Rockies for the greater part of three years; what had really induced me to begin it; what power had kept me sticking to it.

For a little while I sauntered through close-growing pine. Then my trail, shifting me from darkness into light, led out into a meadow encircled by aspens. Here was a flood of moonlight. The transfusion of light from a full moon with yellow, yellow foliage produced gold at meltingness. And this spectacle can be caught but once a year. It is held in store for the few of us who live near timberline; up where evergreens are our only tree friends; these solemn, stately ancient pines and firs and spruces; the conifers that have the quaint power of attracting to themselves the quivering aspens with their round, loosely hung leaves. A clump of windblown little trees met me at the trail's opening and poured forth showers of coin, as from horns of plenty; several tall sisters with slender white-green trunks and branches almost stripped of leaves, took the form of harps with golden strings; but out of the dark green background one exquisite aspen lifted a bole as white and as soft in its curves as a woman's arm. It was thrust out from the forest into the moon's light; the wind shook a thousand glittering spangles from fingertips to shoulder. Ah! The spirit of our valley beckoned me!

Great is the power of this mountain witch. It was many years ago that she laid her spell on me at the time of the September moon. And now it is all months of the mountain year that I love; each in turn holds me till it is done. After September departs in her glory, October holds me in thrall. Fallen leaves lie pale and motionless on dark pools under skies of deep blue. Crispness and

Katherine Garetson feeding the Big Owl chickens. Raising an acre of rye for her chickens was one way she met the requirements for proving up her homestead in the Colorado mountains. (*Estes Park Museum*)

brilliancy of atmosphere dance me through November till I am bound by the snows of December. January is the star month. The February moon shines on snow fathoms deep—it looks so fresh and boundless and without depth! It buries the valley so that the floor sweeps up to the rim of the enclosing mountains. March almost takes me by the throat while her wild winds pile the snow in drifts. Mist and cloud shadows on the range make April as colorful as September but her scheme is blue; and in April the streams are unbound. That is the first boom of the spring orchestra and it is followed by rain on the roof and bird song. May in the mountains broods with low black skies and daily snow storms. Then comes June filled with busy noises; chipmunks and squirrels are out of winter quarters and chattering and barking and scuttling on roof and porch. Big June flies buzz and mumble indoors in swarms, while all manner of birds scream and sing and call and whistle. A thousand different flowers bloom in July (it's the only chance they have). And August sends the hot blood throbbing in my veins—August with a glare of sun and wind that intoxicates me like sea air. . . .

My three years would be up on the twentieth of November. Then I would notify the land office that I had completed my term of residence and would go down with two witnesses to "prove up." . . . The land office was prompt in notifying me that December 7 was the date for me to appear with my two witnesses to make final proof. . . . In Denver, my two witnesses, former neighbors, met me at my lawyer's and we all proceeded to the land office. We each testified in private, and it was over. I knew no one would contest my right to my patent. How could anyone dare to find fault with all my perfect fulfillment of the law? And then I boarded at the train for St. Louis, free of all obligations to the government! A woman who had fought the three-year battle on the land and earned her title.

Homesteading the Big Owl, from Chapter X

. . . About the middle of March I received a big envelope from the land office. My patent, of course. Instead of that, the document declared that the Forest Service contested my right to my patent on the grounds that I had not complied with the Homestead Act in the matter of cultivation. . . .

My family and friends said, "Oh forget it all and settle down here in St. Louis and be a sensible citizen."

If I had had any hopes of being a sensible city woman again, I might have heeded their advice. Three years of life on that claim in Colorado had given me an overwhelming love for the western world. I hated that life in St. Louis, so cramped, so far removed from the natural life, so stupid and dull. I wanted to die rather than submit to such a drab way of living. . . .

I went back to the Big Owl as if the term of residence had never been completed. We put up a fine, four-wire fence, this time with some of the Judge's money, and planted a crop of potatoes and oats . . . there was very little at Big Owl to eat. There was no money. A contested homesteader had no credit.

A neighbor came to her rescue when he hired Katherine to house and feed carpenters he had hired to build cottages near the Big Owl. A.A came out to Colorado to help. Katherine observes that "There was more life at Big Owl in those days and more fun than I had ever known." To everyone's amazement, the oats planted that spring did well and the tearoom at Big Owl did a good business. Although Katherine had decided to stay on her "best loved spot on earth" as long as she could that fall, the influenza epidemic, reaching even into her remote mountain area, caused her to change her plans. Once again she returned to St. Louis for the winter where she worked as a stenographer and at other odd jobs. Her friend A.A. was also in St. Louis that winter and, like Katherine, worked to earn enough money to return to the claim in April. The two women kept the tearoom open for visitors while they worriedly waited to see if her patent would be granted. Katherine recalls the moment when she received the news.

. . . Outdoors was always a cure for my despondency so I went to the Inn for the mail, loitering, watching birds, pretending nothing hurt. As I came home through the Inn yard, I tore open a long envelope without noticing who the sender was.

This was from Washington. I stood stock still, not realizing at first what I was reading. A thrill ran through my body at the sight of Woodrow Wilson's signature. I glanced up and saw Enos Mills standing in the path in front of me. I handed him the document. His eyes danced with delight.

"Congratulations neighbor!" He cried; then, he added gently, "Indeed, you have earned your patent."

Alice Hildreth Zehm, Montana — 1916

Second generation pioneers, school teachers, family cooperation…all these themes observable in the stories of single homesteaders characterize Alice's homesteading experiences. Alice explains she and her sister were "born with a bit of the pioneering spirit" that had led her parents and grandparents to homestead in South Dakota in the early 1800s. With four years of teaching experience behind her, Alice, at twenty-one years of age, set out with her sister in the spring of 1916 for Montana to find a homestead. Her story describes the importance of railroads in providing access to homestead lands, shows how family cooperation insured success, and illustrates once again, how teaching school and homesteading were a winning combination for single women homesteaders. In 1920 Alice proved up on the Lazy Y, as she called her homestead, and soon after married the handsome former schoolteacher, Mr. Zehm. The homestead was their home for forty years while they raised a family of four children (Prairie County Historical Society 1974, 602–603).

From *Wheels Across Montana's Prairies*

My parents and grandparents on both sides of the house homesteaded in South Dakota in the early 1800's. Being born with a bit of their pioneer spirit, we, Stella and Alice Hildreth, decided in the spring of 1916, to go to Montana and file on a homestead. This was not a sudden decision, as we had thought of it for some years, remembering how our Grandfather Hildreth had spoken so many times of wanting to go to "Montaner" as he pronounced it.

I was almost 21 and had been teaching rural schools in Marshall County near Britton, S.D., for four years. My sister was four years younger. About a week after voicing our decision we were on our way to Montana. We arrived in Baker in the morning and found the land office and learned that all available land in that area had been taken. We stayed that night at the Hildreth House. In looking at our train schedule we noticed the name Mildred (our younger sister's name). We decided to go there but when we went to buy our tickets we learned that the train did not stop there, so we settled for Ismay, the next town east of Mildred. There we visited the land office and found a half section of land about nine miles west which was open. We filed on it and in a few days returned to Newark, S.D.

After a few weeks dad and I went out to Ismay and bought lumber and hired a man to haul it out to the claim and build a 10 x 12 shack. Then we returned to Dakota and in the fall I taught a three month term of school near Kidder. Homesteading takes a little money, you see, and we had six months before we had to take up residence.

On December 6, 1916, Stella, Gladys, Roy and I came back to Montana and having nothing but the bare shack on the claim we bought a few necessities and hired someone to take us out with a team of mules. It was getting dark by the time we got to our destination and the bunches of sage brush along the hillsides loomed up as dark objects which we thought might be coyotes. We discovered when daylight came that we needn't have worried.

We had purchased a small laundry stove, a sack of coal, 5 gallons of kerosene, a lantern, ax, a cream can, a few groceries, a 30 inch wide cot, three chairs, a small table, and a thin mattress. Our trunks had not arrived in Ismay when we left town so we went without them. We had all our bedding, some utensils and dishes in those trunks, but being young and foolish we thought it would be fun to really rough it, so out we went.

First thing we did on arriving was to cut a stove pipe hole in the roof of the shack and set up our stove. Then, of course, we needed fuel and water so we all four started out. It being moonlight, we found a creek half a mile away. Here we found dry branches and a small water hole which we chopped open and filled our cream can. We carried it and dragged the branches back to the shack.

Now we figured we would build a fire, cook a bit of supper and wait till morning to fix up our new home. We soon discovered that we had no kettles or frying pans and about all we had to fix quickly was a slab of bacon and some bread, but how could we fry the bacon? Necessity is the Mother of Invention so we used the lid of our water can as a frying pan and soon had bacon sizzling. We were so hungry no banquet would have tasted better that chilly night.

Our little stove had a very small firebox and we knew that it would need firing often so we decided that we would take turns keeping the fire going. We put the mattress on the floor and three of us tried to sleep while the other kept the fire. We had no bedding, just our coats for covers.

We had just settled down for the night when it started to snow and the white stuff came sifting through the cracks in the roof. We knew that would never do, so we took our lantern and with roofing paper and lath that we had brought out from town we covered the roof and fixed the prairie chimney (a short length of stove pipe a wee bit larger at the bottom than the pipe from the stove riveted around a hole in a square piece of metal. This piece of tin was nailed over the stove pipe hole and the stove pipe pushed up into it in place of a chimney). This kept the stove pipe from blowing off and helped some to prevent the roof catching fire.

The next day we got a team from our nearest neighbor (one and a half miles away) and Roy and I went in to Ismay to get our trunks and other baggage. We had forgotten to take our trunk checks and Stella and Gladys discovered them a while after we left. Thinking we wouldn't be able to get the trunks without them, they started out on foot with them. We had managed to get the baggage and started for home. We met the girls about two miles out of town. They had walked over seven miles. As they passed the Shumaker place, several men working on a new barn saw them and had a good laugh, thinking the girls had gotten scared out and lit out to catch us.

The next day we tar papered the shack and Roy and a neighbor went to a strip coal mine and dug a load of lignite. This coal turned out to be mostly frozen slack, but we knew nothing of lignite coal so we piled it up in a nice pile and the following day Roy stayed home and built a sod protection over it while we three girls walked to Ismay to mail some word back home and see if we had any mail.

From the claim we could hear the train to the east somewhere so we thought if we walked in the direction of the sounds we would reach the track and walk on it into town. We walked and walked and walked and got to the railroad just about where it reached Ismay. Coming home we decided it would be dark by the time we got there so we came out by the road which was quite a bit farther. When we got within a mile of the claim, we saw Roy up on a high butte waving the lantern. We soon let him know we were coming but he kept the light waving until we arrived.

Gladys and Roy stayed with us about two weeks until we were pretty well settled and they returned to Newark. We learned what real loneliness and homesickness was after they left, but we determined to stick it out and make the best of it. We liked the wide open spaces of Big Sky Country and had very few dull moments. It took much of our time dragging wood up from the creek and cutting it into small pieces for our little stove, which ate it like hay, almost. Our coal didn't do us much good, as this neighbor had pulled a funny on us, knowing that we were greenhorns.

Many a time toward night when the blues began to bother us we would climb up a flat top butte not far from the shack and tell stories and sing songs. We could both sing like the bird they call the toad so I'm sure we scared many a coyote away.

After Christmas the carpenter who was building the barn for Shumakers asked us to go home with him and stay with his wife and kids for awhile. We very reluctantly agreed and stayed there two months. We were so glad to get back to the "Lazy Y," as we had named our ranch. There is no place like home, even if it is only a "two by four."

When the lambing season came along about the first of April I hired out to help Mrs. Shumaker and Stella went to Ismay to work for Montana Bill and his wife. We earned enough money to go home to South Dakota when our six months on the claim were up.

We spent the summer at home, and returned to Montana in the fall. I taught school about two miles from the claim at the Ash Creek School until about Thanksgiving time when that school was closed and I was sent to teach the Richmond School about seven miles away. There was no school building there but Henry Zehm had offered his cabin for a schoolroom and his new granary as living quarters for the teacher. He moved home with his mother and family nearby.

We discovered that if we came back to the claim weekends we could still claim residency. The school board members insisted that, "Henry Zehm has horses and he'll be glad to take you back and forth each week," Then they added, "He's an old school teacher."

I quickly informed them that no "old schoolteacher" nor anyone else need to take us any place as long as we had a pair of good feet apiece. We used those good feet for the rest of that year. Every Friday night, rain or shine found us on our way back that seven miles over hill and prairie. On Monday morning we returned. We were walking in the dark most of the time.

When we met Mr. Zehm we found that he wasn't old at all and quite good looking but we were too stubborn to let him take us home so we would

"There's no place like home, even if it is only a two by four," said Alice Hildreth Zehm of her claim shack on the Montana homestead she named the Lazy Y. (*Wynona Breen Family Photo*)

sneak out on Friday nights when he wasn't around. One P.M. he had just pulled the binder into the yard by his barn and was taking the canvasses off. We knew that he would offer us a ride so we quietly sneaked off, keeping the schoolhouse between us and him until we got over the hill. Later he told us that he had seen us and thought, "If they want to walk, let them walk."

Those first years in Montana I had to earn my teacher's salary twice, first by teaching my 20 days a month and then by collecting it. One weekend we walked 30 miles to get my warrant, first to the clerk and then to each of the trustees for their signatures and home again.

Our first Christmas in Montana, we spent at Shumakers, because we had only arrived here the first week in December and couldn't go home so soon. The second year I was teaching at the Richmond School so when it closed for Christmas vacation we took our luggage and walked to the claim, stayed overnight and got up the next morning at 4 o'clock to catch the 8 o'clock train for home. We had to cross a creek soon after leaving the Lazy Y and we broke through the ice and got all wet. Our suitcases were heavy but what of it? We were going home to good old South Dakota.

Stella and I were never afraid but once. One night we lay in bed talking and laughing as usual, when we heard something walking around the shack and occasionally rubbing up against it. All we could think of was that the door was unhooked and our only weapon was the ax out on the wood pile. The next morning we looked all around for tracks and although there was snow on the ground we found nothing. We never knew what we heard but the trusty ax was brought-inside nights after that.

We had no cellar under our shack and it froze inside when the weather got bad so the next spring we dug a hole about 6 x 6 by the side of the house and one day a sheep herder friend of ours came by and roped our shack from his horse and pulled it over only the cellar. We cut a hole in the floor and made a trap door. It was about 4 feet deep and by using rugs and blankets to cover things when we were gone we could keep things from freezing there.

I taught the Richmond School at Zehm's for two years. In the summer of 1919 Stella was married to Lee Winder of New York. When I came to Montana that fall our sister Mildred came with me. She was 11. Schools were closed at Thanksgiving time for the Spanish Flu epidemic so we went home and I came back alone.

Henry and I both got schools on Cabin Creek that year. My school closed in December for a scarlet fever epidemic so I finished the term at the Holman School near Browns.

I proved up on the claim on the 20th of March 1920 and on March 27th Henry and I were married. I finished that term of school but I didn't teach again until 1941.

We have four children, Bob, Wynona, Bill and Waneta. We lived on the same place for 40 years. I sold the Lazy Y to Mr. Shumaker. In 1960 Henry and I moved into Terry where I still live. Henry passed away in 1969.

Florence Blake Smith, Wyoming — 1920

Florence's homesteading adventure was announced in the *Chicago Sunday Tribune*, March 21, 1920. Under a photograph of Florence and two homesteading friends, the story reads as follows:

Girls Quit Loop Clamor To Seek Fortune In West:
Leave to Till Wyoming Government Lands

No more smoky atmosphere for Mary and Norah and Florence. No more arising by alarm clocks and choking down a quick cup of coffee and running for the car. No more crowded trolleys and "L" cars for them. No more clamorous loop. No more the dodging of taxis and limousines. No more movies, delicatessens, ice cream parlors, candy shops and skating rinks. No more State street shopping.

Off to the Golden West

Mary and Norah and Florence have bidden adieu to Chicago and turned their faces towards the setting sun. They left last night for Gillette, Wyo. . . .

They left with an assortment of death dealing weapons, agricultural implements, books on chicken raising, old and serviceable clothing, and household goods. Portable houses have gone on ahead of them

Look Boys! 640 Acres Each!

Each of the girls has a 640 acre government claim fifty miles from Gillette, and they mean to work them. So the three 'girls,' two of them still in their teens, have turned pioneers. Mary's friends in the insurance company gave her and Norah and Florence a banquet at the Hotel La Salle last night and ornamented the tables with toy chickens, hoes, rakes, spades, axes, sheds, stables and rail fences. And every body went to the train with the three and shouted good luck after them (Pt. 1, p. 5).[3]

Some forty years later, Florence wrote her own account of that life-changing decision to homestead and of the three-year adventure she had proving up on her claim. Even the unexpected death of her mother just three weeks before Florence's planned departure for Wyoming could not deter her pioneering spirit. Her detailed memoir, *Cow Chips 'N' Cactus*, describes each of the three, five-month periods she was required to live on her land, what supplies she took, how she spent her time, and how she grew to love the landscape and the other homesteaders in her area (1962).

Her account illustrates the importance of twentieth century transportation developments in providing easier access to homestead lands for women. It also provides an example of the professional woman, other than a teacher, who supported her homestead doing work unrelated to the homestead. Florence's memories of her homesteading experience stress how much she enjoyed her time proving up. She was an attractive young woman, much sought after by the World War I veterans homesteading near her and even by rangers she met when visiting Yellowstone National Park. Her memoir tells of visits from family and friends who came out to

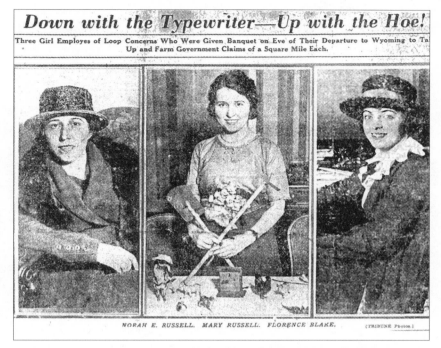

Down with the Typewriter—Up with the Hoe!

Three Girl Employes of Loop Concerns Who Were Given Banquet on Eve of Their Departure to Wyoming to Take Up and Farm Government Claims of a Square Mile Each.

NORAH E. RUSSELL.   MARY RUSSELL.   FLORENCE BLAKE.   [TRIBUNE Photos.]

This *Chicago Sunday Tribune* story told about Florence Blake Smith and her two homesteading friends. (Chicago Sunday Tribune, *March 21, 1920; clipping provided by Robert Blake Smith*)

spend their vacations with Florence. Although her memoir focuses on the lighter moments of homesteading, such as numerous country dances, Florence worked hard not only on her own place but also helping various neighbors with such chores as canning and bread baking. Although Florence had difficult moments in her homesteading, she always took them in stride and they always had a happy ending, in retrospect at least. In the end of her memoir, she has not only proved up but has met the man she will marry, a rancher and widower with three children.

The following excerpts illustrate Florence's experiences at various stages of homesteading: from her decision to homestead the memoir moves chronologically through her three years of proving up. Each year she moved to the claim in the spring and stayed through the fall, then went back to Chicago to work and to save money for the next year's homesteading (Smith 1962).

From *Cow Chips 'n' Cactus*

Dashing down La Salle Street in Chicago one fall day, I ran into a young man I knew, who had just returned from taking up a claim in Wyoming, and as we stood in the doorway of the Rookery Building out of the wind, he explained how one went about doing this thrilling deed. Listening to him and jotting down the several addresses he gave me, it looked quite simple. I "worked" on air for the rest of the day. Since I was free, white, and just twenty-one and female, I decided right there that I could do the same, if he could. All the way home on the elevated train that evening, I figured all my finances, including all the liabilities. It swelled the sum considerable, I was so thrilled, so eager, I could hardly wait for the train to take me home. I hoped my family would take kindly to the idea. (I had momentarily forgotten my brother Bob's love of teasing me.)

Reaching home that evening, I found one of my sisters had brought unexpected guests for dinner, and there seemed no use in going off the deep end about homesteading in the West, at least not for the moment. The more I thought and dreamed about the idea, the further away it appeared. Day followed day without my saying a word to the family of what was consuming my every waking and sleeping thought. There were so many details connected with the project; the distance from home, the many expenses before I could start the trek West. But I gave each one its due respect and consideration. There would be filing fees, locating fees, transportation, price of lumber to build the required habitable house. Also, it seemed, one had to buy posts for fencing and the wire to string between them, all of which added to a prohibitive sum by the mile. Then of necessity you had to eat to live, of course, during the slow process of homesteading. Periodically I gave up the whole idea, only to have it wholly repossess me in an unguarded moment. Then off again I would soar with my daydreaming. I must have been a total loss to the man for whom I worked in the large and busy department of the Federal Reserve. I could think of nothing else but six hundred and forty acres of free, open land, and all mine someday—only for living on it seven months of the year for three years. It looked more like an ideal vacation than a struggle. But of course I was looking through the wrong end of the glasses at the time. For even I was required to improve the land to the extent of $1.25 an acre.

After several days of family criticism because of my loss of appetite and also my loss of interest in the general goings-on of my household and family, I finally confided to my sweet Mother, God bless her. She heaved a sigh of blessed relief that I was in no more serious trouble than a bad case of indecision. We talked far into the night, not only on that first one, but on the many nights to follow, and she told me of an extra bond or two she had tucked away. She also told me she had a little dab of money which she had been saving for some emergency, and to her, *this was that important moment.*

The Federal Reserve Bank had just given us a twenty-per-cent bonus, and never having had that great a sum of money all at one time before in my life, I had invested it in two whole shares of reliable stock. It was purchased at thirty-three dollars and soared to eighty-seven and a half within six months. Not bad. My one and only adventure into the stock market, and that successful. Hard to believe. So it wasn't necessary to hock the family jewels to finance me. (Besides, we had none.) Between my mother and myself, we managed the full amount for the beginning of this "staking a claim in the West." It seemed too good to be true. However, this was only the beginning and plenty of difficulties were to be put in my way.

The first and most important was how to obtain the leave of absence I would need to get out to Wyoming and be located and file my claim. Since this was November, and the Government allowed one six months from filing date to establish residence, which would mean the following spring for me to return there and live, I had to be about things.

Daniel in the lion's den did not feel any worse than I. My boss had one of those concrete exteriors you often find heads of departments have. It protects them against diverse pleas of a raise or a half a day off, against your lame excuse for being late. (What if you did miss the 7:50 Express, or whatever?) He was one of the world's worst, and I dreaded asking for the time off. I was so afraid he would laugh at the idea. Then too, I did not want to share the secret until I knew for sure I would obtain my request. But how else? Whereupon one fine morning when I felt particularly courageous, I walked into the boss's lair. I was scared to death, and had planned on standing up and giving my speech all I had, but my knees shook so I was glad to sit down. Still I was determined to quit if need be, although I hoped that would not be necessary. Even if I was confident I could get another position. *The egotism of youth.* . . .

He let me sit there for a few minutes while he finished writing some secret-code work probably, as his back was almost turned to me. In spite of his lack of interest, I stated my case and made my request. Then I waited, with bated breath, while I watched his usually stern face change to a broad grin. I could hardly believe my eyes. Then he turned around and took one good look at me. Almost gasping, he said,

"Mean to tell me I've had someone in my employ with enough guts to go out West and stake a claim? I'll say you can have ten days off; take two weeks, and if you need any more, let me know. Now tell me all about it."

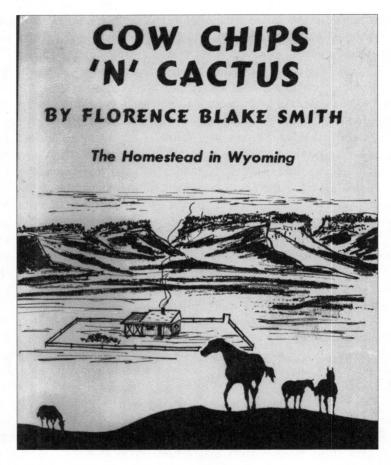

Florence Blake Smith drew this sketch of her "little grey home in the West" and the nearby Pumpkin Buttes for the cover of her book about homesteading in Wyoming. (*Pageant Press, 1962*)

Gosh, he was human, but he had done a good job of keeping it a secret till then.

He showed so much interest and gave me so much encouragement, I was almost overcome. It was not hard to tell him all the details. I could have hugged him. The leave of absence was assured, and I found it would not be necessary for me to quit.

I left Chicago three days later, on a Sunday night. The small town I was headed for was only fourteen hundred miles down the CB&Q track. In reality, it took two and a half days to get there then, and after the first thrill of actually being on my way, the wheels of the train seemed to turn backwards; I felt as if I would never reach the far-distant town in northeastern Wyoming.

After I had answered the questions of an interested couple on the train as to where I was going, they said they felt tempted to go on with me and take up a homestead too. To prove their point, they got off and bought me a couple of boxes of candy and an armload of magazines, besides inviting me to meals while on the train.

Finally I pulled into the depot, a drab red peaked-box affair. Little outside of the daily arrival of the two trains from west and east occurred. The platform was crowded. No one but me got off, and as I looked up the unpaved two blocks of Main street, I could have shouted for pure joy. I had heard so many discouraging accounts of this small town out West, as twenty years before one of my uncles had helped build this same railroad through the West, and had said that this was the "toughest town on the Burlington," trying to stop my mother from allowing me to go. There was nothing tough that met the eye. A few horses were tied to a hitching rail, and all of the men I saw wore cowboy boots with overalls tucked into them, large ten-gallon hats, and a solemn mien. Out of the crowd stepped a typical Westerner, who introduced himself as the locator I had written to. He carried my grip to the small hotel up the street and invited me to supper.

Since I already knew what his filing and locating fee would be, I figured I may as well get my money's worth. We had a Wyoming-grass-fed steak, and to this day, I know of no meat its equal.

Early the next morning after a quick breakfast, Mr. H., with three others seeking homesteads, took us in his car. We were well on the way by 7 A.M., before the warm noon sunshine would thaw the snow, leaving slick gumbo spots. The road, like a shiny ribbon binding the low hills together, was up hill and down. The early morning sunlight painted it pink and rose as we wound our way south the fifty-seven miles toward the homestead. We got stuck several times, and all got out and helped push while the driver guided the car over the better places or stayed in the deep ruts, which were sure to have a solid bottom. We had taken a light lunch, which had been eaten during the first couple of hours, and we were starved. When he decided we could not possibly get down to my land before dark, he decided to take the other three to their claims near-by, which were all adjacent, and promised me we would start out early the next day for mine. But as soon as he had turned the car around, we really got stuck up to the hubs in the thick mud, and I could see us all spending the night right there in the road. The prospect was horrible.

We scanned the hills for a light or sign of human habitation. Mr. H., who knew the country so well, promised us that a ranch was only the other side of the hill. I could see nothing but snow underfoot and darkening winter sky overhead. The wind howled and so did the coyotes. I could swear they were breathing down my neck. He decided to walk over to the dugout quarters of an old man to whom he had introduced us hours before, in the little country store where we had stopped. He told us to walk on up the hill until we came to a road. If the old man could, he would have him drive us over to the nearest ranch, where he thought they would be glad to make room for us to stay all night. It sounded encouraging; we did as he bade us. ...

Being early winter, night descended early. No sunset or after-glow to prolong the day, and there we four gals were—atop a hill, the sky a dark blanket, and not a sign of human habitation in any direction. No one said so, but we were scared to death, with visions of freezing slowly, since we had left our heavy coats in the car. We danced and ran around playing games to keep warm. This country of wide-open spaces was all right for romance in a book, but for stark reality, it had nothing to offer compared to paved streets and lights every twenty feet along the curb. Having more "Irish" than the rest, I walked a couple hundred yards towards a group of darker shadows and came back to report I thought a large ranch was just in walking distance. Glad to find anything, we walked much farther than we thought it ever could be, and came upon several low buildings, corrals, shacks, and a house fenced around, presumably the ranch house. But all was deserted. Not a sign of life. Even an angry, barking dog would have been welcomed. I tried the door; it was unlocked, and inside we could faintly make out a table, a chair, and an old leather couch with a huge hole in the center. We were glad to sink down and give our shaking knees a rest. What to do now? We did it. Nothing. Just sat there till the cold drove us outside to holler and yell and try to attract something or somebody to our rescue. Once we saw a light. Later on, two. It was the car circling the hill and trying to find our "remains." When we yelled at the top of our voices again, we saw the lights stop, then turn and disappear. Unflatteringly, the locator later told us he thought it was coyotes. So, back into the cold house again. If only there had been an old stove, we could have burned the stuffing from the couch, since most of it had been carried away by mice or packrats. The pangs of hunger had us in knots. We learned a lesson then, never leave your coats in a car, even on a hot day, for the nights in Wyoming in all seasons are crisp. One of us took turns watching at the window, while another, spanning the hole in the couch, lay down, flanked by the other two to keep warm. After what

Florence Blake Smith in Illinois before her homesteading adventure. (*Robert Blake Smith, Smith Family Photograph*)

seemed like hours of this, the sentry at the window reported a car appearing again on the hill. This time we all screamed at the top of our voices. Why they did not hear us in town 38 miles north, we'll never know, but pretty soon, after the lights disappeared twice, the car hove to a stop. We were rescued and were we surprised. . . .

Mr. H. had spent two hours trying to get his car out of the mud hole, and then had walked to the top of the hill where he had instructed us to go, expecting to find us huddled together for warmth, but at least there. When he found no sign, he had gone to the old man's dugout, who reported seeing us in wild form dancing around and playing games, or whatever, trying to keep warm. He had then lighted his lamp and promptly forgotten us. Knowing the country better than the four city girls, they presumed we had walked to the nearest ranch in the opposite direction we had taken. So they had bread and coffee before starting out to hunt for us. Arriving at the Sharkey ranch, they learned no one there had even seen, or heard, us. Now which way to go? Three times, he said, they hesitated on top the hill and looked over at the deserted Archibald ranch, but figured four smart city gals could easily see it was partly torn down and deserted... They didn't know us. He even went four miles back to the little store at Savageton, to see if we might have gone there and gotten a ride into town.

Frozen and hungry, but safe, he drove us to a nearby ranch. It was a small house, and they were not prepared for five unexpected guests. We four girls slept in one bed, and a good thing... several times during the night I thought I had frozen to death. I didn't see how I could be that cold and still be alive. Upon retiring, I had removed everything but the heavy underwear belonging to my uncle, which he had advised me to wear in the cold high altitude, but soon I was up and putting on each piece of clothing until I wore my hat back to bed. My spot was on the far side of the bed, and only thought for the kindly woman who was our hostess kept me from wearing my high-laced boots to bed.

While it was still pitch-dark outside, a terrific pounding came to our door, and we were told, in no uncertain terms, "Breakfast's on." Rightly presuming there would be no second call, we immediately got up and prepared to wash, but it was more of a promise that morning than an actual ablution in the icy water. We slid to our places along the bench at the kitchen table just in time to hear the grace before the meal. But what a breakfast! Hot oatmeal; platters piled high with thick pancakes, homemade sugar syrup or runny wild chokecherry jelly, and patties of homemade sausage; steaming coffee, and cream so thick you had to spoon it from the pitcher. This was a nectar and ambrosia to us city folks.

The big, low-ceilinged kitchen with its rafters recently whitewashed; the huge shiny cook stove with the wood box handy, piled high with fragrant chunks of cedar wood; snowy curtains at the windows, darned in many places; and the long, bare pine table scrubbed to velvet smoothness with its

Ironstone dishes and good food—all this made an unforgettable picture, and I was most humble and grateful for the kindness and hospitality. Three shiny and very brushed-looking little girls sat opposite us, now and then raising shy eyes from their plates to stare, then bashfully smile, at the strange people eating with them. It was quite an occasion, but they said not a word through the entire meal. These same youngsters are now beautiful young ladies, with small families of curlyheads of their own. All very attractive and city-bred, having been sent away to a convent for their educations.

After we had finished breakfast, the locator hired saddle horses for us to ride the seventeen miles farther south to the X marked on the map, which was my homestead. The rancher had only four horses that were gentle-broke to ride, and as no one volunteered to stay home, if you counted the locator (and how could you help it—he was six feet two and weighed two hundred pounds and so had to have a whole horse to himself), I offered to ride double with one of the girls. And believe me, to someone who never rode anything but an elevated train that was indeed epic. Naturally, we had to retrace the same seventeen miles to return the horses. Thirty-four miles of my life I could never forget, even if I chose.

It was long after noon when we reached my piece of land, and I would gladly have signed on the dotted line, had it been a lake. It was so good to reach the spot at last and it looked so beautiful to me, particularly the view of the Big Horn Mountains, seventy-five miles to the west. The witnessing thereof by the others, did not take long, and much as I longed to walk over every foot that first day, looking at the gray leaden sky easily discouraged it. So back over our route we went.

I could have filed on "open" land, but it would have been farther away from the place I chose and in what the natives termed "the breaks." Anyhow, I doubt if I would have survived a horseback ride over there. Before boarding the train back for Chicago, I paid the hundred dollars for the relinquishment I bought, one hundred dollars for the locating fee, and about twenty-five dollars for filing fee. The hotel bill, at one dollar a day, ate to the bottom of the barrel, and I was glad my ticket read "round trip."

When I again returned to my job, at the end of the ten days' leave, I was hailed as a heroine, an adventuress, a land-owner. How envious my fellow workers were, who could have done the very same thing had they wished. How strange the urges that drive some and leave another cold. Everything I did from then on took on a glamorous look, for at the back of each thought and the end of each day was the thrill of possession. I was now a homesteader in the West, and a potential owner of six hundred and forty acres of

Wyoming. Although my office hours were from nine in the morning to about three in the afternoon, I seldom got away before five, as there was always an interested person or two who begged for details and the addresses they just might use, if they could only scrape together enough to get them out West to stake a claim. It was a pleasure to me to talk about Wyoming. I did all I could to encourage them, I must admit, with out success...

Good friends were always bringing me something to wear when I got out on the "prairie," like riding boots, a pair of heavy breeches to go with them; a pair of rubber boots and a slicker to wear if it rained; heavy woolen pajamas from a boy friend, whose mother had made them for him when he left Kentucky for the cold of Illinois. I also inherited the heavy woolen hose my Mother had knitted for my brother while he was in the war in France. She also bought me two pale yellow plates, with cups and saucers to match. Thinking I might have company, my sister-in-law gave me a yellow teapot to match and a blue-checked tablecloth. All I needed was a casual visitor. I hoped. I took a little solid-walnut kitchen table, which had belonged to my Grandmother, a sanitary cot, two stout kitchen chairs and a small low rocker, another heirloom, and a regulation sheepwagon stove. These constituted my household goods. The bread can and the wooden boxes with the canned goods, would serve as extra seats if need. I had bought dainty dotted Swiss for curtains, plus a few favorite pictures from my room, and all this had yet to go into [my] trunk. The several handmade rugs and woolen quilts and blankets were wrapped around the furniture. The trunk refused to hold another thing. And there beside it on the floor were my riding boots, my short rubber ones, and a three-pound caddy of that wonderful Darjeeling tea. Oh yes, and my tool chest. Ho hum.

Once more, for the umptieth time, the trunk was repacked, and I decided to have a large wooden box with hinges made to hold the heaviest items. By careful maneuvering, the trunk was strapped, locked, and labeled for Wyoming...

In Chicago, April usually holds a breath of Spring. Not so in Wyoming.

I arrived in a snowstorm. It was not anything like the ones I had been used to, with men in "white" coming along shortly after and clearing it away. This stayed on the ground, and across the tracks of the little town, and far as the eye could see in all directions, the hills were covered with snow that looked as if it had been there for some time and intended to stay awhile. It meant fine moisture in this dry country, and the ranchers and farmers were exulting. The ground was frozen solid and the roads would be rough and rutty, with no C.C.C. camps to work them and no allotments for maintenance of secondary highways. All thought of getting out to the homestead, even if the household goods had been on the track, was out of the question.

Thinking to be on the safe side, I had purchased in Chicago, a portable garage, nine by twelve feet. It was just the size of our living room rug at home, and many's the night I spent moving the furniture inside of it, to acquaint myself with the size of my humble "shack" to be, in the West. It could easily be assembled by a woman. Or so I was told by the affable old man who sold it to me. A generous number of nuts, bolts and screws had been included to prove his point, and to provide complications for the "putter-upper."

Waiting for the roads to their claims to dry up, Florence and two other women homesteaders rented a small house in town and found jobs to pay for their expenses. By mid-May the roads were passable and Florence could finally go to live on her claim.

But I was thrilled when the day came that I got notice to be ready to go out to the homestead. I dashed around madly, hiring two trucks. One for the portable house, which was knocked down, of course, and loaded with care, along with my household effects. The other truck was to come out in back of us, just in case we got stuck in the mud. It carried the extra lumber to be used for the floor, as I wanted a real pine floor and not the heavy, dark, wide two-inch-plank flooring that had come with the garage-house. It took over two hundred feet, as I also wanted a "turlit" and a couple cupboards. The truck driver, whose truck I was riding in, had brought along a man to help him unload, and I had brought along a man I knew, because I did not know the truck drivers. I need not have worried. Within a reasonable number of hours, we had covered the fifty-seven miles south and arrived at Range 43, Longitude 75, Section 2, and X marked the spot where I chose to have them assemble the house. First they put up the diminutive cook-stove outside on the ground. There I cooked our dinner. Putting up the pipe, they discovered they had lost a link. The pipe did the job in spite of it, carrying off the smoke. I cooked for three starving men and me. When did food ever taste so good? That picnic lunch was eaten from the long planks that extended from the rear of the truck, and sitting on the nail kegs, we enjoyed a view of the Big Horn Mountains to the west 75 miles. Midday was very warm and no one wore a coat, although deep pockets of snow lay everywhere in the hills. Hours later, with the house up, the stove was the first thing moved inside, for the wind was now chilly and the heat felt good. Since we had lost the piece of pipe, it was necessary to put it up on the wooden packing box, where it stayed for the entire duration of my homesteading, giving the illusion I was cooking in midair. I never remembered to buy the missing link when I'd go to town, and in fact, I rather liked it. The glowing coals showing through the open front of the stove, as I pulled my chair close, were very cheerful of an evening.

Since I had had the brilliant idea of having the men extend the two garage doors, nailing them together, to make a continuing south wall of a lean-to eight by eight feet, I had two rooms now. It was quite palatial for a mere homesteader's shack, even if I was fifty-seven miles from town and two and a half from my nearest neighbor. Lucky for me I did not take that elderly salesman's advice and try to put the thing up alone. It took three husky men all that day to assemble it, build on the lean-to, and put in the new floor. To say nothing of the "improvements," as we called it, off to one side at the back and on the edge of the draw, yet not too far from the house, and with a wonderful view of the Pumpkin Buttes. After a light supper, they all drove back to town. Later they admitted they surely hated to drive away and leave me standing at the door, for they figured I was in for a bad night. All I can say is that they did not know the Irish. Before the sound of the truck had died away entirely, I was ready for bed, and had a perfect and sound sleep that first night. The day in the open, having begun at 5 A.M., helped. I may have had a few qualms of fear during my stay, but not that night. Before the Coleman lamp had finally sputtered its last, I too had sputtered mine and was asleep. The sky not yet plumb dark.

Next morning I was up again with the sun. I had so many things to do, and the beauty of the sunrise as I ate my breakfast, was a grand privilege to behold. Lucky me. Unpacking my boxes of books, rag rugs, and canned goods took several hours, and before I knew it, I saw by the sun it was noon, and the inner me clamoring for food. I took it out on the little stoop, or porch, the men had built from scraps, and ate a sandwich and some fruit and was back on the job before me. The only thing I had forgotten was scissors, so I cut my material for the curtains with manicure scissors and a sharp butcher knife, sewing each one by hand. They were in place that night at the windows and looking mighty pert, mighty pert.

That second night it was hard to go to sleep. The wonder of possession, the joy of looking out over one's own land, thinking on the dear dead Pioneers' toil and sweat to at last acquire one hundred and sixty acres, which was all they were allowed then, and here was I, with six hundred and forty, an entire square mile obtained by a different kind of sweat, more genteel, as it were....

Having to improve my land, I hired a man to plow and seed forty acres of wheat. He must have planted bird seed. The minute the green stuff showed half an inch above the ground, the ground was black with birds, and the green stuff soon got discouraged and gave up. Why don't birds eat weeds? The crop was a failure. The ground was too rocky and cut up, and I later received credit for my efforts, but no money. It was a dry summer.

I'd always had the wildest yen to write and it looked now that I was homesteading that my big chance had come. No time-clock to punch, no wild dash to and from work. Just the whole day ahead of me to sit and spin the yarns of my imagination into the fabric of a long or short story. But I hadn't counted on the writer's cramp that soon discouraged me. I would put down the pencil, go off for a long walk, sit in a warm sandy hollow and watch a small prairie dog come out from his hole. Paying no attention to me, any more than the sagebrush before me he would dash from one hole to another, as if wrapping at their doors to tell them what a swell day it was and to come on out. Soon the dozen holes would each have a small dog perched on the edge of the entrance, each little animal shaking his tail, which created that funny little bark they made. When a hawk would fly over, they would dash into their holes as one, coming back up to peek out and give the signal the coast was clear. They reminded you of a bunch of kids playing "Run-Sheep-Run," as there was always one on base. I carried a 32 Smith and Wesson revolver whenever I went for a walk, but I wasn't planning to use it on my furry friends. It just gave me a feeling of security as it rested in its holster on my belt. I wasn't expecting to use it on any peeping Toms or morons. No moron was ever known to walk 57 miles from a town to commit his crimes. It was solely to shoot rattlesnakes. . . .

Each night after finishing my easy supper, I would go for a short walk. I would sit cross-legged on my pet rock and watch the sun set behind the Big Horn Mountains and listen to the many birds settling down for the night. The Meadow Larks were singing their last sweet song of the day. The hills were covered with wild flowers and the air was so good and sweet. I would then dash back to my little cabin and light the lamp before it was quite dark. Sometimes I jumped right into bed as soon as I could and before the afterglow of the sunset had even faded. Other times I played my Victrola and sat on the little stoop, hugging my knees and watching the summer moon and stars while the sweet voice of Alma Gluck rang out over the prairie in her memorable song, "Little Gray Home in the West."[4] My little gray home, which actually was painted gray and trimmed with white, was indeed the place of my heart for seven months of each year for the three years I was required to live there. I don't recall ever being lonesome, nor homesick. Scared yes, a time or two, missing my Mother plenty, but I had so many things to read, I could always occupy my time. . . .

Especially those friendly books of David Grayson's which were such a joy and comfort and never to be forgotten.[5] I also had many letters to write, many far spots on my hills to explore over my claim, and loving care to give to each bean vine and plant that survived the furry horde.

The garden was a big pain in the neck. The rabbits ate it as promptly as it appeared above the ground. Learning that the house became filled with flies in spite of the screens, I took them off and placed them around the bit of garden, and only then did I know success in my many seeds and back-aching hours of tender care. A roll of chicken wire took over where the screens left off. Never having planted any seeds before in my life, believe me, it was a thrill to go out in the due course of time and pick a few, well, a few succulent beans, lettuce, and four tomatoes. I picked them, stem and all and hung them from my rafters so I would be sure and have them while they were on the green-ripe side. . . .

Friends visiting Florence from Chicago provided the occasion for a country dance.

A dance was given at a ranch 15 miles away. Everyone owned a pickup or a truck. Don't know as I ever saw a touring car among the country folk in all the while I lived there. But roads were often rutty and rough, and a pickup could be depended on to get there. In the trucks, bales of hay were opened and strewn on the bottom of the biggest truck, and nine of us piled in there, while four rode in the cab. In the full glory of a summer night, the going wasn't bad, but, after dancing the square dances and the waltzes they played over and over until the sun rose a glorious red disk in the east, through one window of the ranch house, as through the other, the silver sliver of the moon fading in the west proclaimed a new day, we could hardly drag ourselves out the door and up into the truck.

The lunch had been served at midnight and was long a thing of the past, but the boiler of coffee was left heating on the back of the stove, and you helped yourself as often as you felt the need of it. As many as a hundred people might attend the dance. Taylor's ranch was a very popular place, and they always drew a big crowd with their kindness and open hospitality.

They were lucky, those who could grab a couple hours of sleep before the chores of the day could be postponed no longer. They had thousands of acres of land and hundreds of heads of cattle and sheep, and em-ployed many cowboys and sheep hands. Along with the several members of their family, it was a small community in itself. Would have made an ideal dude ranch, but they said they had too much work to do to go in for such nonsense. The trip back to the homestead was a silent one. We were dog-tired and freezing cold. The high, rarified air went right through the heavy quilt we had over us, and by the time we got to the cabin, we had to crawl into bed, the four of us, to get warm enough to get up and build the breakfast.

Our escorts and the truck owner had cows to milk and many chores to do. They stopped with engine running while we crawled out from under the hay and fell off the back end as best we might. No one criticized the lack of the social amenities. The driver was Western-born cowboy, lean and long-legged, and had no time for soft talk. He had taken the whole gang in his truck, and had furnished the hay and the heavy quilts. What more did we ask? The answer was nothing.

During her second year on the claim, some of the realities of home-steading dampened Florence's optimism.

My second year of homesteading, I dropped the additional 320 acres, which was known as an "additional homestead." I did not have enough money for the necessary improving of it, necessitating a reservoir. I felt sorely cheated and not nearly as important as I had felt as the landowner of one square mile of land, but terribly rich when the Land Office returned my filing fee on it. ...

When a day would come along, although seldom, when I did not know just what to do with myself, I would open a box of freight items saved for just this sort of mood and be overjoyed to find a real delicacy, like a tin of anchovies with capers, or a can of peeled apricots in heavy syrup, or best of all, that jar of crystallized ginger I had been longing for. Then the day was saved, and I would be content all over with my lot in life. Especially this particular spot in Wyoming. And I would say a silent prayer in thanksgiving. I felt as if I was on a six-months vacation with pay. The wonder never ceased.

I don't know where my Uncle Walt got the idea the town of Gillette, 57 miles to the north, was toughest on the Burlington, or so he said it was twenty years before when he had come to it, helping to build the railroad. I found it was the country that was tough and hard to conquer. Everything you tried defeated you. If you planted crops, the bugs, grasshoppers, and rabbits ate it. If you planted a garden, the birds helped the rabbits. If you dug out the spring, the cattle somehow got through your wired fence and box and tramped it shut, leaving you only a muddy mess, very damp, but no sign of the pure, sweet water you knew from experience flowed underneath. I was expecting to prove-up on my claim at the end of the next year, with a club in one hand and an axe in the other. But I prayed my last year would not be so tough.

By the third year on the homestead, Florence contemplated the choices she must make—to return to her family and job in the city or to start a new life in Wyoming.

Everything that last year seemed to do its level best to make me more sad at leaving Wyoming. I still had two months more, but I knew it would fly. This sinecure would then be over, and I must needs settle down to a business life and make a future for myself in Chicago. I almost burst into tears at the thought. How would I ever be able to stand city life after these past three years, the greater part of each spent in my Lil' Gray Home in the West? I knew there was nothing in the small town. A job as a clerk, if I could get it, or, with my banking experience, a place in the one Bank, if there was a place. It didn't look much like a future there. Sheridan depended on its business of the dudes during the summer, and everything was still as a church once the season was over.

Every day of the following week I spent hiking. I would take a bite of lunch and did not come back to my cabin until hunger drove me. One day I hiked four miles to the foot of the South Pumpkin Butte. I climbed part way up, to a point of vantage, and imagined those early settlers going through in wagon trains, right along the very trail I had taken, and feeling secure so long as they could keep these same Pumpkin Buttes in view. I had some cheap field glasses, but they brought the Pine Ridge, 15 miles away, very close, and the Big Horn Mountains, now covered with snow, even closer. I just put my head down and wept. I could see myself back in Chicago, banging away at a bookkeeping machine or typewriter and this wonderful mental picture of my favorite spot in Wyoming all across the back of my mind.

For some reason, I never saw a living soul for ten days. I could have starved to death, been bitten by rattlers, or broken a leg. Who cared? As luck would have it, I ran out of nothing but matches. It meant I could not read after the sun went down and that I always had to be sure there were a few live coals buried in the ashes of the stove to ignite the shavings in the morning. But it was better than running out of food or coffee as I had done once before in my first year. Another time I was out of sugar, and let me tell you syrup gets awfully tiresome in your coffee.

I lovingly washed and ironed my gingham curtains, which I had made new that year, painted my three chairs, gave my kitchen table a fresh coat of gray paint, with yellow trim, varnished the rocker, and to be using up the odds and ends of paint, gave the flower pots a dab and the wooden boxes nailed near the stove to hold the things I used most often. I ran out of paint when I got to the china cupboard in the lean-to, so it was a very pale shade of gray with a trace of yellow. I planned to give my victrola and my Coleman gaslamp to a friend. Nothing else was of any value, and I thought if I came out on a vacation, I would have things ready to use. I had not counted on those very few people who, once an owner left the premises, figured the contents public property and his by right of find.

I had made plans to lease my pasture for twenty-five dollars for the half section, and as that was the current price, could not expect more.

The nights were getting very nippy, and as I sat outside in the dark of the moon, I would watch the magnificent display of the Northern Lights, or Aurora Borealis, as the books called it. I would wrap a blanket around me, sit on a pillow in my washtub, as it was warmer than a chair, and watch the long streamers of light as they shot from the horizon clear to the zenith. All the constellations in their appointed places, many of them I was not familiar with but shining like diamonds, it was a grand opportunity in astronomy.

I would stand at the window looking into my little cabin and fixing each precious detail of its coziness and warmth in my mind, would feel no shame at the tears, and not realize until I felt the salty taste that I was weeping at leaving all this peace and serenity. I wondered where, when, and from what source of ancestry had I gotten the courage to come out to this vast country. The summer excursions to the country of Benton Harbor or Dowagiac, Michigan, were my only contacts with farms, and I had never had the experience of living alone or miles from a neighbor. It had not been too bad. Perhaps my usually good health had helped me. Being young and strong, nothing was too hard, and the few good neighbors I had, though none of them close, were a wonderful boost to my morale, especially the Brown family. Not only their generous handouts to a lone female, but the good conversation and reading of fine books instilled in their brood, were such a pleasure and contrast, and I was sorry not to have spent more time with them. That night I fell into my bed, pulled up a quilt, and just cried myself to sleep. Not given much to tears, it was a jolt.

Soon after, my old friend Bill Elliott came over and asked me if I would go down and take care of a neighbor woman, who would soon have a baby. Her husband was freighting logs from Pine Ridge to build on another room, and felt he had to do the job while the weather was good. I knew nothing about nursing and less about babies, and prayed she would not celebrate by having it while I was there. It was two miles and a half south of my cabin, and I followed the fence so I would not get lost. A good thing, for their cabin was one large room and a very low ceiling and blended so readily with the hills, I could hardly see its roof, almost even with the hill in back of it, had Bill not warned me.

Caring for and befriending this lonely neighbor woman while her husband was away, helped Florence realize the depth of affection she felt for her Wyoming homestead.

I was dying to go back to my own little cabin. Twenty-four hours a day, not out of someone's sight, seemed a powerfully long while to me, and I flew once I got out of sight of their house, regardless of the milk in the syrup pail or the tea-towel tied and looped over my arm and holding a hand out for my breakfast. Ahhhh, how long it seemed since I had eaten my breakfast in my sunny little kitchen (the hill to the east kept the sun from shining into theirs); if warm enough, the door open the better to hear all the birds and a bit of crust thrown out for the brave ones.

Her words still rang in my ears: "Why does any girl in her right mind choose to come out and homestead in a God-forsaken country like this?" Her ideas were not mine, but then she had been raised on a homestead in a bleak section of Nebraska, and while on this one she had a loving husband for a companion and helper, it seemed almost as bleak. Not to me, it was the most wonderful bunch of land anyplace in these whole United States. I guess liking Wyoming is like spinach, either you hate the sight of it, or you can't explain what there is about it you like.

The year after I proved up, the Tuckers also left Wyoming. One more scar on the face of the prairie, where for awhile human habitation had been, was now no more.

As the last days of her third and final year on the homestead dwindled away, Florence's preparations to leave confirmed her desire to stay. Although she has not told the reader about a marriage proposal, this passage hints that there has been one. Her plans to return to Chicago apparently involve her indecision about possible marriage and a future as a rancher's wife, as well as her sadness at the ending of her homesteading days.

Nights have their way of passing, and soon as I heard the birds up, and the trilling notes of the Meadow Lark, left behind by some freak of decision, I hopped out of bed, and while I fixed the fire and breakfast, got the paint out for the final coat of cream enamel on the Victrola. How nice it looked, how sweet the notes of the favorite records. How blue again, when I realized these were my last weeks on the homestead, and perhaps before another month would be over, I would be back at a desk in bustling, noisy Chicago's Loop. And too, if only I could be sure I wanted to be married and live on a ranch. But return to my family in Chicago I felt I must, to really make sure.

Each time I looked out my west window at the Big Horns, seeming so near in this bright, crisp autumn morning, I would decide all over that I just could not take Chicago's one day of sun and two of shade, although I had lived there most of my life except for a few years in school in San Francisco. But zero in Wyoming was a lot easier to take than zero in Chicago.

I took strips of cloth and wedged them in all the cracks to keep out the snow during the winter. I washed and ironed and put away my funny little

Although she eventually gave up her homestead, Florence Blake Smith kept her adventuring spirit, traveling widely in later life. (*Pageant Press, 1962*)

curtains, these made with Honey's help and a yellow crocheted edge all around, although I knew my cabin would not be occupied by anything but dreams and memories. When the dishes were done, my books packed in their boxes and nailed shut and stacked up along the wall, I got cleaned up and walked over to the Brown ranch to stay for a couple days for the last time. They knew I also wanted to spend a few days with my good friends Inez and Date, so drove me over there. Once more to sleep on my favorite feather bed on the floor, play our precious records, and in all, store up memories to last for the years to come, in case I should not come back. Now that my three years of homesteading were really at an end, I felt lost, deserted, alone and like a ship without a rudder. I did not know exactly which course I wanted to steer. Seems to me we did not laugh as much as we used to, or say as many humorous things as we always used to. I gave Inez the extra key so she could come over when I left and take whatever canned stuff there was and also my lamp and the Victrola and nail some boards across the windows so the horses would not rub them out. When we got to my place, Inez would not get out of the truck; she wanted to remember me as if I might be coming over the hill in a few days to visit again, and if she said goodbye, might just give way to the tears the both of us felt near. As soon as they were out of sight and sound, I frantically packed my trunk, to keep busy. In between my yellow dishes, which had been added to from time to time, were my mementos of three wonderful years on the homestead. The rattle from the first rattler I ever killed, purely by accident and not aim, some bones gleaming white from the carcass of a dead critter I had found from the vertebra, which held a candle and were balanced perfectly. Often I used candles to eat by and still do. A few Indian relics I had found in my wanderings, arrowheads, most of them chipped or broken but artifacts nevertheless of my predecessors on the claim, and the one and only time years later on our ranch, when I really found a good one, I had goose pimples for three days. In my mind I could see the Indians hiding on the South Butte and king of all they surveyed, shooting their arrows at the wild life they lived on, so plentiful then before the white man shot for fun and not food. The fat deer and antelope that roamed over my land, their sleek sides rounded with the short, sweet grass which held so much nutriment in its short, stubby spears, compared to other states.

In my sandy hollow, where I had spent so many pleasant hours, watching the Big Horns and the hills in the distance between the wild sage hens and roosters as they marched almost in formation across the prairie. The nest of pale blue eggs found under a sagebrush and left untouched. All these precious memories, no matter how long I might live or how far away from these acres I might roam down through the years, were as pages in a beautiful and interesting book, with many illustrations made by Nature's master brushstrokes of sun and shadow.

Outside of my little gray house, my bit of fencing, and the comfortable little outhouse, with its view of the country to the east, the prairie was exactly as I had found it. The same wild antelope, coyotes, even horses still roamed its range. How little people were in comparison. I had left no mark of my passing.

There is always a sadness about doing something for the last time. Especially if you have been very happy, as I had been, living in my little gray home in the West, and while deep inside me I knew I would marry and live again in the West, I could not be sure that my family would not talk me out of living so far away, as we had always been close to each other. I had not reckoned with that old bromide, "Absence makes the heart grow fonder." It only needed 1500 miles to convince me where I wanted most to be. Wyoming.

Madge McHugh Funk, Wyoming — 1926

Madge McHugh, a young woman from Wisconsin, wanted to see the "real West." After attending the University of Wyoming, she went to Pinedale to teach school on the suggestion of a friend who promised that the small ranching community in western Wyoming was authentically western. The year was 1926, and the Pinedale region did not disappoint her. Madge lived there the rest of her life, becoming a prominent and colorful figure in its history (Illoway 1983). The following account of her homesteading adventure reveals a typical pattern: a single woman drawn to a frontier community to teach school who sees the opportunity to become a landowner by homesteading.

She took up a relinquishment (an abandoned homestead claim) in cooperation with a local rancher. Madge explains that her reward was the cabin located twelve miles north of Pinedale. In 1941, Madge married Jack Funk, a man more at home in the mountains than town. He is thought to be Zane Grey's model for the protagonist in his book *Man of the Forest*. After their marriage, Jack returned to living in his remote cabin and working for the Forest Service and Madge lived in her own cabin to be closer to her teaching job in town. On weekends, Madge either went to visit Jack at his cabin, or Jack came into Madge's cabin to be with her (Ervin 2000). Madge continued to teach until she was seventy-five and to take an active role in the Pinedale community all of her life. Her cabin has been moved from its remote setting and can be seen on the grounds of the Museum of the Mountain Man in Pinedale.

"And The Mice Kept On Running"

They ran along the log wall right next to my bed, and they scampered all over the bare wooden floor playing hide-and-go-seek with each other, scaring me half to death with their squeals and constant movement alongside my tiny cot. I shuddered and shook in great fear as I tried desperately to get some sleep on this, my first night as a homesteader on 580 acres of sagebrush in western Wyoming. An elderly rancher friend had convinced me that was the way to go because then he would have some much-needed pasture for his cattle, and I would have this little gray home in the West[6] which had been built previously by another brave soul who finally threw in the towel and relinquished his right to the land. The cattleman had neglected to tell me that this dream house was not mouse proof. I could have thrown a cat through the logs. I was informed that it was no effort at all to 'chink' and 'daub' the place. Those were two words I learned to hate before my trials and tribulations were over.

Foolish girl! I had read too many Zane Grey novels that pictured the West as the ideal place to find true romance. Go West, Young Lady, Go West! And so I left my home in Wisconsin and became one of those many so-called school marms who thought that the pot of gold at the end of the rainbow was a ninety-dollar a month job teaching readin', writin' and 'rithmetic to half dozen wild, unruly kids and eventually snaring some dashing, young cowboy.

In desperation, unable to sleep and frightened out of my wits, I grabbed my .22 caliber Colt Woodsman Pistol (which to this day I carry in my car) and fired away at the grey creatures. Of course, I missed my target and plowed a long hole in the floor and managed to demolish the jar of peanut butter, my main source of food for the week. I had no cupboards, so everything was stacked on the floor. My shot only stopped the ceaseless running of those grey pests for just a second.

Then came another strange noise—a loud scraping on the outside of the cabin. Someone had warned me about this. A porcupine likes the salt in wood, so he had decided to use my home for his nighttime feast. Summoning all my inner strength, I grabbed a flashlight in my left hand and my automatic pistol in my right. Slipping outside, I hurriedly blasted away in the general direction of the noise and scrambled back into the house to spend several more hours trying to sleep, but the mice kept on running. There must have been a dozen of them. I was certain that at any minute they would be jumping on my bed.

The full moon came over the hill, and as I had no curtains yet, it shone full blast through my only window, giving the mice more reason to play around and to increase my fright. Would this night never end?

I got out of bed and decided to set some traps. My instructions were to place some cheese on the darn things, light a match to melt the cheese, then set it down very carefully in a corner. Every time I tried to set down the trap, it went off with a loud bang, sending me into orbit.

Once more, I crawled back into bed only to hear a new and different sound. Something was banging against the door—thump! Thump! Thump! I got up, my entire body shaking and quivering. There in the bright moonlight was a young brown bear spanking his little behind incessantly against the bottom part of the door. I piled everything I could find against the door and prayed for daylight to come quickly. When it was light enough to see

Madge Funk's cabin today. It has been relocated to the grounds of the Museum of the Mountain Man in Pinedale, Wyoming. (*Mike Hensley*)

clearly, I crawled out of bed and started a long walk of fifteen miles to my nearest neighbor.

I finally made it to the Forest Ranger Station where my friends lived during the summer. By the time I reached their home, they had gone out for the day. Their house was locked, so I crawled in through the bedroom window and promptly fell asleep on their bed.

Much later that evening, they came home. I heard them come through the door, and I sleepily yelled out, "Hi," Mrs. S nearly had a heart attack.

Somehow, I managed to spend several summers on my homestead. I chinked and daubed and I daubed and I chinked.

Not long ago while rummaging through an old wooden box, I came across a letter from U.S. Senator Joseph O'Mahoney of Wyoming accepting my proof of claim to the homestead. Little did he know what a price I paid.

To this day, a mouse can send me up the wall. Did they ever stop running? No!

6. Rediscovered: Single Women Homesteaders in Historical Records

Historical accounts add yet another dimension to the emerging picture of single women homesteaders' place in history and literature. The majority of single women homesteaders either left no written records or those records have not been preserved, thus the oral histories and personal profiles such as those included in this chapter provide valuable additional information about the kinds of women who homesteaded and the kinds of experiences they had. The writers in this chapter have given voice and recognition to those women homesteaders who for whatever reason (modesty, lack of time, dislike of writing) did not speak up for themselves.

As early as the 1930s women homesteader stories were recorded and transcribed through the WPA Writers Project; however, these oral histories seem to have gathered dust in local museums and state archives, given little notice. Their significance has slowly come to light as the women's movement of the 1970s raised the public's consciousness about women in general, and the revisionist historians of the late 1980s and early 1990s began to question earlier interpretations of the role of women in the West. In the process of documenting their communities' pasts, local historians discovered single women homesteaders' stories, and local and national publications concerned with western history published articles about the stories or the stories themselves. This new interest in western women's history was also evident in increasing numbers of scholarly books about women's experiences in the West.[1] Single women homesteaders were finally receiving some recognition.

Historical accounts share some characteristics with the other genres presented here. Like memoirs, historical accounts provide a distanced perspective on the homesteading experience of single women. From that distance, some details may fade away, while others are vividly recalled. Historical accounts have a more carefully constructed quality similar to articles in the popular press, but they lack the press stories' promotional tone and concern with conveying practical "how-to" knowledge, perhaps because at this point women feel no need to prove the worthiness of their homesteading endeavors. But readers of the accounts must recognize that those who conduct oral histories may filter the narratives of interviewees through their own interests and purposes. Simply put, historical accounts don't tell the whole truth about single women homesteaders' experiences any more than letters, memoirs, or articles in the popular press do. Each genre provides a unique perspective on what homesteading was like for single women.

◊ Oral Histories

In oral histories, the amount of information that emerges may depend on such individual factors as the age of the interviewee at the time of the interview. For example, Mary Culbertson and Helen Coburn, interviewed in their fifties, recall their homesteading days more vividly than does Mary Sheehan Steinbrech who was interviewed in her seventies.

Another consideration is the purpose of the interview. If the interviewer is interested primarily in learning about a community's history, the questions the interviewer asks may not generate many details related to individual experiences.

Excerpts from three oral histories follow. The first two interviewees, Helen Coburn Howell and Mary Culbertson, homesteaded in the area of Worland, Wyoming, in the early part of the twentieth century during the time homesteading for single women was becoming popular. The third, Mary Sheehan Steinbrech, homesteaded near Lander, Wyoming, in the 1930s during the last years that homesteading was possible in the lower forty-eight states.

The oral histories of Helen and Mary are not only unusually vivid accounts of women's reactions to lives in unsettled country, but they offer a unique opportunity for comparison. Helen Coburn Howell and Mary Culbertson came to Wyoming together from Carroll, Iowa, took up adjoining homesteads, and had a cabin built that overlapped their two properties so they could keep each other company while proving up. Helen and Mary's homesteads were in an area of Wyoming under development by the Hanover Irrigation Project as part of the Carey Act (see chapter 3, note 3).

Helen's father, C.E. Coburn, was president of the bank in Carroll, Iowa, as well as president of the Hanover Association, which was developing the Hanover Canal making the land near Worland suitable for homesteading. W.L. Culbertson, Mary's father, was the Hanover Association treasurer. The two men provided the bulk of the capital for the project (Pendergraff 1985). Perhaps as a gesture of their confidence in the project, they sent their daughters out to Worland together to make claims on land the project opened up.

In spite of the fact that theirs was a joint venture, their oral histories show that almost identical circumstances do not mean identical experiences. Both oral histories were recorded in 1936 as part of the Statewide History Project in Wyoming. The person conducting the interviews is identified only by the initials L. L. H. Italicized passages indicate the transcribed voice of L. L. H.[2]

These interviews took place about thirty years after Mary and Helen homesteaded. The women would have been in their mid to late fifties at the time they were interviewed; thus, their stories were recorded at a time when they understood how their homesteading experience had shaped their destinies.

Mary Culbertson, Wyoming — 1905

In 1936, the time of the following interview, Mary Culbertson was living in Worland, working as a secretary to the Washakie Live Stock and Loan Company. Her mother, Mrs. Ruth Culbertson, and her nephew, William L., were living with her. Her good standing within the community is evidenced by the fact that she was the first person elected to the position of county treasurer in Washakie County. Not only was she reelected to the position for a second term, but to circumvent the ruling that no person could serve more than two terms, her brother Roger was next elected to fill the position with Mary as his deputy.

Although Mary eventually left Worland, the town paid tribute to her and her family by naming a street "Culbertson" in recognition of their importance to the town. Long-time Worland residents who knew Helen and Mary say that in their middle years the two women had a disagreement that caused them never to speak to each other again.[3] Mary's oral history recalls her first impressions of Worland and its shockingly rough ways. She explains how she and Helen homesteaded jointly and how they managed such essentials as getting water and having crops planted.

Modes of transportation are an important theme in her story, which describes traveling by train as well as by horse and buggy. Because women in Wyoming, unlike in their home state of Iowa, had the right to vote, voting for the first time was a memorable event recounted dramatically in Mary's story ("Experiences of Miss Mary Culbertson" 1936).

In the oral histories that follow, the voice of the interviewer, identified only as L.L.H., has been retained in italics because he/she provides important impressions and facts that enhance the reader's understanding of Mary's and Helen's homesteading experiences and their status in the community at the time of the interviews.

Experiences in Wyoming of Miss Mary Culbertson

Miss Mary Culbertson, efficient secretary of the Washakie Live Stock and Loan Company of Worland, came to Wyoming in 1905 before the railroad had been built or the present town was established.

She and her companion, Helen Coburn (now Mrs. Ashby Howell), came for the purpose of taking up homesteads under the Hanover Irrigation Project, in which Company their fathers, William L. Culbertson and R.E. Coburn, were the principal investors.

At the time of their arrival, only a few log buildings and tent homes had been erected for the employees of the irrigation projects. These were located on the west side of the Big Horn River directly across from the present municipality, which was established in 1906, a year later, by the Lincoln Land Company on land reclaimed by the Hanover Company. . . .

Miss Culbertson, her nephew, William L., and her mother, Mrs. Ruth Culbertson, make their home together in Worland.

"Everyone in Worland knows Mary and calls her by her first name," Mrs. Culbertson said proudly, watching the capable hands of her daughter cutting and arranging material for a rug. "Mary came here before I did and can tell you more interesting experiences than I can."

Miss Culbertson graciously complied.

My first impression of Worland, I am afraid, was not a very happy one, nor was my opinion very flattering to the place. We arrived by stage from Garland one evening when it was raining torrents. That alone was not conducive to a pleasant frame of mind, but when we drove into the frontier camp with its squatty log buildings and sagging wet tents, and I saw the general desolation of the place, I was overcome by a wave of homesickness that was hard to conceal.

We drove up to the door-step of the only hotel, a three-roomed and lean-to kitchen structure. In the front room were two beds and a baby cradle, a piano, and a large heating stove. A cat slept on one bed and a dog on the other. The rain came through the leaky roof and water splashed with a loud

Worland, Wyoming, in 1905, the year Mary Culbertson and Helen Coburn arrived as single women homesteaders. Both women stayed to see the town grow and both became important persons in the community. (*Wyoming State Archives, Department of State Parks and Cultural Resources*)

din into buckets and pans set all over the place to catch it. While we huddled around the stove to get dry, the hotel keeper's wife came in to say that dinner was about ready and we should go in and eat before the men arrived.

Edwin Conant who was keeping books for the Hanover Company at the time, suggested that it might be better for us to sleep at the Hanover office. We made our beds that night on the office floor, over the wide draughty cracks in the floor boards. A few mornings later the hotel man came out with a big bull snake which he had killed in the hotel. With visions of snakes crawling through the floor onto us, we changed our sleeping arrangements, and there after Helen slept on the office table, and I slept for two miserable, uncomfortable weeks on two trunks, one of them a round-topped trunk. Even from these elevated positions, we started and listened at every sound, dreaming of snakes in our 'nightmarish' sleep.

We continued to take our meals at the hotel. They had a Chinaman cook, and the less said about the food the better. Charlie Worland owned the place, but it was run then by a couple named Mercer. Worland also had a saloon and barber shop in a dug-out in the bank of the hill, called 'The Hole-in-the-Wall.' He kept his cash in a cigar box under the counter, and people could, and did, help themselves almost any time. Poor Charlie never could save anything. He was the biggest-hearted soul in the world and never failed to help anyone who needed anything.

One morning Helen and I went into breakfast at the hotel, and Eddie Conant came in just behind us. When we were going out, we noticed that he was not eating and was looking rather odd. The reason, he told us afterward, was that the biggest bed bug he had ever seen in his life had dropped down into his plate.

There was a typhoid epidemic in the place when we came, and Helen and I were asked to give our services as nurses. It was rather an appalling request as we had had no experience in nursing, but we agreed to do what we could and we made out very well.

All of the sick had been taken to an improvised hospital, a log building which had been curtained off into rooms for the fifteen or twenty patients. The only woman who had had any experience in nursing was a Mrs. Polling, who was in charge. The doctor lived in Hyattville forty-five miles away

So many people were sick, that the well ones were all worn out from the nursing. There was one large family, I recall, living in two or three tents in the most revolting squalor. They were of the ignorant, slovenly type that often followed public works in those days. One little girl had died and the wife of the family was very ill with typhoid. The mother-in-law lived with them and was trying to take care of the sick and do the housework for all of them. There were several men in the outfit, the husband, grown sons, and brothers, who were working on the canals. There were no floors in the tents, no screens, and nothing with which to work. The most terrible, unsanitary conditions imaginable existed. All of the slop was dumped just outside the door. Everything was dirty, piled up, and in a mess, and the flies were so thick you could scarcely breathe. To make things worse, the husband was drunk about three-fourths of the time.

He came in one afternoon where I was sitting with the sick woman and asked me if I had given her some wine. She was delirious most of the time but had been sleeping that afternoon so I did not waken her, thinking the rest might be more beneficial than the stimulant. I told him this, and he picked up the bottle saying he would go into the kitchen and fix it for her. I was suspicious of this sudden solicitude and thought I had better follow him, and, just as I thought, I found him with the teakettle, all ready to fix himself a nice 'hot toddy'. I gave him a scathing look and took the bottle back and gave the wine to the woman myself. Then I hid the bottle where he couldn't get it. The mother-in-law was very angry when I told her about the wine incident, and she told about his ornery trick to everyone she met. Eventually the sick woman was able to be up and around but never did get entirely well.

One of the families that lived down there in tents asked Helen and me to lunch one day. We accepted but the food really was so terrible that we could hardly eat it. The flies swarmed over everything, despite the fact that one of the girls stood over us with a cottonwood branch shooing the flies away.

After I had been here a month I returned to Iowa for six months. Helen and I had taken up our homesteads on adjoining land so that our two-roomed house would suffice for us both, she sleeping on her side of the line and I on mine. I established my legal residence there by staying one night before I left.

In the spring of 1906 I came back to live and stayed on the homestead until we proved up. We had a man and his son to help with the work, and they put in and harvested a fine crop of oats on our land.

We had some amusing experiences with the pack rats while we were on the ranch. We girls were almost frightened to death by the creatures, and they seemed to take a delight in tormenting us. We kept everything that we could closed and out of reach, but they would get at things anyway. At night we hung our clothes and even our shoes on high placed hooks but one morning when I went to take my shoes down—those high topped, laced affairs we used to wear—the rats had gotten into them and filled them with peas and beans. They got into our grain and were very destructive.

That reminds me, I had a phone call the other day from the man who used to live a few miles from us. He had come back after an absence of many years and I hardly remembered him until he reminded me that he and another boy were the ones who used to haul our water for us on the homestead. Most of the people got their water those days from the river. They would take big barrels down to the river, fill them, and wait for them to freeze; then they could easily be rolled off the wagons. We had a platform built on our back porch for the barrel and kept it covered with a tub. When it was forty below zero we used to chop the ice out as needed. We used the water for all purposes except drinking. . . .

Helen and I had been in the state a little over a year and so were proud of being eligible voters. Although we didn't know the candidates or what the issues of the campaign were, the idea of women voting was so novel that we determined to exercise our suffrage rights. This desire to cast our first ballots resulted in an accident that might have been serious.

The boys, Herman Gates and Ashby Howell, had kidded us a lot about influencing our votes, and decided they would take us to the Welling precinct

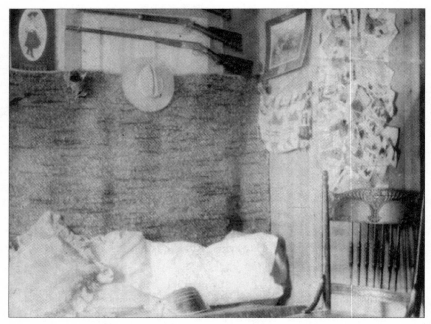

Interior of homestead cabin Mary Culbertson and Helen Coburn shared. (*Howell Family Photograph*)

where we had to vote. They secured a double-seated top buggy and a spirited team of horses to take us, and when we reached the grade at the railroad crossing a short distance from our destination, the horses became frightened and plunged down the embankment and then up on the grade again, tipping the buggy over and landing it on its top. Herman Gates and I were riding in the front seat and were thrown clear out of the buggy, but Helen and Ashby were pinned inside of the rig which went bumping over the sage brush on its top, the horses running as fast as they could go. It happened that S. B. Kimball and Ralph Bair, who were a short distance away, saw the accident and came to their aid, and by some miraculous act they stopped the team with in about an eighth of a mile of the accident.

It seemed to Herman and me, who had picked ourselves up and watched the runaway with horror-stricken eyes, that Helen and Ashby would certainly be killed. We ran to where the men had stopped the buggy and found our companions unhurt except for a few bad bruises. The incident had its humorous aspect too. Herman had been smoking a stub of a cigar and after the excitement was all over, he was still puffing on it. We all walked to a nearby farm and got some tame horses, hitched them to a hay rack, and went on the rest of the way to cast our votes.

We stayed all night at the ranch house, and the next morning we secured a lumber wagon and rode into town. We picked up some skillets of ours on the way, that had been used by threshers, and put them in the back of the wagon. A neighbor threw two cats in also. The first good jolt we went over, the spring seat broke and thereafter made a racket, and with the skillets rattling and the cats yelling we came the fifteen miles into town. When we arrived Herman said, 'Hurry, there is the train, I must mail a letter on it.' We were making so much noise that the horses became frightened and we almost had another runaway. I slid off the seat and stood in the skillets to keep them from rattling while we raced through the town. The cats clawed and scratched my legs, and the people along main street who were watching for us to come back to town after the accident, gave us the merry 'haw! haw!'

For sometime after the railroad came in, in 1906, the trains did not run on regular schedule and the time of their arrival here was always problematical. There was supposed to be one train a day each way, a combination of freight and passenger cars. Many humorous tales have been told concerning the train service in those days, some true and some exaggerated. In the winter time when there was a heavy snow, the trains did not go out for several days.

I shall never forget an experience of my own in waiting for that train. It was on New Year's Eve and a bitterly cold night. Lula Roberson, now Mrs. Shirk, had come out to the homestead to visit us. That afternoon Helen had gone into town with the team and wagon, and we had given her our heaviest wraps.

Two neighbors came over that evening to tell us that all our coal had been used by the threshers and we had better either go to their home for the night or go into town. We decided to go into town. It was about half a mile to the track where we had to go to flag the train. It was not a regular stop and there was no station or shelter. We just stood in the middle of the track when the train appeared around the bend and waved our arms until the engineer gave two short whistles to indicate that he had seen us and would stop. There was deep snow on the ground and it was very cold, but we had put on all the warm clothing we had, and had walked the half mile to the track. We waited and waited, for four long, suffering hours, walking the track, beating our arms, and stamping our feet, trying to keep from freezing to death. It was a ghastly experience which I would not repeat for anything.

Another time, when I was going back to Iowa for a visit, I had to take the train at Toluca. It went across Prior Mountain to Frannie and caught the main line at Billings.

"By the way," Miss Culbertson digressed, *"it is said that the station of Toluca got its name from the incident of a Swede passenger who got off there, as he said, 'to looka.'"*

The agent and his family slept upstairs in the station, and he never would come down at night. On this occasion the waiting room was full of drunken, rowdy Indians. They had most of the seats. Others were lying all over the floor. They had come over for the registration at the time of the opening of the Indian reservation for land. Some of the women who had arrived ahead of me, were fortunate enough to have secured seats, but for seven solid hours I waited with no place to sit except on my suitcase, when I grew so tired from standing or walking the platform that I could not keep on my feet any longer. It was five o'clock in the morning when the train came, and I was never so happy to see one in my life.

In the days of the town's beginning there were no movies available where one could go to spend the evening; no radios to listen to. We couldn't jump into a car and speed off to a neighboring town and be back before bed-time. Our everyday amusements, had to be created by our own ingenuity, and these often took the form of practical jokes on each other.

There was a man here by the name of George Simon who had a café and a soft-drink parlor. One of our favorite tricks was to steal each other's personal belongings, and take them into George's place and 'hock' them for treats for the gang. The owner would then have to come in and pay the charges to redeem them.

Any tenderfoot or stranger had a hard row to hoe, and traveling sales-men, especially, were natural targets for the natives' pranks. One of the favorite stunts was to stage a hold-up for their benefit and scare them out of their wits. While they leaned over the counter talking business, two or three masked men would come in and say, 'stick 'em up' and everyone would duck behind the counter with his hands in the air. When the victim found out he had been 'jobbed' he had to 'set up the drinks.' One time Ord Black-ledge shot a man in the foot when he didn't dance fast enough to suit him.

One of the favorite forms of recreation then, as now, was dancing. Every special occasion was celebrated in this way. In the early days of the town, dances were held in the old hotel. Then when the town was moved across the river, each new home or building completed was initiated by having a dance in it before anything was moved in. Sam Halstead and Perry Williams put up a dance hall about a hundred by a hundred and forty feet in size near the present Worland Laundry building.

Itinerate musicians played in the saloons, and at these dances. I remem-ber in particular one fellow with a peg leg who used to play his fiddle at the dances. There was no set time for the dances to be held, but when it was decided to have one, the news was dispatched all over the country and everyone for miles around would be there. The whole family would drive in, in a lumber wagon, with the baby buggy in the back. Inside the dance hall the buggies would line up in a row along one side of the building. When the older children grew tired they were put to sleep along the side benches, lying on coats and covered with their parents' wraps.

For more 'atmosphere' of the early town, one might recall the old hitching posts, and the long row of dejected looking horses waiting for their masters in front of the saloons. There were several camps near by, each employing quite a number of men—the railroad camp, the ditch camp, and the canal camp. On Saturday nights the men all rode in and celebrated until Sunday evening. Many of them would get gloriously drunk and would ride through the town yelling and shooting their six shooters in the air. . . .

It seemed like a long step from lumber wagon transportation on bridge-less roads, where it was often necessary to camp hours or even days by streams, waiting for flood waters to pass, to paved highways, fast moving automobiles, and modern traffic hazards; from tent houses, kerosene lamps, and water hauled from a muddy river in barrels to water and sewage systems, electricity, gas and well-kept modern homes; from sagebrush flats to productive farms, cultivated with power machinery. From a higgeldy-piggeldy mess of dry goods, groceries and what not, laboriously freighted endless miles over trails which by no stretch of imagination could be called roads, and then dumped in a dugout, which aside from the saloon was the only loafing place in town, to the present well-equipped and attractive stores.

All this and more was accomplished in a few short years. People once well-rooted here are never quite satisfied elsewhere. They often seek more attractive pastures, but most of them return if possible. There is a friendly spirit about the place which grips the heart strings. It is hard to describe. Possibly it is because the stars seem nearer and the fine, clear air is easier to breathe. A few, short years filled with life and interest is certainly well worth living.

Helen Coburn Howell, Wyoming — 1905

In a reminiscence written for her family, Helen explained how she came to be a homesteader:

> My Father was a small town businessman who became interested in development of arid lands in the west under an extensive canal system. It was too big a proposition for small town men and eventually broke him. . . .

One fall day as Mama and I were getting my clothes ready for my second year in college, papa walked in and exploded a bomb by saying, "How would you like to go to Wyoming and homestead, Helen, instead of going to college?" A week later I was on my way in company with the daughter of my Father's partner, some ten years older than myself.

Papa took me to Omaha and bought what he considered the necessary equipment. This included a single barrel rifle, a Smith and Wesson revolver, a handsome pair of high-laced boots to protect me from rattlesnakes and a half-grown hunting dog which I immediately named "Tommy."[4]

Helen continues her account by describing her trip to Wyoming with Mary. They traveled by train by way of Lodge Grass, Montana, where they stopped to visit with one-time residents of Carroll, Iowa, who were now Indian missionaries. During their visit, Helen and Mary were taken to the Indian Fair at the Crow Agency where Helen participated in pony races with the Indian children. A highlight occurred when Helen and Mary met Chief Plentycoups who amazed them by speaking perfect English. After a week in Lodge Grass, they continued on the train to Garland, Wyoming, the town nearest to their final destination, Worland. When they arrived at Garland, the napping girls were awakened by the porter who told them they had only minutes to get off because the train was moving on immediately. Helen recalls: "I scrambled together my baggage—rifle, mandolin, golf clubs, tennis racket, umbrella, handbag and traveling bag, so I practically fell off the train."

The fact that Helen brought golf clubs and a tennis racket suggests how unprepared she was for the living conditions that awaited her in the frontier town of Worland, which in 1905 consisted of only a few buildings and was a long time from having a golf course or tennis courts. To get to Worland the girls faced two more days on a stage coach. They finally arrived at their destination during a rain storm, were taken to a little log cabin hotel where one room "served as office, living room and bedroom." They had supper there accompanied by flies that buzzed like bees. Helen found all this rather amusing but reported that Mary, an "awfully nice, but very sedate" person, did not. After supper, she writes, "the bookkeeper of the Canal company introduced himself and took us to the Hanover Office where we were to sleep—and thus began our homesteading experience."[5]

Helen Coburn about the time she left Iowa for Wyoming. (*Howell Family Photograph*)

Because for Helen, as for many single women homesteaders, teaching school was an integral part of homesteading life, the sections related to her school have also been retained. As in Mary's account, problems of travel are a frequent subject, as are the enjoyable moments, such as dances and the practical jokes played on her by the numerous young men in the region.

Helen's uncle who lived nearby as well as hired men could be counted on for help when problems arose or heavy work was required on the homestead. Not only did Helen and Mary help each other by sharing a homestead cabin, but family and community members pitched in as well.

A newspaper account of Helen's life fills in information not given in the oral history. It reports that Helen and Mary proved up on their homesteads in 1907 after drilling a well, raising a crop, and "paying a certain amount." It's likely the two women paid a specified fee for the land and future water rights as part of the Carey Act, but they might also have taken advantage of the option under the Homestead Act of buying out their claims at a cost of $1.25 per acre.

In March, 1908, after Helen married Ashby Howell, owner of a general store in Worland, they made their home in town. In addition to raising their three children, the couple played important roles in Worland's growth. Ashby was a merchant and developer of the town and Helen was active in community affairs. In 1940 Helen was widowed when Ashby was killed in an automobile accident. She continued to be active in the community until 1959 when she died at the age of seventy-six. The Howell name, like the Culbertson's, is honored with a street name in Worland.

As with many single women homesteaders, Helen's story illustrates how her decision to homestead radically changed the direction of her life, removing her from the civilized and perhaps somewhat restricted life of a young woman in Carroll, Iowa, and launching her into the freedom of the West where her exuberant nature flourished. Her story also provides a good example of the traditional historical view that women were important civilizing forces in western communities.

Helen's granddaughter, Liz Howell,[6] shared the following poem Helen wrote in 1909, which reveals young Helen's love of the state in which she homesteaded:

"If you have breathed the air
of her hills and plains;
If you have watched her
in the gloaming.
If you have felt her pride
when the horsemen ride,
You will drink the toast—Wyoming!"

Mrs. Ashby Howell, Pioneer Worland Woman and
Humorous Stories of her First Years in Wyoming
As School Teacher and Lady Homesteader

"Everyone who has lived in Worland any length of time knows Helen Coburn Howell," informs an admiring friend. "She belongs to the town and is as much a part of it as the canals her father helped to build in the early days, which brought in the people who settled this part of the Big Horn Basin."

No matter what is required, whether it is an idea for a "float" for the Lions' Club parade, a costume for a play, or a place for knitting lessons to be held, they go to Mrs. Howell with their problems, and she solves them all with equal resourcefulness and good nature.

Helen Howell is the wife of Ashby Howell, prominent businessman of Worland. She has earned, by years of unselfish service to the community, the high regard in which she is held. She possesses a dominant personality, coupled with the wise, lovable qualities which make for natural leadership in social and civic affairs, and wins easily and without conscious effort the adherence of her friends in every undertaking in which they are mutually interested.

Meeting Mrs. Howell is an experience. One likes her at once, and succumbs to the charm of her personality. Her eyes are bright blue, expressive of the deep intelligence and the sense of humor that keeps them twinkling while she relates the funny experiences of her early days in Wyoming as a lady homesteader and school teacher. Her complexion, unaided by artifice, has the clear, fine quality of a girl's and belies the silvery grey of her abundant hair.

The Howells keep "open house," and their attractive home is the center of informal gatherings of gay camaraderie—of the "we'll-all-drop-in-at-Helen's-for-Hamburgers-after-the-bridge-breakfast" sort of gatherings, as well as the setting for more formal parties.

Seven or eight of these friends and relatives were gathered about the Howell dining table at afternoon tea, chatting gaily, when Mrs. Howell excused herself from them and came into the living room to obligingly relate many interesting incidents in connection with her first years in Wyoming.

I came by train as far as Garland, and took the stage from there, completing the trip from Garland in two days. I arrived in Worland September 29, 1905, and my companion was Miss Mary Culbertson. Our former home was at Carroll, Iowa, and we came out to take up homesteads under the Hanover Canal Irrigation Project in which our fathers, W. L. Culbertson and R. E. Coburn, were interested.

One of the first persons I met when I arrived in Worland was a tall, good-looking young man with thick, wavy hair, wearing a white wool turtle-neck

Helen Coburn and future husband, Ashby Howell, about 1906. Ashby was one the first persons Helen met when she arrived in Worland to homestead. (*Howell Family Photograph*)

sweater, whose name I soon learned was Ashby Howell. He was from Virginia, and had a Southern accent. I little dreamed then that he was destined to be my husband.

Miss Culbertson and I found typhoid fever raging in the town, and our first impulse was to take the next stage home. They asked us to give our services to the sick as nurses; we protested that we knew nothing about nursing, but we agreed to try it anyway, went to work, and got along very well. There were about fifteen to twenty patients with the fever, housed in an improvised hospital in a old log building, with curtains put up for partitions to give a semblance of privacy. The nearest doctor was at Hyattville, about forty-five miles away; Mrs. Polling was the nurse in charge, and she was just a practical nurse.

There was a little boy in the hospital very ill with the fever, and the father haunted the place, asking to see him, going away to wander in the hills awhile, and back to the hospital again. The little fellow died, and the father almost lost his mind. It was all very pathetic, and I made up my mind then and there that I was never intended to be a nurse.

The town at the time consisted of just a few frame buildings, and was then all on the west side of the river. The hotel where we stayed was a little log cabin shack, called the Worland Hotel, and run by a man named Mercer, who lisped, especially when he said 'soup'. They served mutton meal after meal. The boarders complained that they had eaten so much mutton that they 'bleated'. There was plenty of wild meat to be had, but everyone was too busy to go out and kill it.

Miss Culbertson and Miss Coburn took up homesteads on adjoining land near Rairden, about eighteen miles from Worland, and built their house on the section line that divided them, it thus serving them both for a home. After they had established their residence, Miss Culbertson went back to Iowa for six months, but Miss Coburn remained.

The teacher who had been selected for the Worland school was unable to serve, and Miss Coburn was offered the position as temporary teacher.

There were about thirty pupils in the district, and part of them lived on the east side of the river and part on the west side; to equalize the convenience of the school for all the pupils the Trustees agreed that it should be held four months on one side and four months on the other, the east side winning the first four months. At the end of the first four months, the town moved across the river to the east side, but the school had to be moved to the west side according to the agreement made, which necessitated the teacher's crossing the river twice a day as before.

I had to have a horse to ride back and forth, and thereby hangs a tale. My uncle, Harry Stine, selected a horse for me, and led him straight into the Hanover office one day, and demonstrated his gentleness by walking behind him and under him. I was very much pleased to get a horse so docile. But how that horse's disposition changed! I christened him 'First' then and there.

I rode the horse for a few weeks with a great deal of gratification, and took the best care of him. I 'grained him and curried him' every noon, and he became sleek and rounded out. He increased in spiritedness amazingly from this good care and little exercise.

One day when I was starting out on him and had reached the river, he went into the water just a few feet, then reared up on his hind legs and started back to town. I hardly knew what to do, but I decided if I let the horse have his own way the boys about town would 'razz' me about it. The teacher and her horse were a community joke anyway, and they threatened to follow me about with a ladder. I was more afraid of their kidding than of the horse, so I turned him back to the bank, broke off a good-sized switch from a tree, and forced him to take me across the river.

A few evenings later when I started home after school and went into the stall to get him, I suppose he was still resentful, for he reared up when I put the halter around his neck, and pulled loose the pole to which he was tied. This anchor, thus hung upon him, frightened him so that he struck at me with his front feet. I found myself over in the next stall yelling madly for help, and my eldest pupil came running to my rescue. After the horse had calmed down we led him out, and finally got him saddled and bridled, but whenever I got near to mount him he would rear up again. Finally, I started out walking and leading the horse. I walked for about a mile when evidently he became tired of the slow pace, stopped, and refused to budge. Try as I would, I could not coax him on. He stood there with his head down, apparently ashamed of his tantrum now, gentle as an old cow. Finally I had the courage to mount him, and I rode him down to the river.

I had had an appointment to meet my uncle at the river bank at 4:30 to help me cross the ice. When I didn't come then, he decided that I was staying on the other side of the river for the night and did not wait.

When I started across the frozen river, long cracks shot out in the ice. The horse was afraid and slipped and snorted, and I turned him back to the bank, got off, and sat on a log and held him by the halter, waiting for someone to come along and help me across. It got colder and darker, but finally two men came driving a team hitched to a wagon loaded with hay, and asked me what the trouble was. I got on the hay load and led the horse behind it. I found both men were so full of liquor that I didn't know whether they would make it across or not, but we landed safely, and I got on 'First' and rode on into town.

The horse grew more spirited, and every morning before I could get on him my uncle would have to ride him down. He would rear up in the air, so high that there was danger of falling over backwards, then dash off as hard as he could run. However, I continued to ride him until Christmas, the more so because my uncle offered me another horse to ride and I knew if I changed the boys would say I couldn't conquer the one I had.

During the holidays my uncle found another horse, a young pony that wasn't gaited. I called him 'Second' and kept him only two weeks, for I was not satisfied with him and wanted another horse. My uncle came into the yard one day with a fine bay pony and said 'Here is your horse'. He picked me up and threw me astride the horse's bare back, slapped his flanks and away we went galloping over the hill as hard as he could run with me hanging onto the hackamore for dear life.

I kept this horse and named him 'Charm', because he was the third one, but I was to have still another horse before the end of the term, which I named 'Finish', because he was the last.

The school was held first on the east side of the river in a three-room log cabin about a mile south of the present town, in what was known as the Wamhoff place, now owned by Mrs. Clem. Several men were batching in the house, and in the daytime they rolled up their beds and stored them in a little room at the rear, so the large room in the house could be used for a school room. The furniture consisted of cracker boxes and mended chairs which the boys brought to school. Our books were a conglomerated mess that had been picked up here and there. We had three kinds of third grade readers.

The pupils were from the first grade up through High School. Some of the larger pupils were about as smart as their teacher. It kept me guessing to keep up with them. I remember a most embarrassing algebra problem one of the older boys brought to me to solve. I looked it over and saw I couldn't work it, so I told him solemnly that it would do him much more good to work it out for himself, and to keep at it a day or two, and if he couldn't work it to bring it back. Meanwhile I cudgeled my brain, and took the problem to everyone who I thought might be able to help me, but no one had any better success. The boy kept bringing the problem back, and the situation became more embarrassing. I worried over the thing so much I could hardly sleep,—and, believe it or not, one night I dreamed the solution! To my great gratification, I was able to show the boy how to work the problem and thus save my face.

We had no stove put up, and the first cold morning we all shuddered around in our coats. I went to Charlie Cavanaugh's ranch two miles away to get help to put up the heater. (I tell this as a good joke on Charlie.) Several men were batching there at the time, and Charlie came to the door and stood in it like Horatius at the bridge, barring my way and not asking me in out of the cold. When I knew him better I used to josh him about not inviting me in to get warm, but he'd only look knowing and say, 'That was no place to ask a Lady into!'

One day two young men of the town dropped in to see how the school was getting along. They said they had been looking for cattle. I asked them in, and they sat very still in the seats, but I didn't like the twinkle in their eyes. During the spelling lesson I asked one of the pupils to spell 'Nerve', and looking straight at the two visitors I commanded, 'and spell it with capitals,' but they didn't take the hint, and stayed until the pupils were dismissed. Then they proceeded to climb into the rafters of the building and wrote on the boards "God bless our school marm." They finished by hazing my pony all the way home. One morning when I went to build the fire, the smoke rolled out of the stove instead of going up the chimney, and upon investigation it was discovered that someone had stuffed gunny sacks in the chimney. I suspected these same two boys of being the culprits.

One of my first-grade pupils had great difficulty in learning to count. He seemed not to be able to grasp the difference between one and two. As an object lesson I pointed at another pupil in the class and said, 'Harold, how many noses does Glen have?' The boy answered 'Two'. All the children laughed and Glen, covered with confusion, put his hand over his nose.

When we moved our school to the west side of the river it was held in a tent, through which the cold penetrated as if the canvas were not there. During all the month of February I had to hold classes around the big red 'pot-bellied' stove. The boys would put rubber bands, gum, and other smelly things on the stove, which was very annoying to the teacher, until I found out who did it and then I made it annoying to the pupil.

One evening I had kept a boy in after school to punish him. He was about fourteen years old, and I didn't relish the task of chastising him, but was about to do so when one of the smaller boys stuck his head in the door and yelled 'Hey, teacher, your feller is coming,' which was a very opportune interruption for the boy.

Mrs. Howell had promised her father when she came out West that she would not go to any of the dances. He had the idea that the people here were wild and woolly cowboys and crude Westerners. She found that they were all people from the middle West, like herself, and were from families of good background.

The first dance after she arrived here was to be held on the evening of Thanksgiving Day, and she wanted very much to go. She wrote her father that she was not breaking her promise but just taking it back, as he didn't know the true conditions of the West. The dance was held in a new building which had just been finished for a saloon. These dances were given every time a new building was put up or one moved across the river and were the main form of recreation at the time.

They had just varnished the floor in this saloon building, and it was not quite dry by the time for the dance. We had great difficulty sliding our feet over the sticky floor. The only musician available was the fiddler, Curly Brown, who was usually decidedly tipsy, and this occasion was no exception. He was very much annoyed because I didn't know the figures of the square dances, and he followed me about, pointing the bow at me and trying to make me do the dances correctly. He finally got so drunk that he sat down on his fiddle and broke it, and we had to finish the dance to the music of an old harp, that someone in the crowd was able to produce and play.

Asked to relate more about the homestead and some of the adventures she and her chum experienced, Mrs. Howell said,

Miss Culbertson and I lived together in great harmony the necessary time to prove up, she sleeping on her side of the line that divided our property and I on mine. We named the homestead the C-C Ranch for our initials. We shared the housework and cooked and ate together, and regarded it all as a high adventure. We took our work seriously, however, and while we employed a man and his son to do the heavy work—the fence making, farming, and outside chores—we were far from idle ourselves. We put in a small garden and enjoyed working in it. The men put in a good oat crop, and when it was harvested we girls sewed up the oat sacks. Our furniture was, for the most part, built-in, but we had a day couch piled with the pillows we made and other homelike touches all over the place. We were proud of our guns, and these we had crossed over the front door. An oil derrick was put up in our back yard and a non-producing well drilled.

I must tell you about the time I bought my team and wagon, and the mean trick the boys played upon me. Miss Culbertson and I were the only girls about here for some little time, while there were many young men in the community, engineers working on the canal, young businessmen, cattlemen, and others. Their main form of recreation was playing jokes on each other, and of course, we girls, fresh from the East, came in for a good share of their kidding, and were the natural targets for many of their pranks. I had telephoned from Welling to town to my uncle to buy a team and wagon for us, and I rode in town on horseback to get them. I had gotten a dog while here, which was put on the spring seat of the wagon. When I got into the wagon they handed me the driving reins, a long black-snake whip, the dog leash, and the lead reins of the saddle horse. You can imagine that my hands were rather full, and I hardly knew which line to pull to drive the team. The boys were all lined up on each side of the street watching me get started, fairly bursting with laughter, and all yelling instructions and admonitions. As I started out of town it began to rain, and as I passed the Coulter homestead Mrs. Coulter came running out and offered me an umbrella. She wasn't joking, but I couldn't see where I could handle it, and drove on eighteen miles without its protection.

When I had proved up on the homestead, I sold it at auction and returned to Iowa. In 1908, Ashby came there for me and we were married at Carroll, then returned to Worland, where we have made our home ever since.

Mary Sheehan Steinbrech, Wyoming — 1936

Unlike Helen Coburn and Mary Culbertson who traveled from Iowa to Wyoming to homestead, Mary Sheehan homesteaded close to her home of Lander, Wyoming. Because Sheehan homesteaded thirty years later than Coburn and Culbertson, her story provides an opportunity to compare and contrast women's homesteading experiences at the beginning of the twentieth century with those at the end of the homestead era.

Mary Sheehan received the patent to her homestead in 1939, four years after President Roosevelt withdrew most public lands from private entry through the Taylor Grazing Act (Robbins 1976). Mary explained how it was possible to receive a patent in spite of that. It seems she had filed on the land some time previous to her three-year residency there. A graduate of Lander High School who had taken University of Wyoming classes, Mary was teaching in one-room schools around Lander when she decided to homestead 640 acres on Twin Creek between Lander and Atlantic City, Wyoming.

Her oral history gives only a few clues to her motivation to homestead. The beauty of the land was one of the attractions. In addition, Mary, like Helen Coburn, homesteaded because her family encouraged her to. Possibly she was part of a final rush to take advantage of available homestead land in that part of Wyoming. It would also have made sense to have a homestead nearer to the small schools where she taught rather than commute to Lander. For example, when she taught in Atlantic City in 1938, her homestead was only five or six miles from her school, while Lander was about twenty-five miles away. Living on her homestead also meant that she did not have the expense of boarding with a family or in the town's one hotel, nor did she face the potential risks of driving over the sometimes treacherous pass between Lander and Atlantic City. While Coburn and Culbertson had problems with travel on trains and horses, Sheehan tells of problems with travel by motor car. Like Coburn and Culbertson, Mary benefited from the cooperation of her family while on the claim. In her oral history she does not mention who built her cabin, but she explains that her brothers and a sister helped build the fence around her property.

As in the oral history of Helen Coburn, Mary Sheehan's story of homesteading is intertwined with the story of her teaching, once more illustrating that teaching and homesteading often proved to be a successful combination for single women. Their teaching provided capital needed for improving their homesteads; the homesteads provided them a place of their own and property, which was also an investment in their futures. Mary, whose parents came from the state of New York in 1896 and helped settle the Lander valley, provides another example of a second-generation homesteading woman who followed in her pioneering parents' footsteps.

Mary Sheehan's oral history, conducted by Marjane Ambler in 1984, has been edited to provide continuity to Mary's narrative. Some information not pertinent to her homesteading or teaching experiences has been omitted as have the interviewer's questions; however, Mary's exact words are reprinted (Steinbrech 1983). Perhaps because she was interviewed when she was seventy-two years old, when some memories had faded, Mary Steinbrech's oral history is not as dramatic or richly detailed as those of Coburn and Howell who were interviewed in their fifties. However, her story shows that single women could and did homestead up to the last days of the Homestead Act and that their homesteading experience was an achievement in which they took pride throughout their lives. Home-steading alone taught Mary a valuable lesson about herself . . . that she wasn't "an outdoor person" and that she felt lonely when living alone on her claim. In 1939, shortly after proving up, Mary Sheehan gave up school teaching and homesteading to marry George Steinbrech. They lived in Lander their entire lives, raising two sons, John and James. Later in life Mary was a loved and respected librarian at Fremont County Library.

Oral History: Mary Sheehan Steinbrech

I was born here in Lander, and my maiden name was Sheehan. My parents were Mr. and Mrs. Dan Sheehan. During the 1930s, my sister and I taught school in various little one-room schools around the Lander area. The reason I homesteaded was that it was suggested to me to file on land, so I thought it was a good thing to do and well, it is a really beautiful area. I filed on a homestead up, about 5 or 6 miles from Atlantic City. We built a little cabin, down, kind of in the hollow, because we thought it might be better to have it kind of secluded, where no one would break in. I say, "we" because my sister and my brothers also worked on a fence that we had to build around the homestead. And then we had some help from Mr. And Mrs. Hancock who was Ira Carpenter's brother.[7] They all helped, but I filed on the claim under my own name.

I think it might have been a little unusual for a woman to file on a home-stead, but if you were the head of the family, I think was the way it was, you could do it. When I homesteaded though, that was about the last of the homesteads. I'm not sure just what year it was, but I lived on the homestead for three years, and I filed on it a while before I actually lived on it, so I'm not real sure, but I finally got the patent in 1939. I'd live there every summer, when I wasn't teaching, and I'd live there the rest of the year as much as I could, on weekends, and, oh, when I could get there . . . when the weather was so I could get there. You were supposed to live on your claim seven months out of the year, and it was kind of hard to do it, but I'd do the best I could, and they allowed it. My land was located right around the head of Twin Creek. I'm not sure just how many miles this side [east] of Atlantic City it is, but it's where that loading chute is, that was on my land, and then off to the right hand side as you come toward Lander, was the most of the land . . . it was 640 acres.

At first the highway was down in the bottom. Then, before I left, before I got the patent on the homestead, the county built the road clear up on the hill. That road was more passable than the one down in the valley, but I think people were kind of afraid to drive it, cause there was a big curve on it. That was the road I traveled every day when I was teaching up in Atlantic City. I think it was about five or six miles between the homestead and Atlantic City. When I first went up there that year, 1938, it was after my school closed, and I heard about them wanting a teacher to teach the children who would be there. Some dredge workers and their families had come from California. There were only about five or six little children, but they had to leave their school before it was out, and come here, so they decided to have a summer school for the children. I got the job teaching them. The first time I went up, the weather was real bad, so I rode with the mailman, Fred Cook, and he even got stuck on the way up.

That was my first day at the Atlantic City school and I knew I was going to be there for at least a week, so I stayed at the hotel until the weather cleared up, and I could come back to Lander and have my car. After that I started living in the cabin and the rest of the summer I could always get to the school. The rest of the summer I'd go back and forth from the school in Atlantic City to my cabin, then on weekends I would go to Lander for supplies. I was paid eighty dollars a month, less than a dollar an hour, but schoolteachers weren't supposed to be highly paid people. I don't have a degree. I had mostly gone to summer school and had taken correspondence courses from the University of Wyoming.

People in Atlantic City were very friendly, neighborly . . . very kind, good people. I think they would do anything to help someone, but the thing I liked most about working there was that I could live on my homestead and still go back and forth, and teach. The disadvantage was that it was kind of a lonely place for a younger person. By the time I lived there that long, I decided that homesteading was really not for me. I'm just not the outdoor type. I'd take books along, when I'd go up to the homestead, and go for a little walk and read and maybe go for another walk. Yes, it was lonely.

◊ Profiles

Years after single women homesteaders made their daring moves west, their stories were discovered by family members examining their family trees, communities collecting stories of their past, and researchers probing into the unexplored corners of the West's history. The stories collected here reflect the admiration researchers felt when they discovered that single women actually homesteaded alone. Themes in these profiles of women homesteaders, as in the previous genres compiled in this volume, under-score that women homesteaders looked for adventure, independence, and economic security, and that, in addition to their own initiative, they needed the cooperation of family and community to succeed. The four women whose stories appear next were older than the average age of homesteading women, a reminder that single women of all ages benefited from the Homestead Act.[8] The following remembrances appear chronologically by the date each woman homesteaded.

Nellie Burgess, Idaho — 1908

In 1908 Nellie was a career woman working for the *Chicago Daily News* when she learned of land opening up for homesteading in Idaho. At the age of thirty-five, she may have saved enough money to finance her bold move west and to invest in her homestead. In spite of her urban back-ground, Nellie embraced pioneer life enthusiastically. She planted a gar-den, purchased a horse to ride, learned to shoot a gun, invested in a cow and pig, and roamed about the mountains on hunting and fishing trips with her nephew Glenn who had been sent by the family to protect and help her. The following article was written by her niece, Marjorie Van-dervelde, based on Nellie's journal and letters as well as Marjorie's child-hood memories of visiting her aunt's homestead.

Nellie acquired her land through the Carey Act, which opened arid land primarily in Wyoming, Idaho, and Utah for settlement (see chapter 3, note 3). The fact that Nellie named her homestead Rainbow Ranch sug-gests the optimism she felt about her decision to move west. Nellie seems to have had no regrets about leaving the career of a big-city newspaper reporter for life in the wide-open spaces. Perhaps her maturity and the experience gained in her career had prepared her to approach homesteading life with confidence. During her first days on the claim, Nellie's friend Elise, a coworker at the *Chicago Daily News*, came out to stay with her. Nellie wrote of this time in a letter to her niece Marjorie:

> Elise had never had an opportunity to cook, but had saved rolls of recipes from the *Daily News*. She asked to do the cooking. We burned sage brush and carried the water up a steep hill from the river about 60 feet from the house. We hired a man with a team and wagon to bring groceries etc. from town. The groceries consisted mainly of canned milk, bacon, potatoes and dried apples or other dried fruit (Sudduth 1960, 2).

Nellie's experiences with gardening were more successful than those of many other single women homesteaders. She recalled that "things grew so fast" that she "raised a 40 lb. watermelon the first season" and reported that there were no weeds until later when the irrigation water came (1960, 3).

After six years of homesteading on her own, Nellie married a rancher from the community of King Hill. Her story illustrates that women homesteaders sought adventure, desired independence, and were willing and able to do the work needed to survive on their claims. The happiness Nellie found in her homesteading venture and the respect she earned from her family and friends are evident in the following story, written by her niece, which appeared in *American West* magazine in 1986.

Pioneer Lady Homesteader in Idaho
Life in a Prove-up Cabin: Trapdoors, Swimming Pigs, and a Hardy Spirit
by Marjorie Vandervelde

At thirty-five years of age, Nellie Burgess could have passed for a Fifth Avenue model, willowy and blue-eyed, with curly blondish hair. She was on the staff of the *Chicago Daily News* in 1908 when she noticed an obscure item in the back pages that struck her imagination like a bolt of lightning. Essentially it said:

> In accordance with the Carey Lands Act, a land drawing will be held at King Hill, Idaho, October 23, 1908. . . . Parcels of 40 acres will be drawn by the holders of lucky numbers if they meet certain requirements.

Nell decided to chuck her newspaper career and go alone to Idaho to be a rancher and "help tame that wild west." She was following the example of her father who had joined the gold stampede in California when he was a young man.

As Nell stepped off the Oregon Short Line at King Hill, she was hailed by a rancher in a buckboard pulled by flashy horses. Henry Hafer introduced himself and offered to drive her around to see the land that was up for grabs. He also informed her that she could rent lodgings at his place if she cared to. Nell Burgess lifted her ankle-length skirt just enough to step into the buckboard. Hafer flipped the tips of the lines to his team's backs, and they trotted off for the lands inspection.

As for King Hill, it appeared to be only the Hammett Land Company's shed surrounded by a few other unpainted look-alikes and tents of folks who had come to the land drawing. Altogether, the settlement was like a grouse's brood of chicks hidden in a sea of sagebrush. On one side the Snake River galloped past; on another, a rimrock formation called King's Crown leaned against the sky. Most prospective settlers were eyeing an old lake bed above the Snake, called The Basin. Nell decided she, too, would select The Basin if she had the chance. She knew all about the requirements. An applicant lucky enough to have his number drawn would pay $65 per acre for water, plus 25 cents per acre for land. Filing fee was $1. Another 25 cents per acre would be due after five years, when the patent was applied for.

As the day of the drawing arrived, people from far and near tramped excitedly around the land office. Folks were tense because obviously there was not enough land to go around. An outdoor platform had been erected for the drawing, and a large map of the available lands was posted on a board. Under the direction of a land officer, each participant was given a number, and duplicate numbers were thoroughly mixed in an old wooden butterchurn. When an official drew a number from the churn, the applicant having that number could choose from the lands not already selected.

Nell Burgess's number was the fortieth to be drawn. Since her first choice was taken, she settled for her second choice, forty acres of sagebrush hugging a curve of the Snake River. "I wanted to do some fishing, anyway," Nellie joked to a friend. The drawing was finished at 6:00 P.M., with many people going home disappointed—no Idaho land for them.

Following minimum specifications of the Carey Act, Nell built a prove-up cabin, fourteen by sixteen feet. Her bedroom was in the tiny attic, reached by an indoor ladder leading to a trapdoor. To guard against the occasional misfit who came into the area running from the law, Nell devised an ingenious, person-protection device. A box of black pepper was rigged above the trapdoor so that if anyone pushed it up, he'd get a face full of the pungent spice. The resulting sound effects would give Nell a chance to grab the gun she kept in her bed.

Establishing the necessary thirty-day residence, Nell got down to the business of clearing land for crops. She christened her sagebrush acres, "Rainbow Ranch" and set about transforming it into an oasis. The first plantings were Grimes Golden and Whitney apple trees and three sunflower seeds, a gift from a preschool niece in Iowa. The precious first plantings were pampered with water carried from the river. Nell's first purchases were a riding horse named Flaxie and a .22 rifle. She learned to shoot from the horse, to bring down wild meat for the table. She bought the milk cow "Coffee." And it produced "Chocolate Cream," the calf.

The ranch's first crop was alfalfa. The three sunflower seeds grew like Jack's beanstalk and became a hitching post for Flaxie. Later, there would be wheat, corn, melons, and assorted fruits. But as soon as the land produced, wildlife moved in to help harvest the crops. Jack rabbits nibbled at alfalfa, coyotes liked plums, while porcupines preferred apples, especially the choicest Grimes Golden. Packrats' tastes went to eggs, and magpies also joined in robbing hens' nests. Civet cats tried to help, too, but Nell trapped them in pieces of stovepipe.

Nell had a constant yearning for browned pork chops with gravy. And for spicy sausage to trim pancakes. Idaho was a sheep state and offered wild game such as deer, jack rabbits, quail, and sagehens, with an occasional sturgeon for Friday dinners. After a time, all the thoughts about succulent pork triggered the purchase of Lloyd the pig, who was put in a fattening pen. Lloyd wasn't of a mind to be carved into chops—so he escaped and dashed for the river. Nell told this story:

> We scrambled after Lloyd as fast as we could, fearing he would fall into the Snake and drown. But, alas, our pork-on-legs had vanished. We stood forlornly by the river. A log came floating past. Suddenly it flapped its ears, waved its curly tail, and swam for the far side. Lloyd was alive!
>
> Then another hazard appeared. Across the river a crew was working on the railroad. Of course, we knew those fellows were as honest as the governor of Idaho. But pork chops are pork chops; so we had to hurry. Swim the river? A neighbor offered transportation. Across the river we searched, calling Lloyd and assuring him we weren't even thinking of pork sausage. . . .

Nellie Burgess, taken on her Rainbow Ranch homestead. (*Iowa State University Library/ Special Collections Department*)

Suddenly, Lloyd was there, drowsing in the speckled shade of some brush. The searchers were ready for a foot race with Lloyd, but he walked slowly to the river, plunged in, and swam back to his pen.

One of the early projects of the settlers at King Hill was the building of a community church. Pastors came from various denominations, as the ranchers were willing to give a bit where creed and theology were concerned. When one pastor insisted on baptism by immersion, the congregation obligingly moved down by the Snake. A lad took his fishing pole along. When Nell happened to have a guest at Rainbow Ranch, she and her visitor went to church by the ride-tie method since there was only one horse at first. They started out with one person walking and the other riding. After a mile or so, the rider got off, tied the horse, and started walking. When the first walker reached the horse, he rode a mile or so, the rider got off, tied the horse and started walking. When the first walker reached the horse, he rode a mile or so, then tied up, and took his turn walking. It took a long while to get anywhere, using the ride-and-tie method.

Remember the Iowa niece who gave Nell the three sunflower seeds? Well, there were nine nieces and nephews in that family, and they all wanted to go out and visit the Rainbow. But nephew Glenn Mills, at age sixteen, was lent to Nell, for his parents were concerned about her safety, alone in the Wild West. Nell met Glenn's train in 1912. She rode Flaxie and led Cricket for Glenn to ride. By the time they got to the Rainbow, Glenn had shot enough Jack rabbits to cover Cricket like a horse blanket.

Nell and Glenn made horseback trips to the mountains to pick berries and to hunt deer and elk. Nell's journal tells this story:

> Glenn and I lost our way in the mountains and ran low on grubb. With only a little pancake flour and no grease to fry the cakes in, Glen shot a lean and skinny squirrel. We tried to fry out the sparse fat. . . . At long last we came out at the little town of Soldier [since then it has marched down the road to become Fairfield, Idaho]. We tied up by a restaurant and ordered big meals, including berry pie. We made short work of those meals, and reordered duplicates!
>
> We were still days from home. In true western style we used saddles for pillows, and saddle blankets plus a blazing fire to ward off the mountain cold.

On another such trek the grouse and rabbits were scarce; so, supplies were low again. They came across John and Maggie Rickert, who had taken their stock to high pasture. Nell asked if she might buy hay for Flaxie and Cricket. "No," the craggy mountain couple replied. "Most of ourn washed down river." Undaunted, Nell asked if she might buy a loaf of bread. "Nope," the answer came. So, Nell and Glenn retreated a short distance and broke out the pittance of pancake flour. The next day they came to Camas Prairie. Farmers had harvested the grain fields, and flocks of sagehens were feeding, providing welcome dinner for the travelers.

Glenn fished the Snake, trapped and hunted, looked for Indian artifacts. He chased wild horses back from the river into the desert. Winding past Rainbow Ranch, the Snake River bucked like a nervous mustang. At times there was great splashing, like a horse thrashing under water. Glenn set a sturgeon line—a rope against a hook baited with eel. In May of 1917 he hooked and landed a four-hundred pound sturgeon ten feet long. It provided dinners for the surrounding population, besides being photogenic and furnishing conversation.

One Easter morning Glenn hooked another sturgeon at the same spot in the rollicking Snake. He gave it leash enough to return to a deep hole, then tied the rope to a tree and went to church. He told the Reverend Reese, "I've got a sturgeon hooked, though I don't know whether I should, it being Sunday and all." Reese's eyes twinkled. "The Bible says somewhere, to go and do likewise. I'll get my hat and go down to the river with you." That sturgeon was an eighty pounder.

His Idaho experiences bolstered Glenn Mills when he enlisted in the United States Navy in World War I. His Aunt Nellie was left in good hands, as she married neighbor rancher Dave Sudduth in October 1914.

In 1958 Nell was alone again, a widow, when the few remaining early settlers celebrated the fiftieth anniversary of the 1908 land drawing. King Hill's business district had evaporated, leaving a bedroom town, with most residents commuting to jobs elsewhere. Ranches remained prosperous and productive.

When the sixtieth anniversary of the King Hill land drawing was observed in 1968, Nell Burgess Sudduth was the only survivor of the October 12, 1908, drawing. But Nell died suddenly soon after, a true Western pioneer, much esteemed for her courageous and adventurous spirit. In the grassy mini-park of the Rainbow Ranch, sprayed by the Snake River, is a bronze plaque honoring this Western woman:

Nellie B. Sudduth

1873–1968

Early King Hill Pioneer

Esther Dollard, Wyoming — 1908

Esther Dollard's great-granddaughter, Jean Skaife, is unsure what motivated her great-grandmother to homestead in Wyoming at the age of sixty-three. Possibly one of her sons, James, who was working on a ranch in Wyoming, encouraged his mother, a widow, to come out from Wisconsin to stake a claim on Wyoming land. Esther's history must be pieced together from family photographs of Esther and letters written to her by a son, Gene, who stayed in Wisconsin and two daughters who lived closer, Hettie in nearby Sundance, Wyoming, and Orpha in Line, South Dakota. In addition, the cabin Esther built close to Devils Tower remains on land she once claimed.

Jean's fascination with her great-grandmother began when she and her mother made a pilgrimage to Devils Tower in 1936 to see whether Esther's wish to be buried in sight of Devils Tower had been honored. They were delighted to find her grave marker in a tiny cemetery surrounded by a broken down fence with Devils Tower clearly visible. In 1994, Jean again made the pilgrimage to Wyoming. This time she found the ninety-year-old cabin

In 1908 Esther Dollard homesteaded in this cabin near Devils Tower. (*Jean Skaife, Dollard Family Photo*)

her great-grandmother had built still standing on the rolling grasslands near the Tower and made the acquaintance of someone who remembered Esther. From him she learned that her great-grandmother had been a good horse-woman, a fact corroborated by photos the family had of Esther driving a team of horses (Skaife 1996). Inspired by this search for her heritage, Jean wrote the following article about her homesteading great-grandmother, which appeared in *The Fence Post* regular feature "Parting Shots" (1998).

Parting Shots: From Devils Tower, Wyo.
by Jean Skaife

The Old Store. There it stands like a weathered old face with a wrinkled brow and windowed eyes staring out at the world. Standing in the shadow of Devils Tower, the old store was where my great-grandmother picked up her mail many years ago.

I often wonder what she thought of when she left her cabin, four miles away, and rode her horse, Buster, over the hills for her mail and a bit of shopping. Was it a sunny day with a bright blue Wyoming sky, or was the

Esther Dollard's homestead cabin still stands today in the grasslands of eastern Wyoming. (*Jean Skaife, Dollard Family Photo*)

trip to the old store in blustery snow? Did Buster know where to step so he didn't trip in a prairie dog hole or trample the wild daisies that spread out like a carpet? Maybe there was a letter from my grandfather—Gene, an Irishman who fiddled by ear—telling her that he had played for his last dance. Or did she have a letter to mail—the one in which she said that she would take the stage to Sundance tomorrow, Wednesday, June 1906. Maybe it was a letter to Orpha in Line, S.D., in which she wrote about her neighbors, Mrs. Waugh and Mrs. Boden. Did the Bank in Hulett send notices about her account to the Old Store—Tower Post?

In a letter of Feb. 4, 1917, she wrote to daughter Orpha:

"This letter has been writin a long time now, I will finish it. The weather here is very cold. It seems the coldest I have ever seen since I come out here. I was over to Jamesy's and stayed while he went to Morecroft and he said it was the worst time he ever had and that he never come so near freezing. He took a load of hogs for Mr. Janey. There was four teams, they were taking hogs to ship. They took 80 hogs and Jamesy has a lot more to take but will wait until its warmer.

Esther Dollard, who began her homestead adventure as a sixty-three-year-old widow. (*Jean Skaife, Dollard Family Photo*)

You spoke of my mail box. No there is no rural mail here, its only a box I put there for Jamesy to leave my mail in when they bring it by and the snow is so deep now I never get to the road any more. You said for me to come out this summer. I am coming as soon as roads get good in the spring. I shall just pick up and start, same as I did when I went to Sundance to take care of Hettie. I left a card in the window telling Jamesy that I had gone away for a few days."

Little did she know that the letter to Orpha would be her last letter mailed at the Old Store. She died suddenly a month later.

What really passed through that Old Store Door, so long ago in Wyoming? Letters, family history, family memories. Perhaps it was here that she posted the letter that told how she was among those who chose the land for the "Graves Cemetery." She was the first to be buried there in sight of Devils Tower, her favorite view.

Geraldine Lucas, Wyoming — 1912

In some ways Geraldine Lucas, or Aunt Gere, as she was called, is representative of other single women homesteaders. She was descended from a pioneer family who had moved westward in two previous generations. Her grandfather had established the town of Iowa City; her own father located his large family in Nebraska. Like many other women homesteaders, Gere had an independent character, a career as a schoolteacher, and succeeded in her homesteading venture in part because of family cooperation. Her brothers and a sister lived nearby and her grown son provided financial support.

Historian Sherry Smith sees Geraldine Lucas as representing "the vanguard of changing roles for women not only in the American West but in American society as a whole" for several reasons. After an early and unsuccessful marriage, Gere raised her son alone and attended Oberlin College thus becoming a "single parent" and a "returning student" long before those terms were generally accepted. And the fact that Gere homesteaded as a single woman was further evidence that she was on the leading edge of women's independence (Smith 1994, 21–25).

So it is not surprising that Gere's homesteading story is unique in several ways. Instead of combining teaching with homesteading, Gere, a divorcee with a grown son, homesteaded at the age of forty-seven after a career of teaching in New York City, using her savings to invest in homestead land. Unlike most women homesteaders, she did not need to make a return on her investment. Gere's claim was a scenic, secluded place to spend her retirement years. The land most single women homesteaded was of uncertain value then and is indistinguishable now, rocky mountainsides, arid plains, and even desert areas. But Gere had the good fortune to make her claim in one of the world's most beautiful places. Her homestead was at the foot of the Grand Teton not far from the town of Jackson, Wyoming, on land that is now part of Grand Teton National Park. The public can visit her recently renovated cabins, which are still located on the land that was once hers.

Geraldine Lucas became a colorful character in the history of Jackson's Hole. Her story is told in *This Was Jackson's Hole* by Fern K. Nelson (1994, 271–278).

Aunt Gere: A Character All Right
by Fern K. Nelson

"SHE'S A CHARACTER ALL RIGHT!" Often this was said of Geraldine Lucas—"Aunt Gere," as she was known to friends and relatives. So what sets one person apart as a "character" when they do the same everyday things as the rest of us do? The dictionary defines a character as: "one with a distinctive behavior or personality different from the norm." Well, yes. This Aunt Gere had. She was an independent thinker, self-sufficient and unafraid—in the days when women were supposed to be timorous, dependent, and a mirror of their men-folks in thinking.

Aunt Gere was born November 5, 1865, at Iowa City, Iowa, the sixth in what became a family of twelve children. Her grandfather, Robert Lucas, had created Iowa City as the first capital of Iowa Territory, when he was appointed Governor of the newly-created Territory. Her father, Robert Lucas, soon moved his family to Nebraska Territory, where he built up a large cattle ranch in the Sand Hills. When Nebraska became a state, he was invited to name the county in which he lived. He chose to honor President Franklin Pierce, so it was named Pierce County.

Father Robert Sumner Lucas thought that education for women was a waste of time. Daughter Geraldine wanted to go to college, so go to college she did, working her way to a B.A. degree in Education. She secured work in the school system of New York City, helping her younger sisters with encouragement and money if they also wanted higher education.

While in New York, Geraldine met and married an Irishman named Mike O'Shea. To this union one son was born. They named him Russell L. O'Shea. It must have been a stormy marriage. Aunt Gere would never talk about this period; but she emerged from it with a divorce. It must have been a struggle to divorce a Catholic, and in New York State. She regained the name 'Lucas' for her child and herself, and acquired an abiding hate for all things Irish or Catholic. . . . She was irreligious to the point of atheism.

She worked hard to provide a home and schooling for her son, so it was a great shock to her pride when he ran away to sea. She said, "If that's all he wants, after my working my fingers to the bone, then good riddance!" Fortunately, the captain for whom Russell had become cabin boy took an interest in the lad and encouraged him to get back into school and later into the Coast Guard Academy. Mother and son were reconciled and Russell (she always call him "Razz") soon worked his way up the ladder of promotions to become the youngest man to ever receive the rating of Commander at the time.

Geraldine Lucas surveys the view from the top of the Grand Teton. She made the ascent in August 1924, at the age of fifty-nine with the help of mountain climber Paul Petzoldt. (*Jackson Hole Historical Society and Museum*)

Aunt Gere had two brothers, Lee and Woods Lucas, and one sister, Camelia Seelamire, who had settled in the Jackson's Hole country. When Gere visited them one summer, she fell in love with the country. She soon returned to stay. Picking out a home site at the foot of the magnificent Grand Teton, she filed her homestead claim in 1912. She hired Paul Imeson to put up her homestead cabin. He did a log job which is still a credit to the log-laying art. Gere did not stint with her own labor in clearing brush, carrying wood and water, and cooking for the carpenters. Soon she was ready for the winter.

The first winter was very simple, with one stove (the cook stove), one bed, the table, and a couple of chairs, all in one room. A kerosene lamp, water by the bucket from Cottonwood Creek, and an outdoor privy completed the setup. It was all standard equipment for the country, but a far cry from a New York apartment.

Gere had an abundance of books, and she busied herself braiding rugs for the bigger cabin to come. She learned to use the webs [snowshoes] necessary to get about on the deep snow and visited among the many homesteading neighbors nearby: Jimmy Mangus and his mother; the Brothers Roany and Lew Smith who lived up in Lupine Meadows; the Gabbys; Moritz Locker, who was later to die of a heart attack as he skied over to Kelly and was not discovered until the snow went off in the spring.

The post office for that side of the river was way down at Wilson in those early days. So mail was brought up-country only when someone had the time and energy to ski or web down there and back.

Gere may have had savings, Razz may have helped with money, but her needs were few. Much to the wonderment of the irredeemably nosy folks in the valley, she got along fine with no apparent income from her homestead.

She loved her solitude and independence, but she welcomed the acquaintance of a young girl named Naomi Colwell. At this late date no one seems to know how the acquaintance started, but it developed into a real friendship. Naomi was fascinated with the life Aunt Gere had established, so she filed on the neighboring 160 acre plot and proceeded to build a cabin near their joint property line. They shared the work and mushed around together on their snowshoes. In summer they fenced and did other work to prove up on the claims.

Razz visited the ranch and saw the need for winter transportation. From Alaska, he brought a dogsled, mukluks, parka and a team of Huskies. He brought them overland by train from San Francisco to Victor. Maybe it was on this trip to see his mother, maybe on some other, but the story is that Razz and Naomi fell in love. When Razz left they were engaged. Razz went back to sea; Naomi waited.

Naomi and Gere now rode to the post office (first way down at Wilson; later, only half way, as the post-office of Teton was established near the present location of Teton Village). They also took much longer trips around the neighborhood and brought back more of a load. People really took notice when they saw Aunt Gere, togged out in her outlandish cold-weather gear, mushing about the valley with her dogsled. Proof right before their eyes, if they hadn't known for certain before. She certainly was a *"character!"*

The dogs were quite a chore to feed and exercise—at one point Gere had fifteen dogs. They had to be tied up in the cottonwood grove pretty constantly, as they were not exactly pets, and the neighbors were afraid of them whenever they did happen to get loose and roam.

Katherine Newlin Burt wrote a novel, titled *Cottonwood Creek*, making the heroine an abused young girl who lived with an old curmudgeon of a woman who made her do all the heavy work and abused her mentally, never letting her out of sight. The characters were so blatantly based upon Naomi and Gere's relationship that there was much comment about it in Jackson's Hole. Aunt Gere was so angry to be cast in such a role. And so hurt, because she had regarded Katherine as a good friend.

Not being the type to take a hurt feeling lying down, Aunt Gere sat herself down and wrote a scurrilous poem about Katherine and mailed off copies to all of Katherine's friends. That was the end of a beautiful friendship.

Just how many years Naomi and Gere were neighbors is not known at this late date, but they completed the necessary occupancy and the work required to prove up on the properties. Razz returned for another visit, but the romance had cooled, at least for him. The engagement was terminated. The record shows that Naomi sold her property to Geraldine Lucas in 1922. Did she leave because of a broken heart? Or for the more mundane reason, the necessity to earn her living?

At first acquaintance, Aunt Gere seemed a rather formidable person. She was below medium height and somewhat stocky. Her expression was sober. But there was a glint of humor and intelligence in her grey-blue eyes. She always wore Levis, cut off, gathered and tightened at the knees at knicker length. She made her own denim or chambray pull-over blouses, used black stockings to the knees and sensible shoes.

Books, magazines and newspapers (and later radio) were her constant companions, so she was a quick and intelligent conversationalist, although a trifle dogmatic. She was a martinet to work for, expecting the work to be done quickly and just so, according to her lights. The wood must be ricked just so, that it might be easy to lift out in the winter. The sleds and dog harness must be stacked just so, to be easier to get out and harness the dogs. But exacting as she was, and free with advice and directions, she was always willing to do her share, and was kind and hospitable. She never used "maybe" or "I think so." Hers was a positive disposition

Aunt Gere was to view the Grand Teton as her own particular mountain, so it is no wonder that the urge to climb it, to see the view from the top, to conquer it, grew in her. For many years after the Owen-Shive-Spaulding-Peterson party had scaled the peak, there was little interest in the climb. Then suddenly a new type of visitor found the range. People who had climbed in

Geraldine Lucas' cabin, restored in 2006, is located on National Park Service land near Jackson Hole, Wyoming. (*Mike Hensley*)

Europe came seeking out the Tetons for climbing pleasure. Being right in the midst of the preparation spot, Aunt Gere became acquainted with Paul Petzoldt, a young climber who had made more than one successful ascent. The party that assisted Aunt Gere on her trip up the Grand included Paul, Allen Budge, Ike Powell, Frank Edmiston and Jack Crawford.

The climb took place August 19, 1924. Gere was fifty-nine years old. She freely admitted that the boys had to pull her and even push her up in some places, but still it was the most exhilarating experience of her life. She wore jodhpurs and field boots for this event, with her usual pull-over blouse, gloves, and a bandanna around her head to keep the perspiration and her short-cropped, grey hair out of her eyes. She posed on the top holding the American flag which she had carried all the way. She had her moment of glory.

Aunt Gere, and the whole valley, thought that she was the first woman to scale the Grand. Since there was no Grand Teton National Park, and records were not kept as they are today, it was years before the general public of this valley knew that a Mrs. Eleanor Davis had climbed the Grand, with her husband and others, just the year before. Gere never did learn of it and died believing she was the first.

As might be expected, Gere was no proponent of the Yellowstone Park extension, nor of creating a Grand Teton National Park. She said, 'NO!" many times when approached with offers to buy her land. Finally, she told the agent that if he could offer her a stack of silver dollars as high as the peak, she might consider it.

When Park extension was brought up in her presence, she spoke long and forcefully on individual's rights. "Nobody was going to force HER to sell." When most of her neighbors were selling with a lease back agreement, or just taking the money and going to a more favorable climate, Aunt Gere snorted and pooh-poohed. "No guts to stay and enjoy the winter," she said, although she knew very well that the poor soil and late springs of the area made farming a losing business. "Well, let them take dudes," was her reasoning. And true enough, those who did remain with their homesteads did just that.

Razz would tease her when she got on this subject, saying. "You know you don't really own that place, don't you? You're on it just at the Government's grace. You're paying them rent, in the form of taxes." Stoking her temper, he'd add, "They could take it away from you any time they want."

"Over my dead body!" Gere would respond. "I'm going to stay right here." And stay she did, her health being remarkably good.

She drove a big Buick touring car in the summers, in the winters she used webs to go to the neighbors or out to the highway where she caught a ride to the post office (which was at Jenny Lake during her later years) or to go to Jackson for a few days.

She built a large, more comfortable cabin on the banks of Cottonwood Creek, calling it Razz's cabin. She had a cesspool dug, but no water system was put in in her lifetime. The creek was her water supply; kerosene or gasoline lamps served for light; a privy still sat out back, screened by bushes. Razz's cabin had a big roomy kitchen with wood burning stove, a large living room with fireplace, and two bedrooms, one which was full of trunks which were still full of materials she had brought from New York. A wide porch enclosed two sides of the cabin; glass enclosed the south side. One could sit or work there on sunny days of the winter. The side that faced the Grand had large windows for the view.

She had her piano. "All the Lucases could play something," she said, meaning some musical instrument. The living room was surrounded by bookshelves. The tops of the bookcases and occasional table were covered with exotic things Razz had sent from his travels.

Although Aunt Gere wore her knickers in Jackson and to all functions—even to Dr. Huff's funeral, which shocked some—when she went on a trip outside, she was always beautifully tailored.

The children of Dr. Huff loved to have Aunt Gere come to visit them in town and to go to her cabin at Jenny Lake. She let them crawl in bed with her where she read to them or they recited poems or sang jingles together.

After the dogs became too much for Aunt Gere to keep she disposed of all but one. This one, called old Lum, she brought to town with her when she came in to visit. Most all the children in town got to ride behind old Lum for their first dogsled ride. Finally, Aunt Gere gave old Lum to George Lamb, who had a dog team of his own on his ranch near Snake River Canyon. Since George's dogs were afraid of old Lum, George put them in the lead with him tailing them. Then he'd get a merry, swift ride, with no urging.

Aunt Gere's health gave way in the summer of 1938. She was visiting at the home of Dave and Cornelia Abercrombie when she took sick. She was admitted to St. John's Hospital on August 7 and died August 12. Her ashes were interred under a huge granite boulder on her ranch at the foot of the Grand Teton.

As she said, the Park would get her land only over her dead body. Razz did not sell the place to the Park. Perhaps he respected his mother's stand. However, he did not use the lovely heritage she created for him. Razz's cabins and all the land were sold to Kimball, who had the store and cabins at Jenny Lake. Kimball soon sold the place to the Park.

Aunt Gere would not have liked what happened to her place. The Park furnished it as a summer home for Harold and Josephine Fabian, the Salt Lake lawyer who had handled the legal work for the purchases made by the Snake River Land Company (Rockefeller) for purpose of Park extension. The Fabians used the cabin until 1985. Aunt Gere would much rather it had immediately reverted to nature. Meanwhile, she lies in her meadow, at the foot of her mountain, the Grand Teton.

Emma Peterson, Wyoming — 1919

Like young unmarried women and divorcees, widows were attracted to the potential rewards of homesteading. One such widow was Emma Peterson who at the time she decided to homestead near Newcastle, Wyoming, had been widowed twice. At fifty-two, Emma had built a successful millinery business in Omaha but longed to live the life of a pioneer. A desire for adventure and the need to support herself seem to have motivated her decision to move to Wyoming in 1919. Since Emma had been born in Indiana, then moved to Omaha, this was her second move west. Once in Newcastle, Emma was befriended by another independent woman and millinery shop owner, Mary Lerche, who helped her locate a suitable homestead and gave her work in the millinery shop until Emma's cabin was completed and she moved to her claim.

Emma enjoyed her life on the homestead, working hard but also pursuing her many hobbies such as playing the harp and piano. Although Emma was certainly capable of living alone successfully and seems to have been content doing so, she married a third time. Her third marriage at the age of sixty-nine to a Nebraska rancher required her to leave the Newcastle homestead. Before she moved away she reflected fondly on her simple life on the homestead and the "peace of mind" it had provided. Her story illustrates that successful women homesteaders often were entrepreneurs with a willingness to take risks and that they were women who could adapt cheerfully to changing circumstances and to hardships. Typical of most woman homesteaders who lived alone happily on their claims, Emma had inner resources to draw on. Although women homesteaders were rarely recluses, most did have the ability to enjoy their own company as Emma obviously did (Thorpe 1976). The following article appeared in 1976 in the magazine *In Wyoming: A Bicentennial Interview with Wyoming People.*[9]

A Woman Alone Stakes a Claim
by Elizabeth J. Thorpe

From her train seat, Emma Peterson watched the country flash past. Excited as a young girl venturing into the world for the first time, she didn't care that her friends had said, incredulously, "Go west and homestead? Alone? At fifty-two?" For now the dreary funeral was further behind her with each click of the wheels. Her future and her dreams loomed ahead. She felt young, carefree and convinced she had made the right decision this summer of 1919.

Homesteading, a non-glamorous aspect of western life, offered a peculiar challenge to women. Why? It combined back-breaking labor and torment from the elements with near starvation and often financial disaster. Yet, strangely, many women took homesteads, proved up on them and frequently triumphed doubly by marrying a neighboring homesteader and rancher.

The homestead laws failed to discriminate against females. The "free land" that lured thousands west offered women independence and equal rights. These, on a raw homestead were appallingly equal—equal labor, equal privation and equal failure—or victory. Even practiced farmers failed. Statistically, only one in three managed to remain long enough to get deeds to their farms. The Homestead Act of 1862 provided that any American citizen, or person who had declared the intention to become one, could claim 160 acres of government land. By 1890 all the most desirable farmland had been taken. In the remaining arid and semi-arid lands, later laws increased the acreage necessary for bare subsistence to 320 and 640 acres.

The land toward which Emma rushed so eagerly in northeastern Wyoming was some of the worst for farming. That any homesteaders survived was miraculous; that many were women is incredible, yet some of these valiant ladies endured to find happiness, peace and even wealth. In remembering their struggles they picture a way of life few will ever know and reveal a strength of character (and body) that grew as they tempered their environment to their needs and themselves to its demands.

Emma was born Emma Lawrence in Elkhart, Indiana, in 1867. From a large family, she was married at fourteen and widowed at nineteen. Undaunted, she moved west to Omaha where she set up a millinery shop. A creative young woman, Emma built a successful business which lasted until, in her late thirties, she married Mr. Peterson.

After fifteen years, she again found herself a widow. Childless, her life disrupted, Emma once more chose to follow a dream. She had always imagined living the life of a pioneer. The papers of 1919 featuring stories of an oil boom at Newcastle, Wyoming, helped her make her decision. Stepping off the Burlington late one night in the strange town, she registered at the stone hotel across the street and slept soundly to brace herself for the beginning of a new life.

To her delight, Newcastle was typically western. Wandering its streets, Emma found a kindred spirit in Mary Lerche, the proprietress of the millinery shop. She also, Emma learned, ran a cattle ranch.

Mary, helping Emma locate her land, strode on long legs through sagebrush and cactus, calling back to shorter legged Emma:

"Look out for rattlesnakes and cactus!"

They found Emma's section adjoining the MW Ranch, then owned by John Mead.

It was a dry summer. Grass burned brown and water holes dried up. Emma, staying with Mary Lerche, noticed dish pans on all the top shelves of the store.

"Why are the dish pans up there?" she asked.

"To catch the water when it rains and keep the hats from getting wet."

Rain had been conspicuous by its absence. But one day Mary, whose bedroom was above the shop, asked Emma to work while she went to the ranch. After a hot day Emma went to bed early. She was nearly asleep when lightning blazed and thunder rattled the building. Almost at once rain came in torrents, right through the roof in a dozen places. Emma snatched an umbrella from the corner and stayed in bed with it raised over her head until the rain stopped.

An early and disastrous winter followed. Emma stayed with friends while her cabin was started. The studding was barely completed when winter descended in frenzy, driving the hardiest natives indoors and killing cattle by the hundreds. The next spring, Emma found a dead steer wedged between the studs of her house.

The cabin finished, she settled in. Located in a swale, it was surrounded by hills. Emma could see nothing but sky unless she climbed a hill which, she said, "I did quite often." An added disadvantage was that, after an occasional heavy rain, she would find herself in the middle of a lake and would wait, like Noah, for the waters to go down. Water was, however, more rare than plentiful. In winter she melted snow for her supply; in summer she collected rain water or carried it from water holes in a bucket.

Before putting in a garden, Emma fenced an acre of land around the house. She dug a hundred post holes and set the poles herself. Sam Jennings, the MW foreman, told her the depth did not count as much as the tamping. After digging down a foot in the rocky soil, Emma picked out all the rocks she could, set the posts, tamped them thoroughly and made mounds of dirt around them. She stretched four wires by herself with a hammer. Afterward, a wandering cowboy informed her, "No one but a woman would have set post like that!"

She cleared the acre with pick and hoe, dug out sagebrush and cactus. The sage brush, which made a hot, clean fire, she saved for fuel as there were no trees nearer than Clifton, a flagging station on the railroad five miles away at the foot of the Black Hills.

In addition to the station and station house, Clifton boasted a school house, post office and grocery combined and a few homes. For mail and groceries, Emma walked there and back.

One hot summer day, thirsty and without water, Emma took her bucket and went looking for a water hole. She trudged up and down many little hills before she found one, filled the bucket and started home. After a time, she noticed she had walked a lot without getting home. From the next rise, she located her cabin a mile away in another direction. After that, she marked her trail so she wouldn't get lost.

Tired of isolation, Emma one day decided to visit some neighbors, Mr. and Mrs. Roadifer and their daughter, Lois. It was a five mile tramp through sage brush over the rolling hills, but she started early. The Roadifer's cabin, eleven by twelve, was neat and immaculate. At four o'clock Emma was ready to start home, but Mrs. Roadifer begged her to stay the night, saying that she so rarely had company that she couldn't bear to part with her. Emma, willing but puzzled asked, "Why, Mrs. Roadifer, where will I sleep?" "Don't let that bother you," the lady said.

After a delicious supper, at eight o'clock, Mr. Roadifer pulled a calico curtain across the room at the foot of their bed and brought in a cot for Emma. She slept well and was ready to leave early the next morning. Again, her hostess begged her to stay longer. Emma relented but did start home in the middle of the afternoon.

On her way, she neared a herd of cattle which suddenly thundered toward her. Frightened, she jumped into a deep ditch. When the cattle lost sight of her, they stopped running and began grazing in another direction. Thereafter, Emma stayed a good distance from the cattle, going far out of her way to do it. Later she was told that cattle were used to horsebackers but not to people on foot.

Cowboys habitually stopped at Emma's for a cup of coffee and a piece of pie or cake. Winter or summer she always had something fresh baked for unexpected visitors and appreciated their company. At times, though, in winter, she might not see anyone for weeks. Then she would climb a hill to look at the Black Hills and the MW Ranch. If the snow was not too deep she would walk the two miles to the ranch.

Neighbors were scarce but wildlife was plentiful. Emma often counted as many as forty antelope grazing the hillsides on early summer mornings. Rabbits were abundant, hard on gardens, and good eating. She decided to try her hand at shooting. Everyone, including children, could handle a rifle so she bought a .22 Remington and learned to use it. Practicing one day, she spied a rabbit nibbling grass by her doorstep. She shot at it several times, but it kept on eating. She gave up. Later she improved her aim and feasted on many a cottontail fried in bacon fat. Rattlesnakes, too, she learned to kill and the hoe was her favorite weapon.

In 1921, her sister visited her to see what homesteading was like. One evening she called Emma to watch the dog and puppies playing on the hill. Emma was puzzled because the ranch dogs only came with the cowboys. Not until after her sister left did she learn that they had seen coyotes.

Fond of music, Emma had both a harp and piano on which she often practiced late at night. One night absorbed in some new harp music she was startled by a man's voice outside. She opened the door to Sam Jennings.

"Don't you ever go to bed?" he asked. "It's two o'clock in the morning."

Emma laughed and admitted she had lost track of time. Sam, on his way home from riding after cattle, said her light was a guiding star from many miles away when the nights were dark.

One afternoon as she played her harp on the porch, some cattle ambled along the fence trail. Emma noted that they were lined up and looking over the fence as if listening. Was it possible? She stopped playing. The cattle started down the trail. She waited a few minutes, then started playing "The Last Rose of Summer." To her surprise, they came running back and lined up along the fence again. They stood there as long as she played, so she learned from her experiment that cattle like music.

Among many pleasant experiences, one tragic one stood out in Emma's memory. On a bitter night in 1923, the Barker family invited her to the Christmas program at the Clifton school. The school was dark, lighted by a lantern and a lamp borrowed from the station house. An old organ wheezed out an accompaniment for the carol singers. The twelve children spoke their pieces, after which a husky, nineteen year old lad, just the right age to think himself in love with the teacher, played Santa Claus. Dressed in a red jacket with flowing, cotton trimmed sleeves, Santa spoke to the children, then began lighting candles on the tree. He lit the lower ones first and, as he lit the top one the cotton on his sleeve caught fire. Suddenly the boy was ablaze. Emma said that, until then, she had never understood the meaning of 'panic stricken.' Of the hundred people crowded into the little school house, not one moved. One man yelled, "Run out and roll in the snow!" The boy's mother protested senselessly, "What ever you do, don't let him out!"

Finally, a woman seated near the door came to her senses, tore off the coat she was wearing and threw it on the boy, knocking him to the floor. She rolled him in it and smothered the fire. He was so badly burned it took him a long time to get well. They had Christmas trees in Clifton after that, but no candles were lit.

Tired of walking everywhere, Emma considered buying an old horse to ride. A neighbor said he had just the right one—old, gentle, used to women, priced twenty-five dollars. He brought her over, saddled, for Emma to try. She climbed aboard. The gentleman's insistence on going with her aroused her suspicions, but she started off, the man close behind. Emma, no horse-woman, tired soon and headed back to the cabin. She had about decided to buy the horse when it started to lie down. Remembering a cowboy's warning that, to rid itself of a rider, a horse would get down and roll. Emma pulled a foot from the stirrup ready to leap. The man shouted at the horse. She jumped up and Emma sailed off, landing on her back, seeing stars. After a week in bed she was cured of her backache and of any desire to ride a horse again. Instead, in 1925, she bought a Ford.

After seven years on the homestead, Emma had a two-room log cabin built among the pines on the hillside above Clifton. There she was less isolated than she had been but no less independent. She dug a root cellar a step from her back entry and lined it with stones. This finished, she went into the poultry business.

She hired a man to build a chicken house where she set the hens she bought. In time, she had forty chickens, about two pounds each, almost ready for market. One morning she went out and found forty dead chickens. She consulted both the county agent and a veterinary who pronounced the chickens healthy, though dead. Emma thought of the school teacher's visiting mother. This lady had raised chickens all her life. After a quick examination she announced, "Mites are what killed your chickens." They sprayed everything with coal oil.

After that Emma started over and never lost a chicken. It was a fine business but eggs brought only eight cents a dozen and everyone, including the stores, had more than they could use. She solved that problem by putting them down in salt, lime and water. They kept well for six months.

In the summer of 1933, two pound chickens brought only twenty-five cents apiece and she begged for buyers, but, as she liked raising chickens, she kept on, hoping for better times.

That winter was so mild the water didn't freeze and there was no ice to put up. The only big snow came in March, 1934. Emma swept a large, flat rock, spread ashes on it and let the chickens out to scratch. Before going to bed that night, she examined the ashes carefully and threw a few shovels of snow to be sure there was no danger of fire. Satisfied, she locked the chickens up for the night.

She read for a while, then fell asleep. She woke to what she thought was a beautiful sunrise, coloring the whole room red. Hearing a crackling sound, she looked out the window to find the chicken house and its occupants burned up. Well, she thought philosophically, since she was out of the poultry business, she might as well take a trip east before she started in again.

In the depression years, Emma was a leader in a government funded artists' group in Newcastle. Enthusiastically, she prodded young people's interest in art. One of her students, Elver Barker, now lives and exhibits in the Denver area. He authored *Finger Painting in Oils*, a book describing the varied techniques and materials suitable to this type of painting.

Emma's little income kept her from being as hard up as some but she was well-equipped emotionally for homesteading life, being independent, creative and energetic. In addition to her work, her hobbies kept her from being lonely. She sewed, made hats, braided rugs, painted, played her harp and piano, was an avid reader and an enthusiastic cook. She shared the community life, such as it was, and wrote ballads of important events. She faithfully kept diaries in which she noted for each day the weather, what she baked and had for each meal, her activities and visitors and what book she was reading before she went to sleep. And there was no inhabitant of the ranches tucked in the folds of the hills who was not her friend.

Through her friends at the MW Ranch where she occasionally helped cook during busy seasons, she became acquainted with a rancher named Arisman from Newport, Nebraska. She eventually married him and once more started a new life. Before she moved away, she summed up her feelings:

"Now, after seventeen years, I feel I can sit down in my peaceful quiet cabin among the hills and look back over my homesteading days with a great deal of pleasure. It is true much of it was hard and I am not sure I would want to repeat some of the experiences, yet, in retrospect, I remember most the happy times I had and the pleasant encounters I had with other people who, like myself, were trying to make a home where one had never been before. Homesteading brings you back to the simple life and with it comes a great peace of mind."

Emma died in the late 1950s in Elkhart, Indiana.

PATENT RECORD NO. 4

No. 067430

Sundance — 07617

THE UNITED STATES OF AMERICA

To All to Whom these Presents Shall Come, Greeting:

Homestead Certificate No.....................

Application ....

WHEREAS, A Certificate of the Register of the Land Office at _Sundance, Wyoming_ .... has been deposited in the General Land Office, whereby it appears that pursuant to the act of Congress approved 20th May, 1862, "TO SECURE HOMESTEADS TO ACTUAL SETTLERS ON THE PUBLIC DOMAIN," the acts supplemental thereto, the claim of _the heirs of Esther A. Dallas_ has been established and duly consummated in conformity to law, for the _east half of the northwest quarter and the west half of the northwest quarter of Section three in Township fifty-two north of Range fifty-five west of the Sixth Principal Meridian, Wyoming, containing one hundred fifty acres and eighty-one thousandths acres_

according to the Official Plat of the Survey of the said Lands, returned to the General Land Office by the Surveyor General.

NOW KNOW YE, That there is therefore, granted by the UNITED STATES, unto the said _Claimants_ .... the tract of land above described, TO HAVE AND TO HOLD the said tract of land, with the appurtenances thereof, unto the said _Claimants_ and to _the_ heirs and assigns _of the said Claimants_ forever; subject to any vested and accrued water rights for mining, agricultural, manufacturing or other purposes, and rights to ditches and reservoirs used in connection with such water rights as may be recognized and acknowledged by the local customs, laws, and decisions of courts; and there is reserved from the lands hereby granted, a right of way thereon for ditches or canals constructed by the authority of the United States.

IN TESTIMONY WHEREOF, I, _Woodrow Wilson_, President of the United States of America, have caused these letters to be made patent, and the seal of the General Land Office to be hereunto affixed.

Given under my hand, at the City of Washington, the _twenty-fourth_ day of _May_ in the year of our Lord, one thousand nine hundred and _twenty_, and of the Independence of the United States the one hundred and _forty-fourth_.

BY THE PRESIDENT: _Woodrow Wilson_

By ...., Secretary

...................................., Recorder of the General Land Office

[SEAL] UNITED STATES GENERAL LAND OFFICE

Recorded, Patent Number _750978_

Filed for Record this _24th_ day of _Jan._ A. D. 1923, at _10_ o'clock _A. M._, and Recorded in Book _4M_ on page _538_

By ...., Deputy

Eldridge F. Bell, Register of Deeds

Afterword

◊ Moving On

Now that each homesteader has had her turn to speak in this anthology, I wish I could commemorate the occasion by gathering up all the women for a group portrait. I like to imagine them standing together on the day they receive their homestead deeds. Here is what I see: Each woman proudly poses with a letter from the President of the United States granting title to her land. These are self-reliant women. All but three have had professional careers either before or during their homesteading years. Eight of them are school teachers. One dropped out of college to homestead. Another is a physician. There's also a store clerk, a secretary, a newspaper reporter, a bookkeeper, a telephone operator, and a shop owner. Records show two are widows, one is a divorcee.

Each woman is beaming with joy, perhaps recalling the hardships of the past several years, knowing that the worst of it is behind her. Perhaps she is thinking how naïve she was when she began the venture, how much she has learned. Several are looking forward to marrying men they met while homesteading, others are feeling more confident about their status as single women now that they are property owners. A few are planning to sell their land for a profit and leave, but most will continue to live on their homesteads at least for a few more years. Some eventually will move away reluctantly but retain ownership of their land as long as possible. The homesteads of a few will become a family inheritance handed down through generations. Two will soon die and be buried near their homesteads.

Each of these women possesses 160 acres or more as a result of her homesteading venture. All but Ida Garvin, who will soon lose her battle with TB, are ruddy with the healthy glow of outdoor living. Their hands probably have calluses from hoeing in their gardens, setting fence posts, and chopping wood. Those chores, plus walking long distances to visit neighbors or learning to ride a horse, have made them physically stronger than when they began. Radiant with hope for the future, they must feel that anything is possible. These are the single women homesteaders who succeeded. They deserve our admiration.

As they pose for their group portrait, perhaps the women anthologized here are thinking of a friend who left her claim in discouragement, an acquaintance who wasn't physically or emotionally strong enough to stay the course, or a gal who happily gave up her homestead when she received a marriage proposal. The ghosts of these women hover silently in the back of my mind, keeping their secrets.

Some of the women in this group portrait have already written their stories or have had their stories told by someone else; some will write or tell of their experiences in the future, looking back in wistful wonder at what they accomplished. These independent journey-takers and home-founders, these unconventional entrepreneurs, liberated from the Victorian stereotype of domesticity, will become role models for future generation of adventuresome women. They hold their heads high, satisfied that their stories have finally been heard.

The photographer is ready. He says, "Hold still and smile, ladies."

Snap goes the camera.

"Smile one more time."

Snap, Snap.

"Thank you, ladies."

And so these women homesteaders I've come to know disperse, chatting with their new friends, exchanging addresses, promising to keep in touch. I imagine that they look over their shoulders and wave happily to me. That's how I will remember them, heading bravely into their futures, reminding me that with optimism, courage, a lot of hard work, and a little luck, a woman can not only dream seemingly unattainable dreams, but she can make them come true.

Notes

....

◊ Introduction

1. A particularly fertile time for novels with female journey-takers as protagonists occurred between 1980 and 1992, a break with the pattern of literature in the first three-quarters of the twentieth century, which featured protagonists who were male journey-takers. The following novels are examples: Marilynne Robinson, *Housekeeping* (1980); Doris Betts, *Heading West* (1981); Mona Simpson, *Anywhere But Here* (1992); Jane Roberts Wood, *The Train to Estelline* (1986); Barbara Kingsolver, *The Bean Trees* (1988); Molly Gloss, *The Jump Off Creek* (1989); Judith Freeman, *The Chinchilla Farm* (1989); Sharlene Baker, *Finding Signs* (1990); Lynn McFall, *The One True Story of the World* (1992).

◊ Chapter 1, Single Woman Homesteaders: Their Place in History and Literature

1. I received evidence of this attitude first-hand when a relative of a single woman homesteader approached me after a talk I'd given on single women homesteaders in Powell, WY, April 7, 2000, and commented that her great aunt had indeed homesteaded alone, but the family had always considered her a bit odd.

2. This undated brochure is located in the Colorado History Museum Archives. It lacks publication information.

◊ Chapter 2, Getting Acquainted: Meet the Single Women Homesteaders

1. I arrived at these estimates in the following way. Various statistics from several western states indicate that twelve percent of homestead claims were filed by unmarried women, which would mean that as many as 240,000 single women attempted homesteading. Of the twelve percent who filed a claim, it is estimated that about forty-two percent or 100,800, were successful; however, as most single women homesteaded after 1900, thity-seven years after the Homestead Act was passed, that figure is probably high. To determine a closer approximation of the

women who actually received homestead patents, the estimated number of women homesteaders could be reduced by about one-third to reflect the fact that few of them homesteaded in the first thirty years of the Homestead Act. Although these numbers are admittedly an educated guess, using them puts the estimated number of single women homesteaders at about 67,500. The section, "Numbers Don't Lie," further discusses these statistics.

2. See chapter one, "Myth or Reality?," for a more detailed discussion of why women might have failed to prove up on their claims.

◊ Chapter 3, Heroines of the Popular Press: Homesteaders' Stories, 1911–1928

1. Lares and penates are household possessions.

2. "Grass widow" was a popular term of the day generally used to refer to a woman who was divorced or separated from her husband.

3. The Carey Act, passed in 1894, was an attempt to encourage settlement of arid lands by providing irrigation. The Federal Government "donated" federally owned lands to states, providing the states then found developers to undertake reclamation with private capital. The properties were subdivided into sections, which were sold to individuals. Unlike the Homestead Act, claims made under the Carey Act were available only on land where states had established irrigation projects. Carey Act land could be purchased at a low cost, along with the more expensive water right to the land. A person could claim 160 acres of federal land for 50 cents an acre. The payment would be due in ten years and the land would be theirs, provided the claimant had irrigated 20 acres by that time. Money generated from sale of lands and water rights was used to help finance the building of irrigation projects. Areas of Idaho, Wyoming, and other western states were developed under the Carey Act.

4. The author is describing the provision of the Dawes Act of 1887, which broke up communal tribal land holdings by granting land to individual Indians instead of tribes. After Indian allotments were distributed, surplus land could be opened to white settlement. Although the purported purpose of the Dawes Act was to encourage assimilation of Indians into Anglo-American culture and protect Indian property rights, instead it resulted in more Indian land coming into the possession of whites and increased antagonism between Indians and whites.

5. Honyocker is defined in *The Independent* article by Mabel Lewis Stuart: "The word 'honyocker,' we are informed by a reliable authority, is from the Russian and in that language signifies 'a greenhorn,' 'one new at his business.' It had

been borrowed by the people who already lived in the Western country before it was thrown open for settlement, and applied facetiously to the homesteaders with the meaning perhaps of 'one new at his business,' therefore 'a blunderer.' But far from considering it a reproach our merry enterprising young people on the homesteads claim it as a title of honor and respect. The word is pronounced with both o's short, hon'-yok-er. As a term of contempt it may be curtailed as in the phrase 'only a honyock'" (1913, 133 [footnote]).

6. Mamie Rose and Owen Kildare: Owen Kildare was a small-time gang leader in New York's Bowery district. He found redemption after he met and fell in love with a young social worker, Mamie Rose. She taught him to read and write and under her influence he gave up his criminal past. Kildare became a well-known writer whose tales of life in the slums were popular with *Saturday Evening Post* readers in the early decades of the twentieth century. His biography, *My Mamie Rose: The Story of My Regeneration,* was made into a movie (*Regeneration*) in 1915 (Phillips 2007).

◊ Chapter 4, Please Answer Soon:
   Letters of Single Women Homesteaders

1. In writing this section I am indebted to the insights of Anne Bower in her book, *Epistolary Responses: The Letter in 20th Century American Fiction and Criticism*. Tuscaloosa, AL: The University of Alabama Press, 1997. pp. 1–21.

2. For this information I am indebted to Rene Graf who shared not only the letters she found in her attic but also her thoughts about Julia through correspondence and telephone conversations September 24, 2002, February 11, 2003, February 18, 2003.

3. I am grateful to Julia's daughter Patience Stockton Hillius of Hamilton, Montana, for her permission to reprint Julia's letters.

4, While the term "grass widow" generally referred to a woman divorced or separated from her husband, it was sometimes used to describe a divorced or separated man, as Julia uses it in this letter.

5. Julia inserts in the letter a rough sketch of the layout of her cabin and the situation of her cabin in relationship to Bess's cabin. The sketch shows one corner of Julia's cabin touching one corner of Bess's cabin.

6. Julia is apparently referring to a belief widely held by homesteaders in the late nieteenth and early twentieth centuries that "rain follows the plow." This pseudoscientific theory circulated by promoters of homesteading held that cultivation of the land would actually draw moisture from the sky to the ground. A

period of above average rainfall in Montana about the time Julia homesteaded seemed to prove the theory, but later droughts forced many homesteaders to leave the land.

7. Julia's comment seems to refer to people who deserted their claims ("desserts") and the fact that ownership of those claims could be contested by others. Julia refers to contested claims as "contests" a few sentences later.

8. Julia probably means that they will commute their claim, a practice that allowed homesteaders who could not meet the residency requirement to buy their claims by paying a specified amount per acre.

9. Ida is listed as a widow in the 1920 census. However, family lore suggests that her husband, Norman Garvin, may have visited his grown children after Ida's death. Thus, it is possible that Ida was an abandoned wife rather than a widow. She might have concealed her marital status to qualify for a homestead or because of the stigma attached to being abandoned.

10. Ida's great-granddaughter (Nita's granddaughter), Faith Mullen, generously shared the entire collection of Ida's letters with me and answered many questions about Ida, her children, and other family members through email and a phone conversation in 2003.

11. A relinquishment was property that had been previously homesteaded but whose original claimant had not proved up. Ownership reverted to the government and was made available for others to claim.

12. Ida uses the contraction "John's" to refer to her brother John and his family.

13. Montana had adopted woman suffrage two years earlier in 1914, while in Ohio, where Ida's mother lived, women could not vote until the nineteenth amendment was ratified in 1920.

14. The word "dancey" appears several times in Ida's correspondence. It may be slang for feeling jumpy, agitated, under the weather, or out of sorts.

15. By "the brakes" Ida means the Missouri Breaks, an area along the Missouri River in Montana where Ida's homestead was located. The area is known for its rugged scenery and historic significance (Native American habitation, Lewis and Clark Expedition). In 2001 the area was designated Missouri Breaks National Monument.

16. As World War I was coming to an end, another deadly enemy, influenza, began to erupt world-wide. An estimated 675,000 Americans died of influenza, far more than the death toll of American soldiers in the war (Billings 1997).

17. Ida's concern about the draft was as both a mother and a woman who had grown up in the Quaker tradition (Faith Mullen, interview 10/20/03).

18. Bob was Bob Standish, the child of Mrs. Florence Standish, Superintendent of Nobb Hill Sanitorium. Amer and Bob were playmates when Amer stayed with Ida at the sanitorium in the winter of 1916–1917. (Faith Mullen interview 10/20/03)

19. Great Falls, Montana.

20. These lines begin the third verse of the dialect poem "The Wreck of the Julie Plante: A Legend of Lac St. Pierre" by William Henry Drummond (1854–1907), who made his name writing ballads in the voice of Quebec countryfolk—in English with a strong French-Canadian accent. The actual verse is as follows:

De win' she blow from nor'-eas'-wes',—
De sout' win' she blow too

Ida seems to have remembered the words and the cadence but she has forgotten, never knew, or did not wish to reproduce the dialect.

21. Ida's quote "the happy autumn fields" is from Tennyson's poem, "Tears, Idle Tears." The phrase appears in the first stanza:

Tears, idle tears, I know not what they mean
Tears from the depth of some divine despair
Rise in the heart, and gather to the eyes,
In looking on the happy autumn fields,
And thinking of the days that are no more.

The fact that Ida was familiar with both Drummond and Tennyson is evidence that she was well-read. The fact that she knew this particular poem well enough to quote it might mean that it was especially meaningful to her. In this melancholy poem, the autumn fields cause the poet, and perhaps Ida, to reflect longingly on the past.

◊ Chapter 5, Looking Back:
Single Women Homesteaders' Memoirs

1. Edna Ferber, a noted writer of short stories and novels; Cornelia Otis Skinner, an actress and author; Enos Mills, naturalist, lecturer, and writer. At the time Mills was Katherine's neighbor at Long's Peak Inn. He became known as the "Father of Rocky Mountain National Park" for his efforts to preserve the Long's Peak area as a National Park.

2. "Little Grey Home in the West" was a popular song written in 1911 by Hermann Lohr (music) and D. Eardley-Wilmot (lyrics). Three of the homesteaders in this chapter refer to it: Katherine Garetson, Florence Blake Smith (who apparently had a recording of it that she played on her Victrola), and Madge McHugh Funk.

One can see from the following lyrics why a woman homesteading alone would have identified with the song.

When the golden sun sinks in the hills
And the toil of a long day is o'er
Though the road may be long, in the lilt of a song
I forget I was weary before
Far ahead, here the blue shadows fall
I shall come to contentment and rest
And the toils for the day will be all charmed away
in my little grey home of the west.
There are hands that will welcome me in
There are lips I am burning to kiss
There are two eyes that shine just because they are mine
And a thousand things other men miss
It's a corner of heaven itself
Though it's only a tumble-down nest
But with love brooding there, why no place can compare
With my little grey home in the west.

(Lyrics retrieved June 30, 2007, from FirstWorldWar.com: http://www.firstworldwar.com/audio/littlegreyhomeinthewest.htm.)

3. I am indebted to Florence's son, Robert Blake Smith, for providing a copy of the *Chicago Tribune* article and sharing memories of his mother in interviews. Mr. Smith's account of his mother's experiences appears in "Florence Blake Smith and Pumpkin Buttes," in *From Belle Fourche to Antelope: History of Southern Campbell County* (1991).

4. See note 2 above.

5. David Grayson was the pseudonym of Ray Stannard Baker, an American journalist and popular essayist who began his career as a Chicago newspaper reporter. He also wrote for *McClure's* magazine and various other periodicals of the time. As David Grayson he wrote a series of nine volumes of essays. By the time Florence homesteaded in 1920 he had published: *Adventures in Contentment; Adventures in Friendship; The Friendly Road: New Adventures in Contentment; New Possessions: A New Series of Adventures,* and *Hempfield: An American Novel.*

6. See note 2 above.

◊ Chapter 6, Rediscovered:
Single Women Homesteaders in Historical Records

1. A sample of the books published about women in the West from the late 1970s to the present follows: Susan Armitage and Elizabeth Jameson (Eds.), *The*

Women's West; Sheryl Patterson Black and Gene Patterson Black, *Western Women in History and Literature*; Susan G. Butruille, *Women's Voices from the Western Frontier*; Dee Garceau, *The Important Things of Life: Women, Work, and Family in Sweetwater County, Wyoming, 1889–1929*; Barbara Handy-Marchello, *Women of the Northern Plains: Gender and Settlement on the Homestead Frontier, 1870–1930*; Katherine Harris, *Long Vistas: Women and Family on Colorado Homesteads*; Julie Jones-Eddy, *Homesteading Women: An Oral History of Colorado, 1890–1950*; Sandra L. Myers, *Westering Women and the Frontier Experience, 1800–1915*; Nell Brown Propst, *Those Strenuous Dames of the Colorado Prairie*; Glenda Riley, *The Female Frontier: A Comparative View of Women on the Prairie and the Plains*; Lillian Schlissel, *Women's Diaries of the Westward Journey*; Joanna L. Stratton, *Pioneer Women: Voices from the Kansas Frontier*.

2. The Culbertson and Howell interviews have been reproduced from the transcriptions of the original recordings.

3. Interview with Georgia St. Clair, Worland, WY, Oct. 2001, a Worland resident who knew something of Culbertson and Howell.

4. Helen Coburn Howell, untitled, unpublished manuscript, Howell family papers, 1.

5. Ibid., 4.

6. Liz Howell, interviews December 3–4, 2001, Sheridan, WY. Helen Coburn Howell's granddaughter, Liz Howell, was generous in sharing with me family history and photographs related to her grandmother.

7. Ira Carpenter was Mary's uncle.

8. Elaine Lindgren's study of single women homesteaders in North Dakota, *Land in Her Own Name* (1991), found that fifty-three percent of single women homesteaders were between the ages of twenty-one and twenty-five; seventeen percent were between the ages of twenty-six and twenty-seven. Only thirteen percent homesteaded between the ages of thirty-one and forty like Nellie Burgess did; only four percent between the ages of forty-one and fifty like Geraldine Lucas, and only five percent between the ages of fifty-one and sixty like Emma Peterson and Esther Dollard.

9. This article in the now-defunct magazine *In Wyoming: A Bicentennial Interview with Wyoming People* says nothing about Thorpe's source—whether it was an oral history someone else conducted or an interview Thorpe did. It is also possible that, like Fern Nelson ("Aunt Gere"), Thorpe pieced together the story of a local character from local legend and first-hand knowledge. I am grateful to Elizabeth Thorpe's daughter, Lynn Thorpe, of Belle Fourche, South Dakota, from whom I obtained permission to use the article.

The Wyoming State Archives had no additional information on Emma Peterson although it did have an obituary for Elizabeth Thorpe, which says she was a school teacher in Newcastle, Wyoming, and "an author of numerous historical articles" as well as a "founding member of the Weston County Historical Society" who "belonged to the Wyoming Press Women's Association and received numerous awards" in WPWA contests.

Bibliography

Armitage, Susan. "Through Women's Eyes: A New View of the West." In *The Women's West*, eds. Susan Armitage and Elizabeth Jameson, 9–18. Norman, OK: University of Oklahoma Press, 1987.

Armstrong, Amy. "Homesteading Without a Chaperon." *Sunset*, June 1916, 25–26, 97.

Bauman, Paula M. "Single Women Homesteaders in Wyoming." *Annals of Wyoming* 58.1 (1986): 39–49.

Billings, Molly. *The Influenza Pandemic of 1918*. June 1997 (modified February 2005). Retrieved April 30, 2007, from http://www.stanford.edu/group/virus/uda

Bower, Anne. *Epistolary Responses: The Letter in 20th Century American Fiction and Criticism*. Tuscaloosa, AL: The University of Alabama Press, 1997.

Brush, Mary Isabel. "Women on the Prairies: Pioneers Who Win Independence and Freedom in Their One-Room Homes." *Collier's*, January 28, 1911, 16–17, 21.

Butruill, Susan G. *Women's Voices from the Western Frontier*. Boise, ID: Tamarack Books, 1995.

Byrd, Amanda Blocker. *Reveries of a Homesteader*. Denver: Smith-Brooks, 1916.

Campbell, Joseph. *The Hero with a Thousand Faces*. Princeton, NJ: Princeton University Press, 1986.

Chenery, John A. L. "The Making of Riverton," *Riverton Chronicle*, 1926 [one-time publication].

Dings, Elizabeth G. Introduction to *Homesteading the Big Owl*, by Katherine Garetson. Allenspark, CO: Temporal Mechanical Press, 1989.

Dobler, Lavinia. *Wild Wind, Wild Water*. Casper, WY: Misty Mountain Press, 1983.

Doherty, Thomas P. "American Autobiography and Ideology." In *American Autobiography: A Collection of Critical Essays*, ed. Albert E. Stone. Englewood Cliffs, N.J.: Prentice Hall, 1981.

Ehrlich, Gretel. *The Solace of Open Spaces*. New York: Viking Penguin, 1985.

Erickson, Julia. Selected letters in private collection of Rene Graf. Aberdeen, SD.

Ervin, Zen. "Two Discoveries and a Mystery." Museum of the Mountain Man, Pinedale, WY, 2000. Photocopy.

Everette, Elizabeth Abbey. "Uncle's Gift." *The Independent*, January 1913, 99–100.

"Experiences of Miss Mary Culbertson." Oral history conducted by WPA Writers Project, 1936. WPA File 699 (Folder 209), Wyoming State Archives, Cheyenne, WY.

Fiedler, Leslie. *Love and Death in the American Novel*. New York: Criterion Books, 1960.

Fiske, G. Walter. *The Challenge of the Country: A Study of Country Life Opportunity*. New York: Young Men's Christian Association Press, 1912, 26.

French, Brett. "Reaching Across Time: Letters in the Attic Revive Memories of Homesteading Woman." *Billings Gazette*, 2 April 2000, 1A, 9A.

Funk, Madge McHugh. "And the Mice Kept Running." In *Seeds-Ke-Dee Revisited: Land of Blue Granite and Sage*, ed. Sublette County Artists Guild, 426–427. Freeman, SD.: Pinehill Press, 1998.

Garceau, Dee. *The Important Things of Life: Women, Work, and Family in Sweetwater County, Wyoming, 1880–1929*. Lincoln, NE: University of Nebraska Press, 1997.

Garetson, Katherine, *Homesteading the Big Owl*. Allenspark, CO.: Temporal Mechanical Press, 1989.

Garvin, Ida. Selected letters to Adaline Gwynn in private collection of Faith Mullen.

George, Susanne K. *The Adventures of the Woman Homesteader: The Life and Letters of Elinore Pruitt Stewart*. Lincoln: University of Nebraska Press, 1992.

Hallgarth, Susan. "Women Settlers on the Frontier: Unwed, Unreluctant, Unrepentant." *Women's Studies Quarterly* 17:3–4 (1989): 23–34.

Harris, Katherine. "Homesteading in Northern Colorado, 1873–1920: Sex Roles and Women's Experience." In T*he Women's West*, eds. Susan Armitage and Elizabeth Johnson, 165–178. Norman, OK: University of Oklahoma Press, 1987.

Harris, Katherine. *Long Vistas: Women and Families on Colorado Homesteads*. Niwot, CO.: University Press of Colorado, 1993.

Heizer, Kate. "Via the Homesteading Route: Experience in the Sagebrush of the Uintah Basin." *Sunset*, March 1921, 36–37, 52.

Hine, Robert V. *The American West: An Interpretive History.* 2d ed. Boston: Little Brown, 1984.

Holaday, A. May. "The Lure of the West for Women." *Sunset*, March 1917, 61.

Honey, Maureen, ed. *Breaking the Tie That Binds: Popular Stories of the New Woman: 1915–1930.* Norman, OK: University of Oklahoma Press, 1992.

Hunt, Linda Lawrence. *Bold Spirit: Helga Estby's Forgotten Walk Across Victorian America.* Moscow, ID.: University of Idaho Press, 2003.

Illoway, Lucinda. "Madge Funk: A Biography." Unpublished manuscript based on interview with Madge Funk., 1983 [Oral history collection]. Western Wyoming Community College, Rock Springs, WY.

Jones-Eddy, Julie. *Homesteading Women: An Oral History of Colorado, 1890–1950.* New York: Twayne Publishers, 1992.

Jordan, Teresa. *Cowgirls: Women of the American West.* Lincoln: University of Nebraska Press, 1992.

Kazin, Alfred. "The Self as History: Reflections on Autobiography." In *The American Autobiography: A Collection of Critical Essays*, ed. Albert E. Stone., 31–43. Englewood Cliffs, NJ.: Prentice Hall, 1981.

Kohl, Edith Eudora. *Land of the Burnt Thigh: A Lively Story of Women Homesteading On The South Dakota Frontier.* St Paul: Minnesota Historical Society Press, 1986.

Kuiper, Kathleen, ed. *Merriam Webster's Encyclopedia of Literature.* Springfield, MA: Merriam Webster, 1995.

Larson, T. A. *History of Wyoming.* 2d ed. Lincoln: University of Nebraska Press, 1978.

Larson, T. A. "Women's Role in the American West." *Montana: The Magazine of Western History* 26 (summer 1974): 4.

Layton, Stanford J. *To No Privileged Class: The Rationalization of Homesteading and Rural Life in the Early Twentieth-Century American West.* Charles Redd Center for Western Studies, Brigham Young University. Salt Lake City, UT: Signature Books, 1988.

Lindgren, H. Elaine. *Land in Her Own Name: Women as Homesteaders in North Dakota.* Norman, OK: University of Oklahoma Press, 1996.

Loomis, Metta M. "From Schoolroom to a Montana Ranch." *Overland Monthly*, January 1916, 59–64.

Mansell, Darrel. "Unsettling the Colonel's Hash: 'Fact' in Autobiography." In *The American Autobiography: A Collection of Critical Essays,* ed. Albert E. Stone, 61–79. Englewood Cliffs, NJ.: Prentice Hall, 1981.

Marshall, T. P. "Woman Runs Tea Shop on Side of Mountain." *Dallas Morning News*, 5 October 1924, n.p.

Mills, Enos. "Her Rocky Mountain Homestead." In *A Baby's Life in the Rocky Mountains* by Esther Burnell Mills with contributions by Enos A. Mills, 1–7. Longs Peak, CO: Temporal Mechanical Press, 1999

Mott, Frank Luther. *A History of American Magazines. Vol. 4.* Cambridge: Harvard University Press, 1957.

"Mrs. Ashby Howell, Pioneer Worland Woman and Her Humorous Stories of Her First Years in Wyoming as School Teacher and Lady Homesteader." Oral history conducted by WPA Writer's Project. WPA File 798 (Folder 130). Wyoming State Archives, Cheyenne, WY.

Myres, Sandra L. *Westering Women and the Frontier Experience: 1800-1915.* Albuquerque: University of New Mexico Press, 1982.

National Park Service. "Homestead National Monument of America." 2007. Retrieved July 5, 2007, from http://www.nps.gov/home/

Nelson, Fern K. "Aunt Gere: A Character All Right." In *This Was Jackson's Hole: Incidents & Profiles from the Settlement of Jackson's Hole.* Glendo, WY: High Plains Press, 1994.

Newberry, Alice. Letters. MSS 1202 [Box 1, ff 31,37]. Stephen H. Hart Library, Colorado Historical Society, Denver, CO.

Obbink, Laura A. "In Search of Women's Voice: A Revisionist Reading Gone Awry." Paper presented at the annual meeting of the Western American Literature Association, Albuquerque, N.M., October 1996.

Online Books Page. "Serial Archive Listings for The Overland Monthly. n.d. Retrieved June 20, 2007, from:
http://onlinebooks.library.upenn.edu/webbin/serial?id=overland

Patterson-Black, Sheryll, and Patterson-Black, Gene. *Western Women in History and Literature.* Crawford, NE: Cottonwood Press, 1978.

Peavy, Linda, and Ursula Smith. *Pioneer Women: The Lives of Women on the Frontier.* Norman: University of Oklahoma Press, 1998.

Pendergraff, Roy. *Washaki: A Wyoming County History.* Austin, TX: Saddlebag Books, 1985.

Philbrook, Zay. "My Wyoming Timber Claim: A Woman Pioneer in the Bighorn Mountains." *Sunset*, December 1918, 22-23.

Phillips, Michael W., Jr. *Regeneration.* 2007. Retrieved June 30, 2007, from the Goatdog's Movies Web site:
http://goatdog.com/moviePage.php?movieID=877

Prairie County Historical Society. *Wheels Across Montana's Prairies*. N.P.: Western Printing and Lithography, 1974.

Pratt, Alice Day. *A Homesteader's Portfolio*. Corvallis, OR: State University Press, 1993.

Raban, Jonathan. *Bad Land: An American Romance*. New York: Pantheon Books, 1996.

Reddy, Sheila D. "Yellow Roses by the Doorstep, Apples in the Orchard, Berries on the Fence: Women Homesteaders on the Payette National Forest." Heritage Program, Payette National Forest, Idaho Historical Society, Boise, 1993.

Rehwinkel, Alfred. *Dr. Bessie: The Life Story and Romance of a Pioneer Lady Doctor on Our Western and The Canadian Frontier As Told by Herself and Here Presented in a Running Narrative by Her Husband*. Saint Louis: Concordia Publishing House, 1963.

Riley, Glenda. Preface to *Land of the Burnt Thigh*, by Edith Eudora Kohl. St. Paul: Minnesota Historical Society Press, 1986.

Robbins, Roy M. *Our Landed Heritage: The Public Domain 1776-1970*. 2d ed. Lincoln: University of Nebraska Press, 1976.

Schlissel, Lillian. *Women's Diaries of the Westward Journey*. New York: Schocken Books, 1992.

Skaife, Jean. "Parting Shots: The Old Store." *The Fence Post*, March 2, 1998, 184–185.

Skaife, Jean. "Devils Tower: An Ancestral Marker." *The Fence Post*, December 16, 1996, 102–104.

Smith, Florence Blake. *Cow Chips 'n' Cactus*. New York: Pageant Press. 1962.

Smith, Henry Nash. *Virgin Land: The American West as Symbol and Myth*. Cambridge, MA: Harvard University Press, 1950.

Smith, Robert. "Florence Blake Smith and Pumpkin Buttes." In *From Belle Fourche to Antelope: History of Southern Campbell County*, ed. Harriet Underwood, 134–138. Gillette, WY: Action Printing, 1991.

Smith, Sedonie, and Julia Watson. *Reading Autobiography: A Guide for Interpreting Life Narratives*. Minneapolis: University of Minnesota Press, 2001.

Smith, Sherry L. "A Woman's Life in the Teton Country: Geraldine Lucas." *Montana: The Magazine of Western History* (Summer 1994): 18–33.

Sochen, June. "Frontier Women: A Model for All Women." *South Dakota History* 7 (winter 1976): 36–54.

Sprague, William Forrest. *Women and the West: A Short Social History*. New York: Arno Press, 1972.

Star, Kevin."Sunset Magazine and the Phenomenon of the Far West." (n.d.) Retrieved April 26, 2007, from the *Sunset* Web site: http://sunset-magazine.stanford.edu/html/influences_1.html

Stewart, Elinore Pruitt. *Letters of a Woman Homesteader*. Boston: Houghton Mifflin, 1914; Boston, Houghton Mifflin, 1982

Stewart, Elinore Pruitt. *Letters on an Elk Hunt*. Boston: Houghton Miffflin, 1915; Lincoln: University of Nebraska Press, 1979.

Steinbrech, Mary Sheehan. Interview by Marjane Ambler, June 1984, Fremont County Library Oral History Collection, Lander, WY.

Stout, Janis P. *The Journey Narrative in American Literature: Patterns and Departures*. Westport, CT: Greenwood Press, 1983.

Strange, Joanna Gleed. "The Last Homesteads." *Collier's*, January 1913, 24.

Stratton, Joanna L. *Pioneer Women: Voices from the Kansas Frontier*. New York: Simon & Schuster, 1981.

Stuart, Mabel Lewis. "The Lady Honyocker: How Girls Take Up Claims of Their Own on the Prairie." *The Independent*, July 1913, 133–137.

Suddeth, Nellie Burgess. Letter to Marjorie Vandervelde, 1960. Iowa State University Library, Special Collections Department, Ames, Iowa.

Thorpe, Elizabeth J. "A Woman Alone Stakes a Claim." *In Wyoming*, June/July 1976, 27.

Urbanek, Mae. "Bass, Jennie Paulson: Pioneer School Marm." In *Wind Pudding and Rabbit Tracks: A History of Goshen, County, Wyoming*, ed. Goshen County History Book Committee, Vol. 1, 328–330. Torrington, WY: Platte Valley Printers, 1989.

Vandervelde, Marjorie. "Pioneer Lady Homesteader in Idaho." *American West*, 23.5 (June/July 1986): 50–54.

Warnick, Jill Thorley. "Women Homesteaders in Utah, 1869–1934." Master's thesis, Brigham Young University, 1985.

Webb, Walter Prescott. *The Great Plains*. Boston: Ginn, 1931.

White, Richard. *It's Your Misfortune and None of My Own: A History of the American West*. Norman, OK: University of Oklahoma Press, 1991.

"Women Are Taking Up Much Land in Colorado." *Denver Times*, 16 March 1915, 1–2.

Index

When Marcia Hensley moved to Wyoming as a single mother of two in the 1980s, she took a course in Western history. She also read Elinore Pruitt Stewart's *Letters of a Woman Homesteader* and was troubled by the discrepancy between her college textbook's assertion that women were reluctant pioneers and Stewart's enthusiastic account of homesteading in western Wyoming. She found that Stewart, a single woman homesteader who chose to come West with her daughter, was appreciative of the landscape and the lifestyle.

Hensley identified with Stewart and wondered whether there was a difference in the attitudes of single women who *chose* to go west and those of women who followed their husbands west. She set about looking for other single women homesteaders who had written about their experiences to see which model they fit. The accounts in this collection are the result of a twenty-year search for the answer.

A graduate of the University of Tulsa (M.A. 1966), Hensley was Associate Professor of English at Western Wyoming Community College where she founded and directed the Western American Studies program in addition to teaching composition courses and Western American Literature.

Since retiring she has concentrated on writing and historical research. In 2004 she won the Wyoming Arts Council's Neltje Blanchan Memorial Award for writing inspired by nature. She has served on the Wyoming Council for the Humanities Speaker's Bureau where she presented "Single Women Homesteaders: Lessons in Independence" and with husband, Mike, "If Barns Could Talk: Creating Eden in Wyoming's High Desert." Along with a group of community volunteers, she is compiling an anthology of stories about Eden Valley, Wyoming, to commemorate the Valley's centennial.

Her work has been published in two anthologies of western writing as well as the syndicated newspaper column "Writers on the Range."

❧ NOTES ON THE PRODUCTION OF THE BOOK ❧

This book was simultaneously released in two editions.

A *limited edition* of only 300 copies was Smyth sewn,
bound in Prairie Sage cloth, embossed with burnished gold foil,
and wrapped in a full-color dustjacket.
Each copy is hand-numbered and signed by the author.

The *softcover trade edition* is covered with ten-point stock,
printed in four colors, and coated with a special gloss finish.

The text of both editions is from the Garamond Family by Adobe
and News Gothic by Adobe. Display type is SacreBleu by Adobe
and Border Dingbats 1 by SMC.